DATE D

HERBERT HOOVER
and
ECONOMIC DIPLOMACY

HERBERT HOOVER, SECRETARY OF COMMERCE, 1921–1928

HERBERT HOOVER

and

ECONOMIC DIPLOMACY

Department of Commerce Policy
1921-1928

---

by
JOSEPH BRANDES

Foreword by Lewis Strauss

UNIVERSITY OF PITTSBURGH PRESS
Pittsburgh, 1962

To My Family

FOREWORD

Almost three decades have elapsed since Herbert Hoover, thirty-first President of the United States, left the White House, his true stature obscured from most of his fellow citizens by a fog of misrepresentation and calumny. He was the first target in that high office of certain techniques which had developed with the expansion and control of the media of mass communication. In consequence his exceptional talents, his great works of humanity during and after World War I, and his extraordinary record as Secretary of Commerce, were practically lost to view for the generation which has grown to maturity in the years since 1932.

It was inevitable that the mud which had been thrown would some day fall away and that historians and economists eventually would discover and reveal the facts buried under the strata of political misrepresentation. For this reason, if there were no other (and there are many others), the book by Dr. Brandes would be significant as the forerunner of studies of Mr. Hoover's achievements that will surely appear in the years ahead.

Dr. Brandes was not even of school age when Michelson and his staff contrived an end (as they assumed) to Hoover's public service. Some sense of mission as well as scholarship must have impelled Dr. Brandes to carry through with the impressive amount of research which his book evidences. It is a masterly and thorough survey of the period between 1921 and 1928 when Mr. Hoover headed the Department of Commerce, but the account is not dehydrated and bloodless. In a vital and succinct manner, the author has related the circumstances and recaptured the social, political, and economic climate surrounding important events — some of them not well known even at the time. One such is Mr. Hoover's reiterated warning against the unbridled private speculation of the late 1920's for which, ironically, he was later to be made the scapegoat.

The book will be read by many with a sense of discovery and surprise that the facts as here revealed and documented could have been so perverted in the course of the long-continued, political distortion of Mr. Hoover's career.

Lewis L. Strauss

PREFACE

Herbert Hoover carved out for himself a position of national prominence and power long before the Presidency. His years as Secretary of Commerce, during which he built the Department into one of the most influential in Federal Government, were marked by his significant success as an administrator, a highly effective Cabinet member, and a popular public figure. Hoover's attainment of country-wide and even international prestige during the prosperous period before 1929 represents a sharp contrast with the careers of Presidents Harding and Coolidge, who exercised only local influence in their pre-presidential years. Hoover, more than most of our presidents, brought to the office of Chief Executive experience in the pragmatic functions of national government as well as knowledge of business affairs.

Mark Sullivan, a journalist-historian keeping a sensitive ear to contemporary popular opinion, wrote of the praise lavished on Secretary Hoover's efforts to stimulate continued prosperity in the United States. One contemporary evaluation, for example, credited Hoover with an "annual saving to American business" amounting to the "immense total of $500,000,000." In a typically colorful manner Sullivan reminded his readers that this was five-fold the riches wrested during the Klondike gold rush.[1]

It is not among the purposes of this study, however, either to extol or to disparage the role of Hoover in the 1920's. The first has already been served amply by laudatory biographers; the second may be found, in varying degrees, among critics whose views encompass the spectrum of prejudices. The purpose here is to analyze the development and motivation of Hoover's eco-

1. Mark Sullivan, *Our Times; The United States, 1900-1925* (6 vols., New York, 1926-1935), VI, 648-649.

nomic policies as a major factor shaping America's position in the post-war world.

An examination of the Hoover program in the 1920's necessarily reflects on the decade's economic optimism and business-orientation. It becomes, therefore, a study of the times as well as the man. Few Americans implemented as actively as did the Secretary of Commerce the dominant "middle-class conservative" ideals which prevailed in the era of neo-"normalcy."[2] Economic issues, especially in the field of foreign relations, were invariably affected by Hoover's major role as economic policy-maker and "trouble-shooter" for the Harding and Coolidge administrations.

By focusing on Hoover as a "Depression President," historians have neglected too often those highly significant years in which he stimulated and directed American enterprise at home and abroad. His influence on such major problems as war debts, reparations, the tariff question, branch factories, and new foreign loans, has been under-estimated. Likewise, historical analysts have given insufficient attention to Hoover's campaign against foreign monopolization of essential raw materials, even though much international controversy was aroused over this issue.

It is intended here not only to clarify Hoover's impact on these areas of governmental policy, but to dispel some of the glib assumptions regarding his basic philosophy. For example, while he espoused many of the principles of *laissez-faire,* he set a pattern also for government involvement in economic affairs. This included his Department's manifold services to American business. But quite often, Hoover and the Commerce Department undertook a bolder initiative in fostering trade associations, or struggling for independent sources of rubber "under the American flag." His ambitious program for governmental supervision of foreign loans was even considered too drastic by contemporary Republican and Democratic leaders.

2. Clinton Rossiter, *Conservatism in America* (New York, 1955), pp. 154, 200, *passim.*

These efforts represented more than the platform of one who was the idol and champion of business interests. Throughout Hoover's policies there ran a thread of economic nationalism which envisioned the world's welfare in terms of the long-range prosperity of the United States. Not only did this involve acquisition of strategic raw materials and constantly rising exports of American goods and capital, but the export of American principles as well (such as the virtues of competition and sound fiscal practices).

To implement Hoover's ambitious program, government agencies had to be geared for the new requirements of large-scale American involvement in international economic affairs. This type of bureaucratic expansion was accomplished most successfully in the re-organized Department of Commerce a decade before the New Deal. Under Hoover, there worked an efficient corps of commercial attachés, trade commissioners, commodity chiefs, and bureau heads who aided immeasurably in the achievement of American policies.

In the new order of a world economy there was no eschewing of "foreign entanglements," even if they involved diplomatic tensions. Hoover was one of the first to recognize the implications of America's post-war transformation.

The years after World War I saw the full emergence of the United States as a world power. Much has been written of our failure to join the League of Nations and of the subsequent strength of "isolationism." It is now evident, however, that America's weight was rarely — if ever — absent from the scales of the international economic balance of power. Whatever may have been the failings of our foreign policy politically in the post-war era, this country could not be, and was not, isolated from the wider external currents of trade, finance, and fiscal relations.

Our material progress and advanced industrial status were universally admired, envied, and emulated. America became creditor to the world in terms of the debts owed to us by our war-time allies, a factor of great significance in the international relations of the period. Furthermore, millions of dollars annually streamed abroad in the form of relief aid, loans for European reconstruction and the development of "backward" areas, or in the form of capital for speculative or investment purposes. Most important, however, the billions flowing abroad during Hoover's term as Secretary of Commerce came from private rather than government sources. This provides a distinct historical contrast to the decade following World War II and sets the stage for the problem of loan supervision in the 1920's.

American business and finance, assisted by the Hoover policies, pulsed with the excitement of "foreign opportunities." The prospects seemed promising in terms of more lucrative markets abroad, profitable investment of capital, and direct production and sales by means of branch factories and agencies. In a period of domestic prosperity coupled with a seemingly insatiable foreign demand for American products, financing, and technical assistance, the United States became deeply involved in the economic activities of the world.

*   *   *   *   *   *

The writer can but attempt to acknowledge the debt he owes to the New York University Graduate School of Arts and Science, especially to the faculty in History and in Economics. I am grateful particularly to Professor Vincent P. Carosso, whose devoted interest, understanding, and encouragement are in the best tradition of the great teachers. Historian and mentor, he has been also a friend.

The award of two fellowship grants by the University was of significant assistance, and is fully appreciated.

Beyond the academic field, the confidence and cooperation of my entire family have been an inestimable source of strength. The oft-arduous tasks of research and writing were lightened by the loyalty and devotion of Margot Brandes, my wife, to whom this work is affectionately inscribed.

JOSEPH BRANDES
Paterson State College
Wayne, New Jersey

CONTENTS

SECTION THREE: FEDERAL CONTROL OF
AMERICAN LOANS AND
INVESTMENTS ABROAD

SECTION ONE

MEETING THE CHALLENGE
OF A WORLD ECONOMY

CHAPTER I

THE NEW DEPARTMENT
OF COMMERCE
UNDER HERBERT HOOVER

Organizing the Department

In April, 1926 the top leaders of American business and industry joined to pay tribute to Herbert Hoover, then Secretary of Commerce. This was five years after his accession to that post, and over two years before his nomination for the Presidency of the United States.

John E. Edgerton, President of the National Association of Manufacturers, summarized Mr. Hoover's achievements as "lifting the Department of Commerce from a position of innocuous desuetude to one of indispensable importance to the country's welfare. . . ."[1] Another Hoover eulogist, a past president of the United States Chamber of Commerce and at the time an adviser to the Department of Commerce, pointed to Mr. Hoover's respect for the interests of business and his belief in the "teamplay of government with the leaders of character in the various industries." The speaker continued his tribute, by saying that Hoover conceived "that America was primarily a commercial people — that the Department of Commerce should be a great agency furthering the activities of a commercial people. . . ." In this area, the speaker concluded, "there has been displayed

1. "American Industry Acknowledges Its Debt to Herbert Hoover," *Industrial Management,* LXXI (April, 1926), 199.

3

an energy and resourcefulness in the direction of the Department which has been a revelation."[2]

Needless to say, these opinions, which were to a large degree typical of the business community, were not shared entirely by other groups. Hoover's important position in the Republican administrations of Harding and Coolidge could not but attract the fire of political opposition. On more than one occasion, Hoover was criticized in Congress for using his post to further his own personal ambitions and to aid "big business."[3] Nevertheless, under Hoover the Department of Commerce experienced a period of efficient activity and influence which was probably unparalleled in its history. This is especially true of its activities in the realm of economic foreign policy, one of the leading areas of political debate in the 1920's.

When Hoover became Secretary of Commerce in Harding's cabinet (1921), the Department of Commerce was one of the newer departments of government. At the time, it was considered to be relatively insignificant, even by the officials who worked in it. The new Secretary was determined to expand the Department's functions as broadly as possible, taking advantage of the "wide-open charter" provisions of the enabling act.[4] The prime beneficiary of this drive was the Bureau of Foreign and Domestic Commerce (established in 1912), whose expenditures increased during the Hoover regime from $860,000 to over $5,000,000, while its personnel quintupled.[5]

In its emphasis on the expansion of American trade abroad, the Bureau of Foreign and Domestic Commerce organized a network of fifty offices throughout the world, in addition to district offices in major American cities which maintained contacts

2. Julius H. Barnes, "Herbert Hoover's Priceless Work in Washington," *ibid.,* pp. 196-197.

3. *Congressional Record,* 70 Cong., 1 Sess., pp. 5983, 5994 (April 5, 1928); *New York Times,* Jan. 8, 1926; Feb. 19, 1926; March 20, 1926.

4. Herbert Hoover, *The Memoirs of Herbert Hoover* (3 vols., New York, 1952), II, 40.

5. Merle Fainsod and Lincoln Gordon, *Government and the American Economy* (New York, 1941), p. 107.

with exporters and importers and the various trade associations.[6]
The trade commissioners and attachés, in these offices were required to draw up periodic analyses of foreign "opportunities."
Included in these reports was specialized information on tariffs,
commercial law, and even the credit ratings of foreign firms.
"Not only were our foreign agents hounds for possible American
sales, but they made themselves welcome abroad by helping the
merchants of the countries to which they were assigned."[7] To
aid American exports, surveys were made of the preferences of
foreign consumers. As a part of this effort, American automobile
exporters were encouraged to set up supply and repair centers
abroad to improve their services to the foreign buyer.[8]

What kind of organizational pattern made such functions possible? At the beginning of his term as Secretary, Hoover found
the Department of Commerce ill-equipped to afford the services
which he felt were necessary to keep pace with America's increased, postbellum importance in the world economy. The staff
was small and lacked specialists; organization of the divisions
was along regional lines, each responsible for all trade commodities within its area. One of Hoover's first major reform measures
was to reorganize the Bureau of Foreign and Domestic Commerce along commodity lines, characteristic of the practices of
private American firms engaged in foreign commerce. In the
words of a contemporary business analyst, each of these commodity divisions was "headed by an expert nominated—in some
cases actually voted on—by the trade he knows and represents."[9]

In a 1926 interview Hoover explained his search for men of
"broad economic outlook" and business experience. "I requested
each of the different industries to create a committee to cooperate with the Department in working out the strategy of each

6. This Bureau was greatly weakened under the New Deal, through lower
budgets and the transfer of its Foreign Service to the Department of State,
ibid., passim.
7. Herbert Hoover, *Memoirs,* II, 79.
8. *Ibid.,* II, 80; *Thirteenth Annual Report of the Secretary of Commerce*
(Washington, 1925), pp. 89-90.
9. Donald Wilhelm, "Mr. Hoover as Secretary of Commerce," *The World's
Work,* XLIII (Feb. 1922), 408.

particular commodity. The first duty imposed upon these committees was to select a man from their own ranks who would head the division."[10] These division heads were to keep informed of the latest developments in their specialized areas. By attending trade conventions, contributing articles or other information to trade periodicals, and corresponding with the leading firms in their field throughout the world, these men provided a broad and careful background upon which to determine policy.[11] By synthesizing these reports, from hundreds of commercial agents throughout the world, the commodity divisions could advise more effectively the various American trades concerning the disposal of surpluses abroad, prospective prices of imported raw materials, or the best means of shipping goods to a distant buyer. Altogether, 17 divisions were formed, each representing a corps of experts in a major commodity of world commerce.

In addition to the commodity divisions, several others were organized to deal with the more technical problems involved in economic foreign relations. For example, the Division of Foreign Tariffs supplied invaluable information on customs and import regulations abroad. Particular tariff problems were publicized in *Commerce Reports, The Monthly Summary of Foreign Commerce,* and other publications of the Department. Related to this area was the work of experts in the Division of Commercial Laws, who studied the effects of foreign legislation on American economic interests abroad, especially in connection with American property rights. This Division supplied the Department and the business community generally with the details of foreign tax systems, helped to eliminate "credit abuses" by foreign firms, and encouraged commercial arbitration.[12]

10. Quoted in Isaac F. Marcosson, "Commercial Exploration," *The Saturday Evening Post,* CXCVIII (Feb. 13, 1926), 53.

11. The collection of documents, Record Group 151, of the Bureau of Foreign and Domestic Commerce at the National Archives in Washington, contains the correspondence of the commodity divisions.

12. National Conference of Business Paper Editors, *What the Department of Commerce Is Doing for American Business* (Washington, 1924). Pamphlet, Department of Commerce Library (Washington). Hereafter referred to Commerce Library.

The Finance and Investment Division prepared and distributed to American investors reports on the budgets of foreign governments, financing methods abroad, as well as analyses of foreign exchange conditions. It maintained cordial and cooperative relations with American investment houses. Although a study of this Division's files reveals no apparently obvious favoritism, certain financial firms seem to stand out as beneficiaries of its assistance. In 1923, for example, J. W. Seligman and Company obtained a special report, prepared by the American Commercial Attaché in Paris (Chester L. Jones), concerning delicate financial negotiations between French bankers and the Department of Antioquia (Colombia). Details of this proposed loan flotation included provisions "covering the pledge of the major portion of the mineral and industrial resources of that State." Information of this type illustrates the very valuable data supplied to American bankers competing with European interests in the international security market.[13]

Another American banker despatched to the Finance and Investment Division a set of questions to be used by commercial attachés in determining the foreign market for American securities. Gratified with the results of the "questionnaire which I wanted to have sent out to your foreign representatives," the banker asked later whether "it might be valuable to send the questionnaire to the chief South American countries as well as to Europe." In reply, Division Chief Grosvenor M. Jones was "pleased to say that arrangements will be made to send the questionnaire on the foreign securities markets to the chief Latin American countries."[14]

Correspondence with American firms in connection with the Department's services was kept confidential in order not to re-

13. Grosvenor M. Jones (Chief, Division of Finance and Investment) to J. W. Seligman and Company, April 7, 1923. Records of the Bureau of Foreign and Domestic Commerce, National Archives, Record Group 151:640 (Dominican Republic). Hereafter records in the National Archives will be designated by the symbol NA, followed by the record group (RG) number and classification.

14. Clare M. Torrey (Blyth, Witter and Co.) to Grosvenor M. Jones, Dec. 12, 1923. Jones to Torrey, Dec. 22, 1923, *ibid.*

veal the operations of these firms to their competitors. At times, the information provided by the Department involved United States treaty relations with foreign governments. For example, in October, 1926 a telegram from W. A. Harriman and Co. inquired whether the Dominican Republic had authorized a new dollar loan, and how this matter might be related to the condition of the Republic's finances. Only one day after it received the Harriman telegram, the Department of Commerce replied with a thorough report, emphasizing the fact that the projected $10,000,000 loan would require State Department approval under the 1924 United States treaty with the Dominican Government. An analysis of the Caribbean Republic's finances, listing revenues and expenditures, as well as recent deficits, concluded with some blunt advice by the Division of Finance and Investment: "In general it must be said that the condition of the public finances is not entirely satisfactory. . . . It is doubtful that the plan of the Minister of Finance in the manner indicated by him can be effected."[15]

To coordinate the research work of all the divisions, Hoover formed the Division of Regional Information with Louis Domeratzky as Chief. Domeratzky played an important part in publicizing the activities of the Department by contributing to *Foreign Affairs* and other periodicals. His staff produced some excellent studies on such subjects as international economic change, cartel movements, American branch factories abroad, and foreign markets for American products.[16] These specialized monographs were prepared under the supervision of the capable Dr. Julius Klein, Director of the Bureau of Foreign and Domestic Commerce and a trusted adviser of Secretary Hoover. Klein was well-informed of progress in important current economic research; moreover, he never lost direction of the activities of his Bureau. An excellent administrator, Hoover was in a

15. W. A. Harriman and Co., Inc. to Jones, Oct. 29, 1926; reply from Jones, Oct. 30, 1926, *ibid.*

16. See Bibliography for specific titles. For the development of this type of research see: Sanford Schwarz, *Research in International Economics by Federal Agencies* (New York, 1941), pp. 19-21.

position to give credit to deserving staff members, which he did publicly on more than one occasion.[67]

In dealing with his widespread staff, Hoover sought to develop a "departmental spirit" of friendly cooperation and efficiency. As a first step, unfit political appointees were removed in favor of qualified personnel. American business was tapped for the Department's appointments and it became a prime source of many new staff members. After a suitable period of government experience many of these men found that their future services to private business increased materially. Consequently, Hoover could explain that he had "little difficulty in obtaining good young men, as service with us [in the Department of Commerce] became a stepping stone [for them] to a job outside the government. Their subsequent success in life is proof both of their capacity and of their opportunity."[18]

The emphasis on business-oriented personnel was applied to central headquarters in Washington and also to the commercial attachés who headed the Department's overseas staff. On one occasion, the very able chief of the strategic Berlin office of the Commerce Department was roundly criticized by his superior in Washington for giving too much responsibility to "bright young assistant trade commissioners" with no business connections. He was reminded that "the confidence of the [American] manufacturer can be retained much more easily if they are [sic] represented in your office by men from the industry who know their [sic] language." Failure to follow this recommended policy would impair "the confidence of the [commodity] divisions, and especially of the exporters," in the reliability of the Berlin Attaché.[19]

17. Herbert Hoover, *The Future of Our Foreign Trade* (Washington, 1926), p. 6. Commerce Library pamphlet (address of March 16, 1926). See also Herbert Hoover, *Memoirs*, II, 79.

18. Hoover, *Memoirs*, II, 43.

19. From O. P. Hopkins (Acting Director, Bureau of Foreign and Domestic Commerce) to Commercial Attaché F. W. Allport, Sept. 13, 1927, NA, RG 151:235.1 (Germany).

Publicizing "Foreign Opportunities"

The vast network of commerce agents and research writers brought forth tangible results in the publications of the Department of Commerce and in the assistance given to Americans interested in foreign trade or finance. Hoover was convinced that it was both profitable and desirable for America to take advantage of the foreign opportunities which were beckoning.[20] As Secretary of Commerce, he mobilized his Department's resources to awaken the country to such opportunities and to aid those willing to participate in foreign economic activity. Consequently, it was almost inevitable that the glare of publicity should fall upon the Secretary and his Department and on the ideas they were presenting. With the aid of friendly journalists and the political admirers of Hoover and Republicanism, both received national attention.

Much was made of the democratic nature of the assistance given by the Department of Commerce in the foreign field. One publicist proclaimed: "Now, the little man, like the big man, is a unit in a national manufacturing, exporting, and selling scheme, and the Department of Commerce is his sales organization in a sense."[21] Although these facilities were utilized primarily by relatively large industrial, financial, and merchant groups, Hoover was anxious to prove their value for the entire American economy, especially for the farmer. In this connection, the Department launched an educational campaign emphasizing the influence of agricultural exports in maintaining a prosperous America. As part of this program, a slick-magazine pamphlet was produced in 1923: *How the United States Department of Commerce Serves the Farmer.*

This official publication illustrates the manner in which the services provided by the Department of Commerce within the framework of the world economy were explained to influential sections of the American public. The pamphlet emphasized the

20. An excellent indication is the tone and content of the *Annual Reports of the Secretary of Commerce.* See especially those for 1925 and 1926.
21. Wilhelm, *op. cit.,* p. 408.

assistance given to agriculture by the commodity divisions. For example, the Textile Division was shown working "closely" with "farmers' cooperative cotton marketing associations" and with the wool growers, in supplying useful information on certain market conditions abroad. The Chemical Division watched over the imports of Chilean nitrates and German potash, essential fertilizers, to prevent price "gouging." At the suggestion of the Secretary of Commerce, $20,000,000 worth of corn was bought in the United States in 1922 for the purpose of famine relief in Russia. This philanthropic measure was credited in the pamphlet with helping to maintain corn prices at a crucial time. The wheat farmer too was aided by the successful efforts of the Division of Foreign Tariffs [headed by the energetic Henry Chalmers] in alleviating the effects of a European embargo on American wheat.[22]

Hoover's term as Secretary of Commerce began in the midst of the primary post-war depression, when agriculture and the export trade were particularly hard-hit. Even then, he did not hesitate to make his opposition to government stimulation of the economy by deficit financing in such forms as unemployment and relief payments. Hoover felt that an essential answer to the crisis, and one more consonant with American tradition, lay in assisting agriculture and industry to compete with foreign producers. In calling the Economic Conference of September 1921, Hoover asked for measures "to promote business recovery, for the only real and lasting remedy for unemployment is employment. . . . It is not consonant with the spirit of institutions of the American people that a demand should be made upon the public treasury for the solution of every difficulty."[23] Following his lead, the Conference formed a committee on credits for expanding American exports. By then unemployment had risen to five million, but Hoover expected only the private sector of the economy to play a significant part in solving this problem.[24]

22. Herbert Hoover, *How The United States Department of Commerce Serves The Farmer* (Washington, 1923), pp. 7, 9, 10, 14, Commerce Library.
23. Hoover, *Memoirs,* II, 45.
24. *Ibid.,* p. 46. Herbert Hoover, *American Individualism* (New York, 1923), pp. 44-45.

Throughout Hoover's term as Secretary the Department of Commerce spared no effort in acting on the policy that exports were a key to business stability and thus to American prosperity. Agriculture — a weak line in the American economy even after the brief post-war depression — was not ignored in the campaign conducted by Commerce officials and friendly journalists. The Department was credited with helping to increase agricultural exports from the pre-war average of one billion dollars to twice that sum in the period 1922-25 and in finding, when the prospects looked dim, new markets for surplus products such as tobacco and raisins.[25] In what was proclaimed as a "Coal to Newcastle" miracle, the California Rice Growers' Association and a number of lending institutions were saved from disaster when the Department of Commerce found a market in Japan for California's huge rice surplus of 1922. The Commerce Department emphasized that this was no losing operation. Thanks to the efforts of its agents, these surpluses were sold at good prices.[26]

By 1925 Hoover pointed to the fact that American foreign trade had increased by one-third over that of 1913 and boasted that "at least some part of our foreign trade in recent years may fairly be attributed to the increased activity of the Department of Commerce . . . the growth of our service in the promotion of overseas trade." Between 1921 and 1925, Hoover noted, there was a "ten-fold [rise in] demands for services from exporters, merchants, bankers, and others interested in foreign trade." As many as 18,500 firms were "currently receiving foreign-trade service from the department. . . . As an illustration of the results obtained through these services it may be noted that 175 firms to which the department rendered material assistance during 1925 obtained business which reached a total value of $73,000,-000."[27] In an even more generous vain, the National Conference

25. Marcosson, *op. cit.*, p. 50. For an explanation of declines in some agricultural exports see the *Fourteenth Annual Report of the Secretary of Commerce* (Washington, 1926), p. 50.

26. Hoover, *How The United States Department of Commerce Serves The Farmer*, p. 7.

27. *Thirteenth Annual Report of the Secretary of Commerce* (Washington, 1925), p. 39.

of Business Paper Editors (1924) estimated foreign business secured by American firms through the efforts of the Bureau of Foreign and Domestic Commerce at $529,000,000 in the 1923-24 fiscal year — "an ample return to the taxpayer for the $2,600,000 which he invested in the Bureau that year."[28]

Statistics of this type were favorites of those who publicized the efforts of the Department of Commerce. One writer called it "the silent sponsor of our international economic expansion. . . . Through its efforts American overseas business was increased by not less than $500,000,000 during the past twelve months." The same writer also quoted an unnamed Englishman's plaint that "our competition is not so much with American industry as with the American Department of Commerce."[29] One of Hoover's biographers paints the typical commercial attaché as "a super-salesman for American trade in general," speeding to service one of the 2,400,000 inquiries made to the Bureau of Foreign and Domestic Commerce in 1927.[30] More scholarly analysts of the period agree that "during Mr. Hoover's secretaryship from 1921 to 1928 [the] Bureau of Foreign and Domestic Commerce had become a great agency for the promotion of American trade."[31]

At a time when the prevailing Republican emphasis was on curtailment of government expenditure, Hoover succeeded in increasing the Congressional allocations for the foreign activities of his Department.[32] A good part of the explanation for his success here lies not only in his personal reputation for efficiency and integrity, but also in the wide appeal his policies for expanding American influence in the world economy had at the time. The Secretary and his assistants continually stressed the vital

28. *What The Department of Commerce Is Doing For American Business,* p. 4.

29. Marcosson, *op. cit.,* p. 8.

30. Will Irwin, *Herbert Hoover: A Reminiscent Biography* (New York, 1928), pp. 266, 268.

31. William S. Myers and Walter H. Newton, *The Hoover Administration* (New York, 1936), p. 540.

32. For background discussion, see Arthur M. Schlesinger, Jr., *The Age of Roosevelt; The Crisis of the Old Order, 1919-1933* (Boston, 1957), I, 77-87.

services of the overseas field staff which "supplies information and advice . . . conducts investigations . . . adjusts commercial disputes between foreign officials and firms on the one hand and American firms on the other . . . facilitates contacts . . . warns of any illegitimate phases of foreign competition or any possibly discriminatory proposals."[33] There was a practical and urgent appeal in Hoover's final analysis that "only in this way can our exporters be assured of a genuinely secure and permanent position in the world's markets."[34]

Hoover succeeded in combining the business orientation of the times and the popular feeling of national economic self-interest with the broad socio-economic appeal of trade as a source of prosperity for all Americans. The result, at times, was a paradoxical mixture of liberal and restrictive policies. Although the Secretary of Commerce could preach the need for fostering "the increased consuming power of the world . . . [not] supplanting the other fellow,"[35] his Rubber Division worked zealously to develop independent sources of crude rubber under American control and to increase the share of American manufacturers in the sale of tire and rubber specialties abroad.[36]

To a large degree the Department of Commerce measured its success in terms of the expansion of American exports. When it noted an "exceptionally great increase" in the ratio of *imports,* the Department tended to explain this in terms of the country's prosperity and its demand for foreign luxury goods. The high prices charged by foreign combinations for imported raw materials and the low prices of American exports resulting from higher efficiency were also cited by the Department in an attempt to explain away what it considered to be high import ratios.[37]

33. *Thirteenth Annual Report of the Secretary of Commerce,* p. 88.
34. *Ibid.,* p. 42.
35. Hoover, *The Future of Our Foreign Trade,* p. 8.
36. "Exports of U. S. Rubber Manufacturers Set New High Record," *Commerce Reports,* III (July 6, 1925), 20; "Gain in International Tire Trade," *Commerce Reports,* III (Sept. 28, 1925), 739-740; Special Agent Harry N. Whitford, "Rubber and the Philippines," *Foreign Affairs,* IV (July, 1926), 677-679.
37. *Fourteenth Annual Report of the Secretary of Commerce,* p. 50.

Proud mention was made in its official reports whenever the Department "rendered substantial assistance" to American firms desiring government contracts for railroad equipment in Colombia, for example, or when it aided American builders in getting any significant overseas construction awards.[38]

Working with Organized Business

It was Warren G. Harding, however, who helped to set the popular tone of the new administration just before his election as President. In an article, well-summarized by its title, "Less Government in Business and More Business in Government: The Need for a Closer Understanding Between American Government and American Business, and the Economic Benefits that Will Follow It," Harding set down the administration's theme. "We must give government cooperation to business, we must protect American business at home and we must aid and protect it abroad."[39] This principle was executed scrupulously and energetically during Herbert Hoover's tenure as Secretary of Commerce.

Hoover had his own somewhat idealized views of the importance of business in the American economy. He saw it as a manifestation of the traditional "American Individualism," which meant not only efficient production, but also "a constant militant check upon capital becoming a thing to be feared."[40] Secretary Hoover saw in business not only the practical explanation for the highest standard of living in the world, but also the American ideal: "Upon this soil grow those moral and intellectual forces that made our nation great."[41]

Dr. Julius Klein, Director of the Bureau of Foreign and Domestic Commerce, supplemented and helped to carry out the ideas of his chief. Klein's views of the contributions of business

38. *Thirteenth Annual Report of the Secretary of Commerce*, p. 101; *Sixteenth Annual Report of the Secretary of Commerce* (1928), p. 123.
39. Warren G. Harding in *The World's Work*, XLI (Nov. 1920), 25-27.
40. Hoover, *American Individualism*, p. 38.
41. Quoted by Dr. Julius Klein in "Business" in Charles A. Beard, ed., *Whither Mankind* (New York, 1929), pp. 84-85.

were even broader, for he wondered "how much of Western civilization would have been possible . . . [without] the material prosperity" brought by private enterprise. He recognized also the unique achievements of *American* industry in providing employment for an ever-growing labor force and flooding the world's markets with superior goods, services, and credit facilities.[42] Klein considered it particularly significant that the United States after World War I had displaced England as the world's creditor nation. The official Commerce Department interpretation of this fact for the future of America was that just as England had been the center of world trade because of her financial predominance, so the United States would now assume and maintain international economic leadership.[43]

But the emphasis of the Commerce Department under Hoover was not on encouraging world trade in the English liberal economists' sense of stimulating "comparative advantage." If such theories were applied to American trade policy, the United States would buy freely the specialties of foreign producers so that the latter could purchase those commodities in which American producers excelled. Hoover, however, favored a protective tariff to stimulate further domestic production by restricting imports. He was confident that "we can dismiss the fear that our increased tariff would so diminish our total imports as to destroy the ability of other nations to buy from us."[44] The comparison with England of the nineteenth century was further negated by the Department's efforts to bring about American self-sufficiency or to influence world supplies of such major import categories as rubber, sisal, potash, nitrates, camphor, and even coffee.[45]

The work of the Department of Commerce in guiding and assisting American business along the lines of Hoover's policy pronouncements was facilitated by the growing decline of com-

42. *Ibid.*, pp. 96-97, 101.
43. Klein, "How Uncle Sam Stands on Foreign Trade," *System: The Magazine of Business*, XLIX (Feb. 1926), 206.
44. Hoover, *The Future of Our Foreign Trade*, p. 12.
45. Hoover, *Memoirs*, II, 82-83.

petition within the American economy. Hoover recognized, without disapproval, that "business organization is moving strongly toward cooperation. There are in this cooperation great hopes that we can even gain in individuality . . . and at the same time reduce many of the great wastes of over-reckless competition in production and distribution."[46] Hoover's opinion that by a perfectly natural process "we are passing from a period of extremely individualistic action into a period of associational activities" was echoed by Dr. Klein, who praised the manner in which modern business associations "are concentrated upon the modification of the destructive elements in our business life."[47]

Trade Associations were of particular importance in dealing with foreign countries, where the individual American businessman might otherwise have lacked the resources or the information necessary to compete successfully, particularly in those commodity areas where foreign government controls were the major problem   (e.g., Brazilian coffee and Malayan rubber). The Department also took a friendly interest in the organization of these business associations and maintained close contact with their officers. Playing an important part in their respective industries, the associations could not be ignored, either in the routine activities of the Department, or in its special publications.[48]

One example of this type of business-government cooperation is the correspondence between Dr. Klein and Felix Coste, Manager of the National Coffee Roasters Association, concerning an all-embracing coffee-trade association. Director Klein thanked Coste for "the good news that your plans for the National Coffee Council are making progress." He continued: "I just showed the letter to Mr. Hoover, who was much encouraged by it . . . especially if you follow the original proposal of having one

46. Hoover, *American Individualism*, p. 44.
47. Klein, "Business" in *Whither Mankind, op. cit.,* p. 104. Dr. Klein quotes the statement by Hoover.
48. Everet G. Holt (Chief, Rubber Division), *Marketing of Crude Rubber (Trade Promotion Series,* no. 55, 1927), p. 195. All volumes in the *Trade Promotion* and *Economic Series,* as well as the *Trade Information Bulletins,* are publications of the Bureau of Foreign and Domestic Commerce in Washington.

spokesman of the labor element and another from the larger women's organizations [as] representatives of the consumers."[49] The latter suggestion had been made by Hoover and Klein as a wise public relations measure to help dispel the feeling among some consumers that the new association might result in price gouging.[50]

The Department of Commerce, in fact, helped provide the impetus for the creation of a national coffee association. In 1926 a major coffee importer and an active member of the National Coffee Roasters Association wrote to Hoover's office to commend the stand taken by the Secretary of Commerce in favor of cooperative American coffee purchasing as a weapon against Brazil's coffee valorization scheme. He deplored the disunity within the American coffee trade and proposed that a United States coffee syndicate, aided by Federal credit, be formed to fight the Brazilian coffee price-pegging. The reply from Hoover's assistant, J. H. McLafferty, was cool to the credit idea, emphasizing that little could be achieved without unity in the ranks of the trade. "As a rule, the Department of Commerce can not take up controversial trade matters unless a large percentage of the trade is agreed as to what should be done and asks for the type of help which a government department can give."[51] In this and other cases the Department spurred the coffee trade to unite against foreign price controls.

When British restrictions had raised the price of rubber for American importers — and consumers — Hoover held numerous conferences with representatives of the rubber, auto, and oil industries. Moreover, he spearheaded the national campaign to fight British rubber controls, advocating American acquisition and ownership of the raw sources of supply. He also promoted conservation and the use of substitutes wherever pos-

49. Klein to Coste, April 5, 1926, NA, RG 151:351.1 (General).
50. Hoover to E. A. Kahl (Green Coffee Association), San Francisco Chamber of Commerce, March 12, 1926, *ibid.*
51. A. A. Young (National Coffee Roasters Association) to the Department of Commerce, Feb. 2, 1926; J. H. McLafferty to Young, Feb. 19, 1926, *ibid.*

sible.[52] Under his leadership the Rubber Association of America and the heads of the major rubber and tire companies formed "the Unofficial Committee to cooperate with the crude rubber investigation" to find alternate sources of rubber.[53] Long before these measures were adopted, The Rubber Association of America had been receiving, "for guarded dissemination," confidential Commerce reports on such subjects as British and Dutch Government views concerning rubber restrictions.[54]

Advice on the rubber "emergency" flowed from the Department of Commerce through the newspapers, its own publications, and especially the business press. The influential trade journal, *The Rubber Age,* always gave prominent notice to press releases by "Secretary of Commerce Herbert Hoover, who instigated the conservation [of rubber] campaign and has steadfastly maintained his interest in it." In an editorial, filled with praise, the journal cited "Secretary Hoover's opinion [that] the saving in rubber, due to the resistance of American consumers to the high prices caused by British restriction legislation, amounted to no less than 72,500 tons [in 1926]."[55]

Hoover's approval of the idea of legalized American import combinations of commodities controlled by foreign governments was consistently championed by *The India Rubber World,* another important trade publication. The latter also backed enthusiastically the Department of Commerce's search for American-controlled sources of rubber.[56]

In the pages of an outstanding business magazine Director Klein himself lectured American exporters on advertising, packing methods, and other means of attracting the foreign buyer.

52. Draft of Hoover's address to the Cleveland conference of rubber, auto, and oil industry leaders, May 6, 1924, NA, RG 151:621.2 (Rubber Investigation).

53. H. H. Whitford (Chief, Crude Rubber Section) to A. L. Viles (General Manager, The Rubber Association of America), May 13, 1924, *ibid.*

54. P. L. Palmerton (Chief, Rubber Division) to A. L. Viles, Feb. 19, 1923, NA, RG 151:254.

55. Both quotations from *The Rubber Age* (New York), XXI (April 10, 1927), 9.

56. *The India Rubber World* (New York), LXXIII (Nov. 1, 1925), 63; LXXIII (Feb. 1, 1926), 254; LXXII (Sept. 1, 1926), 709-712.

He warned that "implicit guarantees of delivery and service" were often more important than price cuts; American exporters must continue to offer "quality" and new business techniques.[57] Klein's general tone displayed the national optimism of the Department of Commerce: European recovery will not interfere with the expansion of American export markets. "Markets . . . can be found and in fact are being found every day for American industries, large and small, through the agency of the Department of Commerce."[58]

The publications of the Department offered a wealth of business information at nominal cost, or no cost at all. *Commerce Reports* presented detailed surveys of economic opportunities abroad by geographical areas and by specific commodities; to these was added the valuable monthly supplement, *Survey of Current Business. What The World Wants* featured requests for American goods, especially from foreign buyers of manufactures. On the other hand, agricultural interests were served by the periodical publications, *Foodstuffs Around the World, Foreign Notes on Meats, Fats, Oils and Live Stock,* and *Trade and Crop Notes.* Of most lasting value are the more ambitious publications — such as the occasional *Trade Information Bulletins,* regional handbooks, the *Monthly Summary of Foreign Commerce, etc.* Nor can the direct contacts with business provided by the *Exporters' Index* of the Department of Commerce be ignored. This *Index* included the names of thousands of American firms receiving from Commerce confidential information valuable in dealing with foreign firms (such as carefully revised lists of foreign firms facing bankruptcy or liquidation).[59]

System: The Magazine of Business, a leading business monthly of the 1920's, paid the Department of Commerce an appropriate compliment when it summarized some aspects of its functions on behalf of the business community. The magazine reserved

57. Klein, "How Uncle Sam Stands on Foreign Trade." *op. cit.,* pp. 205-206.
58. *Ibid.,* p. 308.
59. Hoover, *Thirteenth Annual Report of the Secretary of Commerce,* p. 127.

for the Commerce Department a regular feature titled "What Washington Offers Business This Month," repeating in each issue the following explanation: "It [the Department of Commerce] is 'the business man's department of the government' so completely staffed that you need to spend nothing for many services and varied types of information."[60] When a new Secretary of Commerce took over the Department in 1929, he could well comment on the "better relations between government and business . . . due to the man who was the head of this Department for nearly eight years — and who is now our President."[61]

60. *System: The Magazine of Business,* L (Dec. 1926), 712, contains typical illustrations of the Department's work in aiding American exports, ranging from the market for lamps in India to the export of automobiles with right-hand drive to Europe.

61. Secretary Robert P. Lamont, quoted by Theodore G. Joslin, "Eighty Thousand Weekly," *The World's Work,* LIX (July, 1930), 108. The article's title refers to the number of inquiries made of the Department of Commerce.

CHAPTER II

THE SECRETARY OF COMMERCE IN THE NATION AND IN THE CABINET: BUSINESS AND AMERICAN WELFARE

A National Figure

While this study does not intend to present either a political or biographical treatise of Herbert Hoover's career, some brief comments on his place in the American scene of the 1920's should help to explain the impact of Hoover's policies in the Department of Commerce. This becomes especially apparent when one considers the political repercussions of his two major contributions in the field of international economic relations — the struggle he led against price controls in essential raw materials and his formulation of a policy to regulate the flow of American capital abroad. The man who was elected President in 1928 by "an overwhelming majority" — and without a "personal political machine" — did possess the advantage of eight years in the national limelight as Secretary of Commerce.[1]

Indeed, Hoover's prestige dated back to his efficient administration of American relief in Europe during and after World War I. Long recognized as an outstanding international engineer and businessman, his activities during the war gained for him as well almost universal appeal as a humanitarian. A much-

1. Eugene Lyons, *Our Unknown Ex-President* (New York, 1948), p. 235. This "Portrait of Herbert Hoover" is rather favorably colored. Hoover's work as Secretary of Commerce is usually summarized in glittering generalities by all of his biographers. No scholarly analysis of Hoover's role as a Cabinet officer has been published to date.

quoted comment by John Maynard Keynes, who attended the Versailles Peace Conference, testified that "Mr. Hoover was the only man who emerged from the ordeal of Paris with an enhanced reputation."[2]

It was small wonder that in becoming a "household name in the United States" before the 1920 presidential elections, the American Relief Administrator should attract the attention of political scouts.[3] The Hoover enthusiasts of 1920 were primarily Democrats and liberals, who looked to the forthcoming elections with growing pessimism. Typical of the progressive elements which worked for Hoover's nomination for President was Vernon L. Kellogg, a science professor from the West, and an official of the American Relief Administration. Kellogg drew a picture of political Washington tied in the bonds of inertia and expediency: no wonder the Washington politicians did not want Hoover, he said, for he "is very clearly not one of them, nor is he a man to be controlled by them."[4]

At a time when Americans were conscious of the upheavals in Germany and Russia, Kellogg could see the United States "entering on our own particular revolution" in which men of Hoover's caliber — efficient and above politics — would replace the tradition-bound politicians, those "personifications of our own indolence and intolerance." Viewed in this manner, Hoover's "independence" and "common sense" represented to liberals like Kellogg the nobler side of America, the "personification of our impatience with the old, all too old, order" of circus politics. Hoover, promised Kellogg, would do away with "those mysterious draperies from which the illusionist-politician extracts white rabbits and full dinner pails."[5]

2. Quoted in Herbert Corey, *The Truth About Hoover* (Boston, 1932), pp. 5, 131; Arthur M. Schlesinger, Jr., *The Roosevelt Years* (Boston, 1957), I, 81; see also Lyons, *op. cit.,* p. 197.

3. Schlesinger, *op. cit.,* p. 80.

4. Vernon L. Kellogg, "Washington Five and Eight O'Clocks," *The Yale Review,* IX (April, 1920), 458.

5. *Ibid.,* pp. 459-460. For a more ambitious propaganda effort, see Kellogg's biographical *Herbert Hoover, the Man and His Work* (New York, 1920), a study which led the way for other Hoover biographers in the 1920's.

Acting on their belief in the Hoover appeal hopeful Democrats in Virginia and California organized "Make-Hoover-Presi-
dent-Clubs." But Virginia's Carter Glass, a politically wise
ex-Congressman and Wilson's Secretary of the Treasury, commented dourly that Hoover would not be nominated by either
party because he had no definite political affiliations.[6]

Other Democrats were more outspokenly in favor of Hoover.
For example, Franklin Delano Roosevelt wrote early in 1920:
"I had some talks with Herbert Hoover before he went West
for Christmas. He is certainly a wonder, and I wish we could
make him President of the United States. There could not be
a better one."[7] Franklin K. Lane, Louis D. Brandeis, and other
prominent figures favored Hoover, too, especially when he
declared for ratifying the Versailles treaty without serious reser-
vations. The liberal press participating in the pro-Hoover movement was well represented by Herbert Croly's New Republic,
as well as the New York World.[8]

Hoover permitted his name to be entered in a few presidential primaries of both major parties, but one might well argue
with the conclusion of Samuel H. Adams, a serious analyst of
the 1920's, that he "made quite a showing."[9] The Republican
Convention of 1920 gave him only six votes after he declared
himself a Republican.[10] It may be true that "Hoover's humanitarian work . . . had endeared him to thousands of his fellow
countrymen. . . . Had the issue been left to the mass of the
voters, he might well have been the nominee in 1920."[11] The
fact is that his organized support came from groups which were

6. Carter Glass, quoted in Rixey Smith and Norman Beasley, Carter Glass
(New York, 1939), pp. 204-205.

7. F. D. R. letter to Hugh Gibson, Jan. 2, 1920, quoted in Frank Freidel,
Franklin D. Roosevelt (Boston, 1954), II, 57.

8. Lyons, op. cit., p. 199; Schlesinger, op. cit., I, 81-82.

9. Samuel H. Adams, Incredible Era (Boston, 1939), p. 153.

10. William A. White, A Puritan In Babylon (New York, 1938), pp. 201,
211; Freidel, op. cit., p. 60.

11. Samuel H. Adams, op. cit., p. 134. Claude M. Fuess, Calvin Coolidge,
The Man From Vermont (Boston, 1940), p. 248, cites the 1920 Literary Digest
poll showing Hoover as one of the most popular Presidential candidates in that
year.

none too powerful in American politics of 1920. Hoover himself objected to some of the efforts of his "politically amateur friends" who refused to recognize that he "could not be nominated by either party."[12] The image of the Quaker engineer as a potential candidate for the White House remained, however, a potent one throughout the 1920's. That image influenced both the defenders and the opponents of his policies.[13]

That Hoover could expand the functions of the Department of Commerce and assume a leading cabinet role was possible because of the very fact that he was a prominent national figure, even before the "Prosperity Decade" began. In his ideology of individualism and in his national outlook, especially in foreign relations, Hoover reflected the shifting patterns which prevailed in the United States of the post-war decade. He also represented the success of American business methods through his own personal example and as a result of his proclamation that America's leadership in material progress meant "equality of opportunity" for all. In that sense, one might agree with Edwin Emerson that "He is an exemplar of his age. . . ."[14] Herein lay much of the strength of Hoover as Secretary of Commerce.

Hoover In The Cabinet And In The Eyes Of The Nation

Warren G. Harding, basking in the glow of the Republican landslide which followed his easy front-porch campaign for a return to "normalcy," was perfectly aware of Hoover's popularity and ability. His precise motives for appointing Hoover to the Department of Commerce, however, cannot be determined readily. Harding's best biographer, Samuel H. Adams, explained the selection of Hoover on the grounds that "for once Harding was sensitive to public opinion and opposed to party

12. Hoover, *Memoirs*, II, 34.
13. *Congressional Record*, 68 Cong., 1 Sess., pp. 7624-7626 (May 1, 1924); 70 Cong., 1 Sess., p. 5996 (April 5, 1928); *The New York Times*, June 17, 1928.
14. Edwin Emerson, *Hoover and His Times* (Garden City, New York, 1932), p. xi; Hoover, *American Individualism*, p. 47.

pressure . . . [and] sincerely admired him."[15] Arthur M. Schlesinger, Jr., in his own analysis of "The Old Order," wrote that Hoover was offered a choice of the Department of Commerce or the Department of Interior as a reward for supporting the Republican ticket: "Hoover chose Commerce on condition that he would have a voice in all important economic policies, whether in the field of business or foreign affairs."[16] Both views appear to be essentially correct; a man of Hoover's stature undoubtedly could be counted on to strengthen the new Administration.

Segments of the liberal press explained Hoover's acceptance of a cabinet post under Harding in terms of the selfless devotion to duty of a man who would not surrender his ideals for the honors of office. "The conditions laid down by Mr. Hoover for his acceptance of the Secretaryship of Commerce," declared *The Weekly Review,* "will come as a shock to the professional politicians who conceive of all men as eager for office and who can not understand the attitude of the man who thinks first of all of its responsibilities and opportunities." Internationally-minded Americans hoped that Hoover would bring engineering efficiency into government for the purpose of achieving the reconstruction of the world. With his broad experience in foreign enterprises, he was expected to bring a spirit of cooperation into the world's economic affairs.[17]

Some "progressives" even continued to feel that Hoover "represented, if anyone did, the liberal sentiment" in the Republican cabinets of the 1920's — as somewhat of a counter-balance to the conservative Andrew Mellon, Secretary of the Treasury.[18] Only Hoover and Mellon remained in their respective posts throughout the Harding and Coolidge administrations. Hoover, Mellon, and Secretary of State Charles Evans Hughes were

15. Adams, *op. cit.,* p. 205.
16. Schlesinger, *op. cit.,* I, 82. Hoover, *Memoirs,* II, 36, supports this conclusion.
17. "Hooverizing the Department of Commerce," editorial in *The Weekly Review,* IV (March 9, 1921), 216.
18. William A. White, *op. cit.,* p. 250.

often mentioned as the only "indubitably strong" members of Harding's cabinet.[19]

Far from becoming the cabinet spokesman of progressive ideas or of internationalism alone, Hoover played a sincere and loyal part in helping to determine and explain the policies of Republican "normalcy." For one thing, his disillusionment with European conflicts, the horrors of World War I, and the vindictiveness of Versailles, caused him to re-affirm the ideology of American nationalism. Hoover believed "that there is a world of difference between the principles and spirit of Old World individualism and that which we have developed in our own country. We have, in fact, a special social system of our own . . . [which] abhors autocracy . . . [and] aims to provide opportunity for self-expression, not merely economically, but spiritually as well."[20] This pattern of American ideals could only be threatened, according to Hoover, by the "malign social forces . . . both of reaction and radicalism" coming from abroad.[21]

These opinions were contained in a significant little book, *American Individualism*, written by Hoover in 1922; it reflected the values of the "American way" which were to guide the new Secretary of Commerce. Before the book's publication, Hoover warned of the potential dangers posed by a powerful League of Nations to the traditional American ideals of self-sufficient individualism: "I see no reason why such a body should have any power that leads to supergovernment, or that in any way minimizes the very essential principle of nationalism upon which our patriotism and progress is founded."[22] This stand alienated some of his "internationalist" supporters. Soon, as an outstanding member of the Harding administration, Hoover was also to be included in the liberals' criticism of Republican policies on inter-allied debts.[23]

19. Claude M. Fuess, *op. cit.*, p. 288.
20. Hoover, *American Individualism*, pp. 12, 37.
21. *Ibid.*, p. 67.
22. Hoover during the 1920 campaign, quoted in William S. Myers, *The Foreign Policies of Herbert Hoover, 1929-1933* (New York, 1940), p. 20.
23. "An Opportunity Missed," editorial in *The New Republic*, XXVII (July 27, 1921), 229-230.

Republican insistence on the repayment of debts due from America's wartime allies was censured by "liberal-international- ist" opinion as an unjustifiable hindrance to European recovery. Did the Republicans fear "to tweak the money nerve of the American people," who might think "that our government had let itself be worked by the British"? So chided the *New Re- public,* which believed Americans would prefer to assure the cause of peace, rather than "cling to this very dubious mass of paper [the European war debts]."[24] But the new Secretary of Commerce concluded that the repayment of these obligations to the United States was quite feasible. Moreover, he deplored the over-generous attitude of "many Americans who loved Europe more and America less."[25]

As head of the Department of Commerce, Hoover was in a strategic position to carry out these views. Hoover's European Division Chief, Alan G. Goldsmith, seemed to echo the pre- vailing nationalistic mood in the country and in the Department when he criticized the efforts of an American banker to ease the Government's war-debt policy: "In my opinion," wrote Goldsmith, "Mr. [Fred I.] Kent [Bankers' Trust Company, New York; Federal Reserve Board official, and representative to the Reparations Commission] has too much the European point of view and is perhaps willing to use their [sic] methods to an extent that the average American would not tolerate."[26]

On the issue of war debts and in other major areas of public controversy, Secretaries Hoover, Mellon, and Hughes worked together to execute the Republican policy.[27] There was thus no "liberal" dissension within the cabinet. Hoover thought highly of most of his colleagues; some of them, like Mellon and Hughes, he considered to be qualified "above the others," and

24. *Ibid.*
25. Hoover, *Memoirs,* II, 179.
26. European Division Chief Alan G. Goldsmith to Assistant Secretary of Commerce Christian A. Herter, January 5, 1923, NA, RG 151:640 (United Kingdom).
27. Secretary of State Charles Evans Hughes to Herbert Hoover, Jan. 5, 1925, NA, RG 151:640 (Interallied Debts); Secretary of the Treasury Andrew Mellon to Herbert Hoover, January 8, 1925, *Ibid.*

several "went out of their way on many occasions to further [his] work."[28]

Bolshevik Russia very early provided another basis for some disillusioned liberals to criticize Hoover and the Administration. Editorially, *The Nation* accused Hoover of concealing from the American people the real need for relief in Russia by suppressing the cables of his own representative in Moscow. Apparently, most of the contention stemmed from a report by the Secretary of Commerce that Russia had a grain surplus for export; the report, claimed *The Nation*, "almost stopped receipts of the independent relief agencies."[29]

Hoover's supporters replied by citing the inadequate cooperation given by the Communist authorities to American relief missions, an argument which was promptly denied by the liberal opposition. Hoover himself proclaimed that American relief had saved "the lives of ten million" Russians, but emphasized that endless charity was not enough. Russia, he said, must find a lasting solution to her problems by restoring the "productivity . . . destroyed in her social experiment."[30]

In spite of his abhorrence of the Soviet's "social experiment," Hoover had opposed the economic blockade of Russia. This attitude stemmed from his belief in "cold economics" as a salve for the world's ills and a feeling that it would do good "for the world to lift the curtain on this new experiment in economics."[31] As early as 1922, he acted as intermediary with the State Department on behalf of several American companies which were interested in resuming business activities with Russia. Replying to a Hoover note, Secretary of State Hughes mentioned his own

28. Hoover, *Memoirs*, II, 40.
29. "Mr. Hoover Stabs Russia," editorial in *The Nation*, CXVI (March 21, 1923), 327.
30. Herbert Hoover quoted in David Hinshaw, *Herbert Hoover: American Quaker* (New York, 1950), p. 405. This book offers an excellent and convincing account of Mr. Hoover's valuable relief work. It contains useful appendixes including, among others, the text of the resolution of thanks to Hoover by the "Council of Commissars" and a letter of thanks from Maxim Gorky.
31. Hoover quoted in *ibid.*, p. 405.

personal misgivings about the venture, although he considered the firms free to act at their own risk.[32]

Another issue which involved Hoover in controversy throughout the 1920's was the old, traditional one of American politics: the tariff and America's international balance of payments. A committee of the Council on Foreign Relations oversimplified Hoover's economic foreign policy when it concluded that increasing "the opportunity for profit of American business abroad for its own sake, without other ulterior objective . . . has been the motive especially associated with the activities of Mr. Hoover."[33] Actually, in assisting the export of American goods and capital, Hoover espoused a much broader "ulterior" objective — that of augmenting the prosperity and national standing of the United States. This goal could be achieved, according to Hoover, within the framework of "American Individualism" by adding to the latter a feeling of "public service" and "public responsibility."[34] One of the means of implementing this broad policy of national self-interest was the protective tariff, to which Hoover assigned no small credit — for America's prosperity.[35] Republican tariff protectionism, though it was criticized by some at the time as a restraint on economic freedom, was explained by Hoover in terms of the compensation and benefits it yielded to workers, farmers, and business.[36]

There was yet another form of government protection defended on the grounds of national interest, one which depended much more on Hoover's initiative and support than did the protective tariff. This type of intervention involved the creation of machinery to regulate foreign security issues in the American

32. For additional details and the text of the Hughes letter see: Merlo J. Pusey, *Charles Evans Hughes* (New York, 1951), II, 526.

33. James W. Angell (for the Council on Foreign Relations), *Financial Foreign Policy of the United States* (New York, 1933), p. 126.

34. Hoover, *American Individualism*, p. 43; Walter F. Dexter, *Herbert Hoover and American Individualism* (New York, 1932), pp. 180-181.

35. Hoover, *The New Day* (Stanford, 1928), p. 138.

36. Ray L. Wilbur and Arthur M. Hyde, *The Hoover Policies* (New York, 1937), p. 181. Although this is primarily a study of Hoover as President, there are many useful references to his Secretaryship.

market. Setting the tone of administration policy as early as 1921, Hoover demanded definite standards to govern the approval of American loans to foreign borrowers. In 1922 he wrote Hughes of his conviction that the federal government had certain unavoidable "governmental and moral responsibilities toward these operations, and that our bankers [had] certain internal responsibilities to our commerce."[37]

In making proposals of this type Hoover generally received the backing of his cabinet colleagues and of President Harding. Machinery for governmental approval of foreign loan issues was centered in the departments of Commerce and State, although the loan controls then in existence were more moderate than those originally proposed by Hoover.[38] President Coolidge, whom Hoover considered "a real conservative, probably the equal of Benjamin Harrison," weakened the Federal apparatus of credit restraints.[39] But his Secretary of Commerce continued to wield great pressure on behalf of controlling foreign loans, through public addresses, press releases, and the every-day functions of the Commerce Department.[40]

Warren G. Harding was wont to consult Secretary Hoover frequently on all economic problems. Characteristic of the attitude of the professional politician toward the engineer-businessman in his cabinet was Harding's comment that "Hoover is the damnedest smartest man I have ever met."[41] When Calvin Coolidge first became President, he also stated publicly his respect for the Secretary of Commerce:

37. Hoover, *Memoirs,* II, 14, 86.

38. *Ibid.,* II, 47, 88; Herbert Feis, *The Diplomacy of the Dollar* (Baltimore, 1950), pp. 8-9, presents a succinct analysis of this issue.

39. Hoover, *Memoirs,* II, 56.

40. A valuable review of the problems involved in passing on foreign loans is contained in the lengthy report from Secretary of State Frank B. Kellogg to Herbert Hoover, Jan. 9, 1928, NA, RG 151:640 (General). Pertinent details on the parts played in foreign loan machinery by Hoover, other Cabinet members, Harding and Coolidge, are also contained in Hoover, *Memoirs,* II, 47, 56, 85, 89, 177; Wilbur and Hyde, *op. cit.,* p. 353; George W. Edwards, "Government Control of Foreign Investments," *The American Economic Review,* XVIII (Dec. 1928), 684-701.

41. Quoted in Hinshaw, *op. cit.,* p. 136. See also Lyons, *op. cit.,* p. 227; Hoover, *Memoirs,* II, 36.

Measured by accomplishment and ability Herbert Hoover holds com-
manding rank. If five Americans were to be selected on the basis of merit
and ability to devise remedies for the present condition of the world—
Herbert Hoover's name would head the list.[42]

Nevertheless, Coolidge resisted some of Hoover's more ambitious projects, partly from fear of tampering with the "Coolidge
Prosperity," partly because of his conservative ideas regarding
the limited functions of government.[43] It is also possible to spec-
ulate that political rivalry between the two men toward the close
of Coolidge's last term lay behind his sarcastic characterization
of the Secretary of Commerce as "the wonder boy . . . the
miracle worker."[44]

Whether or not Coolidge actually hoped to be "drafted" for
a new term in 1928 is debatable, but on the question of the
relationship between the President and his cabinet, Coolidge
was far more explicit. He said: "The Presidency is primarily an
executive office. . . . The ideal way for it to function is to assign
to the various positions men of sufficient ability so that they
can solve all the problems that arise under their jurisdiction."[45]
This dictum applied rather well to Herbert Hoover's career as
Secretary of Commerce. His energy, tireless zeal, and acknowl-
edged ability always made themselves felt in government policy
of the 1920's. He was not hampered by any narrow interpretation of his "jurisdiction," whether it be made by the Chief Executive or by the Congress.

Hoover stood out among the other Cabinet members as a
man of positive opinions and a man with a record of efficiency
to uphold. To many he was the "incarnation of Prosperity";
some opposed him as the symbol of a time when "the economic
élite and political leaders were closely identified."[46] But Hoover

42. Quoted in Hinshaw, *op. cit.,* p. 136.
43. Lyons, *op. cit.,* 229; Hoover, *Memoirs,* II, 226, 230.
44. President Coolidge quoted in White, *op. cit.,* p. 353.
45. Calvin Coolidge, *The Autobiography of Calvin Coolidge* (New York,
1929), p. 196. See also: Schlesinger, *op. cit.,* I, 87.
46. Alpheus T. Mason, in Foreword to Prothro, James W., *The Dollar
Decade; Business Ideas in the 1920's* (Baton Rouge, 1954), p. vii. See also the
excellent analysis in chapter VII of George Soule's *Prosperity Decade* (New
York, 1947), volume VIII of Henry David, *et al.,* eds., *The Economic History
of the United States* (New York, 1945 — in progress).

proclaimed that "American Individualism" was vastly different from the "capitalism" of the nineteenth century. It differed
specifically from the *laissez-faire* doctrines of Adam Smith's fol-
lowers. As proof of this he pointed to the regulatory and anti-
trust legislation whose purpose was to prevent an "autocracy
of economic power."[47] The objective of American government,
Hoover preached, was not to aid a favored class but to assure
"social justice" and "opportunity" to all Americans.[48]

In Hoover's scheme of things, government had a specific and
constructive part to play in broadening the "opportunity" for
every American to improve his position. But, in the economic
sphere, he defined "opportunity" in terms of self-help. "Aided
by the guiding hand of public officials, private enterprise was
to be fostered and added opportunity offered to more and more
persons in the field of competition."[49] The Secretary of Commerce saw good coming from government action along these
lines only as long as it was not "destructive of individual
initiative."[50]

Illustrations of this kind of government activity were not lacking under Hoover's Secretaryship. In numerous addresses he
proudly cited the "assistance which the government has given
to the great expansion of our export trade through searching out
opportunity for American goods abroad." The work of his Department of Commerce in answering a multitude of requests for
aid by American business was singled out by Hoover as a proper
"index of what the Federal Government's contribution has
been."[51] Business-oriented publicists never tired of explaining
how the Bureau of Foreign and Domestic Commerce had become the "chief information agency of the American exporter:
It was reorganized by Secretary Hoover so as to function in

47. Hoover, *American Individualism*, p. 53.
48. *Ibid.;* Edgar E. Robinson, *The Roosevelt Leadership* (New York, 1955), pp. 30, 37.
49. Robinson, *op. cit.*, p. 36.
50. Hoover, *Memoirs*, II, 174.
51. Hoover address in Boston, October 15, 1928, *The New Day*, p. 122.

closer harmony with the key industries and trade bodies of the country."[52]

The managers of industry were fully appreciative of the fact that "Secretary of Commerce Herbert Hoover has given constructive government leadership to American business, and has been able to bring about confidence on the part of all groups in the business community in the real desire of the government to promote their interests in a broad and practical way."[53] But it would be gross injustice to Hoover to conclude that he was the servant of entrepreneurial "class" interests. His Department's services were offered for the good of the American nation as Hoover saw it. Not only was "business" implicit in the very name of the Commerce Department, but it was also the basis for American "standards of living and comfort." Hoover emphasized that "capital" was increasingly becoming democratic and, in some measure, even the property of the "people" through such modern developments as mass ownership of stock.[54]

It was a prime objective of the Hoover policies to fortify American self-reliance in a world that often appeared hostile. For example, Hoover consistently worked "for strengthening the private merchant marine as a measure of defense." To meet foreign competition, he proposed Federal outlays totalling as much as $10,000,000 to "make the difference between profit and loss for most of our trade routes."[55] Only in this way could Hoover consider the United States safe "from discrimination and from combinations which would impose onerous freight rates."[56] He cited at least twenty sea routes as merely extensions of inland American waterways. These routes, he felt, should be served by "very substantial shipping under the American flag"; the private operators were to be assisted through more liberal government

52. National Conference of Business Paper Editors, *What the Department of Commerce is Doing for American Business* (Washington, 1924), p. 16.

53. Charles Clifton (President, National Automobile Chamber of Commerce) quoted in *Industrial Management*, LXXI (April, 1926), 200.

54. Hoover, *American Individualism*, pp. 39-41, 57.

55. Letter from Hoover to President Coolidge, Nov. 21, 1927, quoted in William S. Myers, *The Foreign Policies of Herbert Hoover*, pp. 111-112.

56. Hoover, *The Future of Our Foreign Trade*, p. 13.

mail contracts.[57] By thus aiding business, Hoover maintained, America would also strengthen her national defenses.

In the Congressional hearings on foreign "monopolies," held in 1926, the Republican majority agreed with Hoover that the United States must seek sources of essential raw materials "under its own flag." Otherwise, they concurred, Americans would be at the mercy of foreign manipulators.[58] This policy of encouraging independent supplies of imported commodities was not, however, divorced from the traditions of private enterprise championed by Hoover and by the Republican Party. The Congressional investigators of 1926 agreed that "the governmental facilities of the United States should freely assist," but they left it to private American capital to achieve the cherished goal of national self-sufficiency. Harvey S. Firestone's rubber plantations in Liberia were cited favorably in the Committee report as an illustration of this principle.[59]

The Hoover policies as Secretary of Commerce met with little opposition from the Republican majorities in Congress. But Democrats like Representative Ralph F. Lozier (Missouri) continued to attack Hoover for ignoring American "monopolies" while criticizing the controls exercised by the British rubber combination. Lozier's burden of complaint was Hoover's affinity for the interests of organized business: "In Mr. Hoover, versatile, adroit and sagacious, we have the greatest diplomat that ever served big business."[60] Democratic Representative Ashton C. Shallenberger (Nebraska) made Lozier's charges even more specific by claiming that Hoover's fight against British rubber controls played into the hands of American tire manufacturers who raised their prices to an exorbitant level. They were encouraged to do so, according to Shallenberger, by Department of

57. *Ibid.;* Hoover, *A Merchant Marine Policy* (Washington, 1925), pp. 4-5, Commerce Library pamphlet (address of Nov. 16, 1925).

58. House Committee on Interstate and Foreign Commerce, *Preliminary Report on Crude Rubber, Coffee, etc.,* Report #555, 69 Cong., 1 Sess. (Washington, March 13, 1926), p. 13.

59. *Ibid.,* p. 13-14.

60. Ralph F. Lozier, quoted in *The New York Times,* Feb. 19, 1926.

Commerce publicity which impressed the public with the gravity of the rubber shortage.[61]

There was even, though numerically small, a *Republican* anti-Hoover faction among the representatives of the farm states and within the feeble remnants of the older "progressive" bloc. To some degree, this opposition stemmed from the fact that American agriculture found itself in a depressed condition amidst the general economic prosperity of the 1920's. It is not surprising, therefore, that the farmer should have felt neglected by administations which repeatedly refused to accept such farm relief measures as those proposed by the Farm bloc in Congress, (for example, the McNary-Haugen bills). Much of this resentment was turned against Hoover, who seemed intent on aiding industry, commerce, and finance, but not agriculture. Republican Representative Edward J. King (Illinois), on occasion, would excoriate Hoover as "the master adviser of mass money," and a traitor to the rest of America.[62]

Congressmen from the farm areas also feared foreign retaliation against American farm products, if Hoover's proposal to permit American buying pools in imported raw materials were enacted. In the Congressional debates, many representatives from the farm areas often expressed their distrust of Hoover and his proposals.[63] Perhaps this explains why there was so little strength in Hoover's candidacy as a possible "progressive" nominee for President in 1928.[64]

In truth, there was not much that Hoover could do for the American farmer (aside from supplying information and research services). In sharp contrast with business, American agriculture was still characterized by a multitude of independent and unorganized producers. Short of drastic legislative relief, little could be done to alleviate the effects on the American farmer of

---

61. *Ibid.,* March 16, 1926.

62. Edward J. King, quoted in *The New York Times,* March 20, 1926. For the problems of agriculture in this period, see: George Soule, *Prosperity Decade,* chapters V and XI.

63. *Congressional Record,* 70 Cong., 1 Sess., pp. 5980, 5983, 5984 (April 5, 1928).

64. William Allen White, *A Puritan in Babylon,* pp. 339-340.

world market and crop conditions. Official Commerce Department publications did present useful agricultural data, and issues of *Commerce Reports* repeatedly expressed concern over the decline in farm exports. Widely distributed pamphlets like *How The United States Department of Commerce Serves The Farmer* (1923) illustrated the excellent public relations efforts of the Department in this area. More substantial action on behalf of agriculture, however, had to await Congressional action.[65]

It was easier for the Department of Commerce under Hoover to emphasize its assistance to the large manufacturers of agricultural machinery and to publicize its achievements on behalf of the American consumer of *foreign* agricultural products. As early as 1922 the Department's Agricultural Implements Division, organized by Hoover, was actively seeking buyers abroad for American-made farm equipment.[66] In addition, the well-organized campaign of the Department of Commerce to protect the American consumer of rubber against British price controls paid rich dividends in popularity for Hoover and his Department. Similarly acclaimed were the Department's successful attempts to stop the misbranding of coffee by South American planters, a practice which, according to estimates of the Commerce Department, had cost the American consumer millions of dollars over a period of years.[67]

In the spring of 1927 nation-wide publicity was again focused on Secretary Hoover as he directed the battle against the "unprecedented" Mississippi flood. About 1,500,000 people were made homeless in an area covering a half-dozen states. As a result of his efforts, Hoover could report that "only three lives . . . were lost after we took charge."[68] His efficient relief and

65. Soule, *op. cit.*, p. 249.

66. Article by George Bell (Chief, Agricultural Implements Division), *Commerce Reports*, Feb. 26, 1923, p. 543. For an illustration of information services to the non-industrial economy, see: Department of Commerce, *Survey of Current Business*, Jan. 1923, pp. 49, 51.

67. *Thirteenth Annual Report of the Secretary of Commerce*, p. 101; letter to Hoover from William H. Ukers (editor of *The Tea and Coffee Trade Journal*), Jan. 18, 1926, NA, RG 151:351.1 (General).

68. Hoover, *Memoirs*, II, 125.

rescue work in the Mississippi Valley recalled the vivid picture of
the humanitarian American Relief Administrator of World War
I days, giving of himself to save the lives of millions. Before the
end of his term, Secretary Hoover and his policies had achieved
a firm and largely favorable position in the American mind.[69]

In the same year (1927) Hoover received more favorable attention in the eastern cities for his criticism of the data on which
the National Origins Immigration Act was based and the principles on which it was to operate. This law restricted immigration into the United States on the basis of quotas assigned to
foreign countries which were limited to two per cent of their
nationals living in the United States in 1890. Hoover implied the
need for a more equitable and judicious formula for regulating
immigration.[70]

Hoover also obtained in 1927 a personal vote of confidence
from the influential Kansas Senator Arthur Capper, who asked
that the government-owned shipping lines, then operated at a
loss, be turned over to the management of the Secretary of Commerce. Hoover declined this offer, pleading that he was as concerned with the welfare of the private merchant marine as with
the success of the government lines; he could not, therefore, devote himself exclusively to government shipping. The affair
caused the editor of *Commerce and Finance* to comment caus-
tically that "if this tendency to pass the buck to Hoover continues
at the present rate, President Coolidge may soon be able to close
all the other departments in Washington in the interest of economy."[71] There is no doubt as to the very significant influence of
Hoover on the American scene even before 1928.

One of Hoover's colleagues in the Harding and Coolidge administrations, S. Parker Gilbert, an Under-Secretary of the
Treasury and Agent-General for German Reparations, appropri-

69. Emerson, *Hoover and His Times,* pp. 207-210; White, *A Puritan in
Babylon,* p. 340; Hoover, *Memoirs,* II, 125-131.

70. Emerson, *op. cit.,* pp. 238-239; John Higham, *Strangers In The Land*
(New Brunswick, New Jersey, 1955), pp. 322-324; Robert A. Divine, *American Immigration Policy, 1924-1952* (New Haven, 1957), pp. 31, 40-41.

71. Quoted in Emerson, *op. cit.,* p. 264.

ately remarked that Hoover was "Secretary of Commerce and Under-Secretary of all other departments."[72] Hoover made excellent use of the vast publicity resources available to the Secretary of Commerce to bring attention to those policies which he felt were necessary to the welfare of the United States. James L. McCamy, in his scholarly study of government influence on public opinion, wrote that "administrative publicity in its contemporary scope is generally said to have reached maturity under the secretaryship of Mr. Hoover." McCamy also noted that Hoover "became president, some say, on the foundation of a reputation which was not damaged in any way by the Department of Commerce press agents."[73]

72. S. Parker Gilbert (Under-Secretary of the Treasury and Agent-General for German Reparations), quoted in Schlesinger, *op. cit.,* I, 84.

73. James L. McCamy, *Government Publicity* (Chicago, 1939), p. 12 n.; Schlesinger, *op. cit.,* I, 87: "Every item released by the Department of Commerce enhanced the picture of the master organizer, the irresistible engineer, the omniscient economist."

CHAPTER III

CONFLICT AND COMPROMISE WITH THE DEPARTMENT OF STATE

The Commerce Department's activities in the field of foreign economic policy were to bring it into frequent contact with another and more venerable executive office, the Department of State. The latter had an old and well-established Foreign Service whose many functions included also the protection of American business abroad and the compilation of economic data. Admittedly, the Department of State was not specifically organized to aid American business, and unlike Hoover's Commerce Department, it had no commodity specialists, no comparable periodicals publicizing "foreign opportunities," and far less intimate rapport with American business. Each embassy or legation transmitted its dispatches, interspersed with a variable amount of economic data, to the regional divisions in the State Department. The Office of the Economic Adviser to the Secretary of State culled this information, providing the Secretary with whatever he required to guide him in making foreign policy decisions.

Hoover and his men, on the other hand, stressed the need for the kind of specialized machinery which he had organized in his Department. His staff officials were expected to have at least some degree of business knowledge and experience. This was reflected in the quality of their reports on world trade and finance. But the people who defended the Department of State and its prerogatives (such as Frank L. Polk, former Under-Secretary of

State) criticized Hoover for expensive duplication of work which consular and embassy officials had been doing for years. The critics stressed also the fact that most problems in foreign trade or finance involved the kind of political and diplomatic skills which, in their mind, the Commerce staff did not possess.[1]

These criticisms soon created certain jealousies and frictions which hampered the work of both departments. This struggle was conducted in Congress, within the executive branch, and through the media of public opinion. On the whole, Secretary Hoover gained the upper hand in this test of strength, which is in itself a significant corollary to the public's view of the achievements of his Department.

Only a few weeks after the inauguration of President Harding, former Under-Secretary of State Frank L. Polk proposed that all Federal commercial personnel abroad be placed under the supervision of the State Department. This was a counterblow at moves by the Department of Commerce to take over some of the functions of the consular officials. Polk hoped that "Hoover would recognize the danger of interfering with the [State] Department's control of the political functions of the Consuls . . . [because] most trade questions are political."[2] The issue was carried into Congress the same year when Representative John Jacob Rogers (Massachusetts) introduced a bill which, if made law, would have given general jurisdiction to the Secretary of State (then Charles Evans Hughes) over all American government activities abroad.

A memorandum drawn up for Hughes by Ambassador Henry P. Fletcher throws some light on the inter-departmental wrangling which occurred at the beginning of the new Administration. The memorandum referred specifically to negotiations between Hoover and Consul General Robert P. Skinner. Hoover was sufficiently disturbed by the Rogers bill that he threatened to resign from the Cabinet, if it passed. He expressed concern

---

1. Letter of Frank L. Polk to Secretary of State Charles Evans Hughes, April 9, 1921, records of the Department of State, NA, RG 59:110.78/79.
2. *Ibid.*

over delays in processing important economic information because of "red tape" in the State Department. Skinner, on the other hand, assured Hoover that in the future "nine-tenths of the reports" would be made available to his staff within "twenty-four to forty-eight hours after they reach the [State] Department."[3]

It seems that the Hoover-Skinner conversations were none too productive, for Skinner concluded that

Mr. Hoover is playing up the situation for the benefit of his presidential aspirations four years hence and is making his present position help the personal campaign he intends to make later on when he will make the most of the way he has stood for the protection of American commercial interests while the State Department did nothing.[4]

Here was a clear and rather hostile re-statement of the oft-repeated charge that the Secretary of Commerce was motivated primarily by presidential ambitions.

At the end of his first year in office Hoover still had to insist that as an interested Cabinet member he was entitled to receive State Department reports on the reparations problem. He maintained vigorously that the political aspect of reparations could not be set apart from the economic phases which were the concern of the Commerce Department.[5] The early defeat of the Rogers bill at this time, however, represented a prime set-back for the State Department forces. Before his death in 1925, Congressman Rogers weakened the original proposal to extend State's control to all the Foreign Service and, in the Congressional debates of 1924, he adopted a more favorable attitude to the Department of Commerce.[6] His widow, Edith Nourse Rogers, took his place in Congress and, as late as 1928, tried actively to improve relations between the two departments.[7]

3. Memorandum of Henry P. Fletcher, June 6, 1921, *ibid.*, RG. 59:110.78/80.

4. *Ibid.*

5. Herbert Hoover to the Department of State, Dec. 15, 1921, NA, RG 59:462.00 R 29/2172.

6. Hoover to Secretary of State Charles Evans Hughes, Feb. 28, 1925, NA, RG 59:110.78/126.

7. Nelson T. Johnson (Assistant Secretary of State to Hughes) wondered whether Mrs. Rogers had political motives in coming to the aid of the Bureau of Foreign and Domestic Commerce (at the time under the direction of Dr. Julius Klein), April 5, 1928, NA, RG 59:110.78/163.

Throughout Hoover's entire secretaryship efforts were made to achieve cooperation between the foreign representatives of the departments of State and Commerce in the face of recurring Congressional and public outbursts of stormy controversy. The most successful of these conciliatory measures were initiated specifically in behalf of American business, especially the export trade.

Hoover's research chief, George B. Roorbach, took a practical step in this direction early in 1922 when he notified the Consular Service that *Commerce Reports* would be pleased to publicize their dispatches concerning business opportunities abroad and that the consular officials who compiled the information would be credited suitably and in the same manner as the commercial attachés or trade commissioners of the Department of Commerce. Subsequently, American businessmen who benefited from this economic intelligence service and etsablished contacts with foreign buyers were asked by the Commerce Department to "furnish the American consul, attaché, or trade commissioner who sent in the report a copy of their letter to the foreign merchant." This practice, they were advised, "should work out to the distinct advantage of American exporters as it will enable . . . [the] representatives of the Government to follow up the matter personally."[8] Assisting American business became the primary function of the Commerce Department's Foreign Service, but the State Department was by no means excluded from gathering relevant economic data.

Roving trade commissioners of the Department of Commerce availed themselves frequently of the existing consular facilities abroad. Particularly useful was the knowledge and assistance of State Department officials in places which were unfamiliar to the average trade commissioner. A pertinent example of this is the aid given by Consul David H. Miller, in Seoul, Korea, to

8. George B. Roorbach (Chief, Division of Research, Bureau of Foreign and Domestic Commerce) to Wilbur J. Carr (Director of the Consular Service), March 27, 1922, NA, RG 59:110.78/81.

Trade Commissioner William I. Irvine, who was investigating the market for American automobiles in the Far East.[9]

On several occasions Director Klein of the Bureau of Foreign and Domestic Commerce took the initiative to ask that consular officials supply foreign price indexes and other statistics, "in view of the closer cooperation which we are endeavoring to effect."[10] He also suggested better liaison facilities between the two departments so as to aid the Department of Commerce in using the economic reports prepared by consular agents. The respective Liaison Offices were indeed strengthened, in spite of the suspicions of some State Department officials.[11]

Where economic legislation by foreign governments hampered American business abroad, it was essential to obtain the State Department's cooperation to remove such restrictions or to lessen the severity of their enforcement by foreign administrations. Thus, Hoover worked closely with Secretary of State Hughes in a successful effort to aid American automobile manufacturers by securing the removal of a 30 per cent Swiss Surtax on imported cars.[12] On another occasion, Assistant Secretary of State Leland Harrison apprised Hoover of State's successful negotiations with Costa Rica to provide adequate safeguards for American sales representatives in that country. At the request of the Department of Commerce the State Department also helped to clarify that country's tariff regulations. The resulting agreement with this Central American Republic provided for local customs courts where American firms could use the services of the United States consul or trade attaché in presenting their appeals.[13]

Hoover's Department of Commerce sought also to utilize the

9. David H. Miller to the Secretary of State, June 13, 1922, NA, RG 59:110.78/95.

10. Klein to Wilbur J. Carr, September 23, 1922, NA, RG 59:110.78/96.

11. Klein to Carr, April 19, 1923, NA, RG 59:110.78/108, with attached note by Carr's assistant, Addison E. Southard, April 28, 1923.

12. Department of Commerce memorandum to the Department of State, July 12, 1922, NA, RG 59:654.113 Au/14.

13. Leland Harrison to Hoover, Jan. 22, 1926; Hoover to Harrison, Jan. 26, 1926; Louis Domeratzky to the State Department, April 13, 1927; memorandum by Wilbur J. Carr, April 23, 1927: all in NA, RG 59:618.11247/12-15, 618.113/1.

services of consular officials, even when they returned to the United States on leave. They were asked, where possible, to lecture on "foreign opportunities" to groups of American businessmen. When the Consular Service, on one occasion, announced the "arrival and availability in the United States" of consuls from Ecuador and Germany, Director Klein wasted no time in relaying the information to "four hundred manufacturers and exporters in New England" and invited them to interview the visiting officials.[14]

In spite of many instances of cooperation between the Commerce and State departments, no end to inter-departmental frictions and jealousies in their activities abroad occurred during the 1920's. Consul Edwin C. Kemp in Budapest, for example, offered to show that his office could easily perform the functions of commercial attachés and trade commissioners. All he asked was additional funds to conduct his "interesting experiment" to prove that the Foreign Service of the Department of Commerce was quite unnecessary.[15] In a similar vein, the Paris Consul (Ernest L. Ives) protested against the impression given by some "misleading" published statements that the quality of official economic reports had improved since their preparation was "turned over from consuls to the agents maintained by the Department of Commerce abroad." The same official later complained that he was not receiving the cooperation of the local trade commissioner.[16]

Perhaps the most sensitive area in which the cooperation of the two departments seemed to be threatened was in the supervision of capital exports from the United States. One of the principles established by Hoover and Hughes was the need for discouraging American loans to countries like France, which had not yet negotiated an agreement concerning her American World War I debt. In 1924, however, prospects for such a settle-

14. Klein to Carr, Aug. 5, 1922, NA, RG 59:110.78/98.
15. Report of Consul Edwin C. Kemp, Dec. 28, 1922, NA, RG 59:110.78/105.
16. Reports of Consul Ernest L. Ives, June 7, 1923 and Oct. 25, 1924, NA, RG 59:110.78/110, 125.

ment with France appeared good. She needed dollars desperately in order to stabilize her currency.

American financiers could not ignore the profits which they would derive in large-scale lending to the French, nor could American foreign policy disregard the political consequences which might arise from the financial collapse of the continental "kingpin." Before the end of 1924, Grosvenor M. Jones (Chief, Finance and Investment Division) notified Hoover of the final provisions which had been made between J. P. Morgan and Company and the French Government, whereby the Morgan firm would make a $100,000,000 short-term loan to France.[17]

At the same time, several financial groups in the United States were interested in extending credit to French corporations and public agencies. This gave rise to a demand for reliable data on French finances, a demand which Consul Charles D. Westcott in Paris felt competent to satisfy with periodic reports to Harvey E. Fisk of the Bankers Trust Company and to other financiers. His efforts unloosed a storm of protest from the Department of Commerce. Oliver P. Hopkins, Acting Director of the Bureau of Foreign and Domestic Commerce, pointedly reminded the State Department that only his agency was the "legal channel" for supplying financial information.[18]

Hopkins's severe criticism of the Westcott reports stressed the delicate nature of the data on French budgetary conditions, especially in view of their bearing on the forthcoming war debt negotiations. Hopkins contrasted the Consul's "unsolicited letters" with the careful system of preferences by which the Commerce Department decided which interested bankers should receive confidential information. In addition to such general principles, Hopkins found fault specifically with Westcott's optimistic conclusions regarding Finance Minister Joseph Caillaux's program for stabilizing the *franc*. He saw in these conclusions a by-

17. Grosvenor M. Jones to Hoover, Aug. 29, 1924, NA, RG 151:640 (France).

18. Oliver P. Hopkins to Wilbur J. Carr (Assistant Secretary of State), Sept. 19, 1925, *ibid.*

product of inadequate financial knowledge, not to mention downright statistical error.[19]

A half-year later Commercial Attaché Chester L. Jones wrote from Paris to Director Klein that he was "still unable to identify Consul Westcott's figures" contained in the reports sent to American bankers. Attaché Jones and his staff had even sought the aid of "the [French] Treasury [which] declared itself unable to explain the basis on which Consul Westcott's report was calculated."[20] Jones continued to add to the "definitive" collection of statistics on French finances which Commerce had been compiling even in the years before Westcott's initiative backfired against his own Service. The Department of Commerce, it appeared, was much better equipped to exert leadership in the field of international finance than was its diplomatic counterpart.

Perhaps because of the more intimate knowledge they possessed of world financial conditions, the officials of the Department of Commerce tended to be more cautious than the State Department in approving foreign loan flotations. In the 1920's, for example, they did not hesitate to present the doleful budgetary conditions of Colombia and Chile, or to point out that Bolivia had already borrowed beyond her means.[21] Although their purpose was to bring to America's attention the business opportunities which existed abroad, Commerce Department publications usually emphasized objective and measurable conditions, even at the risk of discouraging prospective investors. While it is true that often the facts presented were overwhelmingly favorable, at least they could be cross-checked with other sources. These publications of the Commerce Department generally did not reflect an official bias.[22]

The activities of the Department of Commerce in connection with the floating of foreign loans in the United States during the

---

19. *Ibid.*
20. Report of Commercial Attaché Chester L. Jones, March 29, 1926, *ibid.*
21. Senate Committee on Finance, *Hearings to Investigate the Sale of Foreign Bonds or Securities in the United States* (Washington, 1932), pp. 724, 725, 825, 846, 1610-1615.
22. James W. Angell, *Financial Foreign Policy of the United States*, p. 105.

1920's received national attention in the 1932 election year. One of the issues at the time was the question of losses American investors suffered by participating in these foreign loans. In testimony before the Senate Finance Committee investigating this problem, Grosvenor M. Jones and other Commerce officials dispelled effectively every accusation indicating that these losses were the result of fact-finding failures by the Department. Jones spoke of the warnings issued by his Division at the time Hoover was Secretary. He mentioned how he indicated that several Latin American countries were "going wild on borrowing"; that Chilean revenues were too much dependent on the uncertain income from export taxes; that some states of Brazil were poor financial risks, etc.[23]

Sometimes the investment bankers heeded the facts presented by the Department of Commerce; on several occasions they did not. The (1932) Senate Committee hearings did bring out, however, the point that these official investment reports were available even to small investment bankers and to individual investors. Everyone, of course, was then free to exercise his own judgment.[24]

It appears that the wrath of some of the Senate investigators was turned mainly against the State Department's "failure" in the 1920's to control loans to Latin American countries, particularly those with which the United States had special treaty relations. For example, Senator William H. King (Democrat, Utah) claimed that under the provisions of the Platt Amendment the State Department was duty-bound to restrain the "wasteful extravagance" of Cuba's Machado regime. This could have been accomplished, according to King, by withholding Government approval of any further loans by American bankers to Cuba.[25]

23. Senate Committee on Finance, *Hearings,* 1932, pp. 727, 745, 848.
24. *Ibid.,* p. 745; For a partial list of those receiving the reports see pp. 826-844. A former commercial attaché in Peru did testify that he was forced to resign after the Department took issue with his "pessimistic" presentation of Peruvian finances (*ibid.,* p. 1616). He implied that the Commerce Department was too eager to "sell" foreign investments to the American public.
25. *Ibid.,* p. 1847.

Senator King was not unfamiliar with the field of Cuban-American relations and the manner in which they were influenced by the investment and loan policies of the State and Commerce departments. In 1926 he introduced a resolution demanding that the American Government take all necessary measures to protect American economic interests in Cuba under the Platt Amendment. This proposal not only disagreed with the approach adopted by officials of the State Department, but also brought protests from the American Chamber of Commerce in Cuba. The Chamber appealed not so much to the State Department as to Secretary of Commerce Hoover, asking him to express publicly his opposition to the King resolution. In their message to Hoover, these Americans in Cuba defended the administration of General Machado as "honorable and upright" in politics and favorable to business; they attacked the proposed Senate resolution as "inopportune and detrimental to the existing friendly relations between the Republic of Cuba and the United States."[26]

Hoover's reasons for opposing the King resolution can be ascribed to several factors. By this time, Hoover already had begun to develop his own "good neighbor policy" with regard to Latin America; thus, he rejected the idea of political interference in Latin America by the United States.[27] In addition, Hoover could be expected to sympathize with the views of organized American business overseas. Dr. Julius Klein, Hoover's right-hand assistant in the Department of Commerce, presented still another explanation. He described Senator King as "one of the very few sharp critics of our service," and a relentless foe "of our Foreign Service Bill."[28]

Klein's memorandum asserted that King's opposition to the

26. J. D. Frisbie (Secretary, The American Chamber of Commerce of Cuba) to Hoover, June 26, 1926, NA, RG 151:640 (Cuba).
27. Samuel F. Bemis, *The Latin American Policy of the United States* (New York, 1943), p. 222; John F. Madden, *et al., America's Experience as Creditor* (New York, 1937), p. 239; Alexander De Conde, *Herbert Hoover's Latin American Policy* (Stanford, 1951), *passim.*
28. Julius Klein to Frederick Todd (Commercial Attaché, Havana), July 15, 1926, NA, RG 151:640 (Cuba).

Department of Commerce was "animated entirely by personal reasons, namely his very bitter antagonism to Mr. Hoover, which goes back to the Food Administration days." The Senator's allegation that commercial attachés were merely duplicating the work of consular officials was dismissed on the grounds that the Senator had relatives working in the Department of State. Otherwise, according to Klein, "such a belief [would] long since [have] been dispelled, particularly since the President's Executive Order of April 4, 1924" assigned to the Commerce Department's agents the prime responsibility in economic matters and provided for the cooperative exchange of information among all American agents abroad. Klein then proceeded to describe King's "unreasonable" attitude in criticizing some of the Commerce Department's offices he had seen on an overseas inspection tour.[29]

This rather unflattering portrait by Hoover's Director of the Bureau of Foreign and Domestic Commerce was not meant in malice, but was really an attempt to prepare the commercial attachés stationed in Cuba for a forthcoming inspection by Senator King. The latter, warned Klein, was "quite hopeless so far as logic, reasoning, or the acceptance of evidence is concerned, and any attempt *on our part* to show him the error of his ways will be worse than useless, if not irritating." Consequently, the commercial agents abroad were advised to make use of their contacts with American businessmen, so that *they* would convince the Senator of the valuable work done by the Department of Commerce. A judicious campaign was thus planned by the Department to confront the impending threat.[30]

Director Klein did not exaggerate the seriousness of Senator King's opposition to Hoover and to his Department. This hostility flared up in 1924, when King led the fight against the Senate proposal to raise the Commerce Department's appropriation to $24,027,105, an increase of about 10 per cent above the sum voted by the House. His arguments, based on the need for econ-

29. *Ibid.*
30. *Ibid.*

omy in government, criticized Commerce personnel abroad for the "wasteful duplication" of duties which could have been performed by consular and diplomatic officials alone. In an implicit attack on the public relations of the Commerce Department, King pleaded that its work was "not as important to the business and commerce of our country as some connected with it affect to believe."[31] Senator Kenneth McKellar (Tennessee) joined in the attack by proposing that the old Rogers Bill be amended to place all commercial attachés under the unified control of the ambassador or minister in each foreign country.[32]

Once more, however, the Department of Commerce emerged victorious over those who tried in vain to transfer some of its functions to the State Department. The influential Senator Reed Smoot (Republican, Utah) denied King's charges of duplication and inefficiency. On the contrary, he stated that he "felt like congratulating Secretary Hoover upon the class of men he had in Europe." Senator Lee Overman (North Carolina) reported that businessmen were clamoring for more commercial attachés to "travel from one place to another, soliciting business for America, giving American manufacturers information about business opportunities." His colleague from the state of Washington, Wesley Jones, praised the testimony of Hoover and Klein, who had affirmed that difficulties with the State Department had been "planed out," and that Commerce agents had proven themselves better adapted than the men from State to carry out frequent and informal expeditions on behalf of American business.[33]

At the same time, however, the State Department did not relax its own campaign for Congressional preference. Testifying before a House committee, Wilbur J. Carr proposed that his Consular Service be permitted to receive the type of business training given to Department of Commerce personnel. Consul General Robert P. Skinner testified that "there is undoubtedly

31. *Congressional Record*, 68 Cong., 1 Sess., p. 7624 (May 1, 1924).
32. *Ibid.*, pp. 7624-7625.
33. *Ibid.*, p. 7625-7626.

duplication" in the work done by consular agents and commercial attachés. He saw no reason why the Consular Service could not be solely responsible for economic activities abroad. Hugh Gibson, Minister to Poland, cited the valuable service given to American firms by his own staff: "In this phase of our work our duties are as constant as though we were the legal business representatives of an American company, retained by the year," he proudly declared.[34]

Even foreign governments were brought indirectly into the conflict between the two departments. In 1923 one of the issues of *Commerce Reports* included a pessimistic article under the headline "Danish Economic Conditions Unfavorable." This was shortly after the crash of the Danish *Landmansbank,* just at the time when that country was striving to achieve a durable economic recovery.[35] Subsequently, Denmark's Foreign Ministry protested vigorously that this kind of publicity was "prejudicial to the interests of Denmark" and could injure the country's credit rating abroad. Relaying the protest to Washington, the Chief of the American legation in Copenhagen warned that the position of all United States representatives abroad would be weakened greatly unless "more moderate headlines could be employed" by the Department of Commerce publications.[36]

From the other side of the world, Consul Wilbur Keplinger, in Bombay, complained of errors in the Department of Commerce report on "The Bombay Phonograph Market." What's more, he charged the Department with tactlessness in treating the protests of influential native dealers.[37] Consuls in Latin America complained that they suffered "great embarrassment" when confidential information which they had reported to commercial attachés was printed in Commerce Department publications.[38]

34. House Committee on Foreign Affairs, *Hearings on the Foreign Service of the United States* (Washington, 1924), pp. 46-47, 130, 198.
35. *Commerce Reports,* Feb. 26, 1923, p. 530.
36. Dispatch to the State Department from John D. Prince (American Legation in Copenhagen), May 8, 1923, NA, RG 59:110.78/109.
37. Wilbur Keplinger, July 24, 1925, NA, RG 59:110.78/131.
38. Reports to the Latin American Division, April 9, 1925, etc., NA, RG 59:110.78/129.

Other State Department officials protested against Commerce publicity which failed to give them credit for aid given to American business. Robert P. Skinner was especially outspoken in minimizing the Commerce Department's claim, among others, that it alone prevented the passage of legislation abroad which would have excluded American automobiles by making the left-hand drive illegal.[39]

All of the tension between the two departments was neatly brought to the public's eye in Consul General Tracy H. Lay's book published in 1925, *The Foreign Service of the United States*. This was an intensely loyal study of the State Department's Foreign Service. Adding to the book's appearance of official sanction, the Foreword contained a generous commendation by Secretary of State Charles Evans Hughes. The book in effect represented a well-written defense of the State Department's role abroad and attempted to demolish the arguments of its enemies — particularly that upstart competitor, the Department of Commerce. The battle soon was joined. Its tumult carried into the Cabinet and into the press.

The burden of Lay's argument was that the Department of Commerce, by expanding its overseas functions at the expense of the State Department's Foreign Service, had caused "friction at home" and "friction abroad." Lay made public the previous charges of "duplication and overlapping of functions" aimed to discredit the Commerce Department. Apparently, what irked him most were the foreign activities of commercial attachés and trade commissioners who, instead of possessing the virtues of diplomatic training combined the qualities of salesmen, statisticians, and government agents. In Lay's opinion,

this seemed to cross the wires of diplomacy; to bring into the diplomatic machinery an extraneous element in the form of a representative who bore no responsibility in matters of international policies and yet was free to work through official channels in direct relation with foreign governments.[40]

39. Reports of Robert P. Skinner, June 17, 1925, NA, RG 59:110.78/13C.
40. Tracy H. Lay, *The Foreign Service of the United States* (New York, 1925), pp. 201-203.

Searching through legislative precedent, Lay failed to find any justification for the octopus-like expansion abroad of the Department of Commerce. He admitted that under the Act of July 16, 1914 the Secretary of Commerce could appoint commercial attachés and roving trade commissioners to investigate business opportunities abroad. But, he concluded, this did not change the intent of the original Commerce Department Enabling Act of 1903, which specified clearly that information from abroad should be channeled through the Department of State. Lay quoted his own Department's old ally, Representative John J. Rogers, to the effect that Congress never intended "the Department of Commerce to extend its activities in just the way it has sought to extend them." In several other passages Lay recalled Rogers's praise of the State Department's work and the Congressman's opposition to "a new foreign service [being] established and built up" by Hoover's Department.[41]

Elsewhere in the book, Lay propelled his frontal attack by drawing from a monograph of the Institute for Government Research which charged that the Department of Commerce "has not paid any particular attention to domestic trade problems," the implication being that this was the result of its concentration on the foreign field.[42] A somewhat similar complaint, based on Lay's arguments, appeared editorially in the New York *Journal of Commerce*. The editors praised the book for having revealed "the ridiculous character of the present situation." They then proceeded to criticize the Department of Commerce for unspecified cases of "inefficiency or blunder." What justification could be presented, they asked, for the Department's attempt to assume "a practical control over the consular service" which could demoralize the "conservative members of our . . . diplomatic staffs" and threaten American relations with foreign countries?[43]

The *Journal of Commerce* editorial became "exhibit A" in the lengthy memorandum which was drawn up by the Department

41. *Ibid.*, pp. 157-158, 160.
42. *Ibid.*, pp. 156-157.
43. New York *Journal of Commerce*, Feb. 24, 1925.

of Commerce in protest against Lay's book. Addressing himself to Secretary of State Hughes, Hoover deplored Lay's "destructive attacks upon the work of the Department of Commerce . . . the misrepresentations and half-truths." It might have been possible to ignore these attacks, Hoover wrote, had it not been for Hughes' approval of the book. Lay's draft, Hoover indicated, should have been cleared first through appropriate channels of intra-Cabinet liaison. Had that been done, then the author's "partisan" accusations that the Department of Commerce was "paternalistic and tending to break down the individuality of American commerce" would not have appeared in print.[44]

Hoover saw in these accusations a threat to the continuance of his four years' cooperation with the Secretary of State. "Under the circumstances," he concluded, "I think that there is due to this Department some disavowal of the statements in question, and I am confident that I can rely on your spirit of fair play to deal with the matter promptly and effectively."[45]

Charles Evans Hughes, who was about to resign as head of the State Department, replied immediately — in the calm tones of moderation which were typical of his statesmanship.[46] He explained that in his Foreword to *The Foreign Service of the United States* he had not undertaken to vouch for the author's accuracy. The book was unofficial, and the views were solely those of Tracy H. Lay. Hughes concluded by hoping for "a continuance of harmonious relations" with Hoover.[47] One month later, the State Department purchased copies of *The Foreign Service of the United States* for distribution among all consular officials, to "improve their morale and . . . guide their unofficial as well as their official activities."[48]

44. Hoover to Secretary of State Charles Evans Hughes, Feb. 28, 1925, NA. RG 59:110.78/126.
45. *Ibid.*
46. A good analysis of Hughes's role in the 1920's is contained in Dexter Perkins' *Charles Evans Hughes and American Democratic Statesmanship* (Boston, 1956).
47. Hughes to Hoover, Feb. 28, 1925, NA, RG 59:110.78/126.
48. Unsigned memorandum by the "Assistant Secretary of State," March 30, 1925, *ibid.*

While it may be true, as Merlo J. Pusey states, that "mutual admiration as well as mutual interest in foreign trade brought Hughes and Hoover frequently together,"[49] it is equally true that their respective departments repeatedly vied with each other in frequent jurisdictional disputes. In a 1922 address Hughes stated his sincere intention to cooperate with the Secretary of Commerce: "I am glad to say that we are achieving at this time a very gratifying measure of co-operation among the departments; in particular the relations between the Department of State and the Department of Commerce are most cordial and mutually helpful." The Hughes statement continued to emphasize that the two departments "are working with each other and endeavoring each to aid the other in its recognized field of effort."[50] The last phrase in this statement proved to be the stumbling block in the path of these good intentions, for both agencies jealously sought to expand their "field of effort."

The evidence of friction caused by the ever-growing scope of Commerce personnel appears to deny the conclusions of Pusey and others that "long-existing conflicts between the State and Commerce departments concerning foreign representation in commercial matters quickly subsided under their [Hoover's and Hughes'] co-operative techniques." Even if the two Secretaries did agree that economic information services were to be provided by the Department of Commerce, as Pusey claims, they could not or would not restrain the conflicting departmental loyalties of their respective staffs. These conditions continued, though less strikingly, under the new Secretary of State, Frank B. Kellogg (1925-1929).

Now, as a senior member of the Cabinet, Hoover, in the last years of his term, could strengthen his Department's position even more, while Kellogg was preoccupied with political rather than economic programs for international cooperation. The De-

49. Pusey, *Charles Evans Hughes,* II, 427.
50. Charles Evans Hughes, *The Pathway of Peace* (New York, 1925), address of May 18, 1922, p. 265.

partment of Commerce continued its valuable work with the State Department on such questions as assuring Americans equal access to the oil of the Near East and finding markets abroad for the growing American aircraft industry. But now, more than before, publicists like Isaac F. Marcosson (*The Saturday Evening Post*) persisted in their campaign to portray the Department of Commerce as the sole repository of expert information on foreign economics. They explained that an American businessman would need to write to as many as nineteen consulates in China, for example, to get information which he could receive from one commodity division in the Commerce Department. As a result of publicity like this, bills were presented to raise the budget of the Commerce Department and to safeguard its expanded functions by new legislation.[51]

These developments were not countenanced casually by the old-line diplomatic Foreign Service. The State Department's representatives abroad did not cease their complaints against the commercial attachés and trade commissioners. Some of these complaints present interesting aspects of the friction between the Commerce and State departments which persevered under the Secretaryship of Frank B. Kellogg. The conflicts were lessened significantly because of the impressive predominance of the Commerce Department in assisting American business abroad by compiling economic data. But the problem of inter-departmental cooperation was to remain a serious challenge even shortly before Secretary Hoover's nomination for President in 1928.[52]

Under Kellogg consular officials complained that Commerce Department representatives were generally uncooperative and too often revealed confidential economic information.[53] Some-

51. "Strictly Confidential" dispatches from the American Embassy in London, Jan. 6, 1926, NA, RG 59:840.6176/67; Isaac F. Marcosson, "Commercial Exploration," *The Saturday Evening Post*, CXCVIII (Feb. 13, 1926), 9, 50; State Department memorandum, Nov. 10, 1926, NA, RG 59:110.78/136.

52. Wilbur J. Carr (Assistant Secretary of State), April 6, 1928, NA, RG 59:110.78/164.

53. Consul George P. Shaw, June 20, 1927, NA, RG 59:110.78/147.

times, the zeal of commercial attachés in pursuit of economic ends became a source of unbearable annoyance to diplomatic officials. A dramatic example of this is contained in the correspondence of Consul Daniel C. Berger at Tientsin during the Chinese civil war.

Amidst strife and chaos Berger and his staff were working feverishly to find missing Americans and to help American missionaries and merchants to leave threatened areas. At this time, Berger reported, the Commercial Attaché in Shanghai was "Mr. [Julean H.] Arnold," who sought to gather as much favorable data as possible for the benefit of "American individuals and firms interested in [the] China trade, with a view to overcoming or counteracting 'the effusion of startling news' regarding conditions in China." In a sarcastic reply to Arnold's personal requests for cooperation, Berger wrote: "The Consulate General regrets to inform you that the 'startling news' regarding conditions [in China] is so real that it has no time to devote to trade promotion activities."[54]

Notifying the Department of State, Berger announced that he could not agree to work with the "Commercial Attaché" because "Mr. Arnold endeavors to portray normal business conditions and a promising business outlook in China . . . ignoring the data that runs contrary thereto." In case the Department of Commerce should object, Berger explained, he wished to make his own position clear. He would not consider supplying "information that might be used to mislead American exporters by minimizing the present chaotic state of affairs." In effect, the memorandum amounted to a categorical refusal by a State Department officer to participate in what he regarded as a deception by an official connected with the Commerce Department.[55]

54. Reports of Daniel C. Berger (Consul in Tientsin), April 6, 1927, NA, RG 59:110.78/142, including quotations from correspondence with "Mr. [Julean H.] Arnold" (Commercial Attaché, Shanghai).

55. Ibid.; Who's Who In America (1928-29) described Arnold as the first American student interpreter in China, commissioned by Pres. Theodore Roosevelt (1902). Beginning in 1914, Arnold was a commercial attaché in China, and headed the United States delegation to the China Tariff Revision Commission (1926-27).

The Department of Commerce, on the other hand, registered its own complaints against the State Department. Toward the end of 1927 Secretary Hoover was concerned about rumors of an impending European chemical cartel agreement whose reported goal was the "destruction" of the American chemical industry. Reports from the American Consulate in London indicated that the negotiations between I. G. Farben and the British chemical interests were aimed to form a "European Chemical Trust." Similar reports filtered into the press on both sides of the Atlantic. Denials and confirmations flowed in confusion from American agents abroad.[56] On December 9, 1927, the New York *Herald Tribune* printed on the same page an article citing the claim of the American Consul in Paris that *no* Franco-German chemical combine was in prospect and another from the Commerce office in Paris which confirmed the *success* of the cartel negotiations.[57]

Director Julius Klein notified the State Department of this confusion and asserted firmly that the Chemical Division of his Bureau of Foreign and Domestic Commerce should have been consulted before the consuls' statements were given to the press. This, he admonished, would have avoided such embarrassing conflict of opinion by the two Federal agencies.[58]

Late in 1927 the Department of Commerce already was acting as the Administration's official spokesman on economic foreign policy. Assistant Secretary of State Wilbur J. Carr replied to Klein's protest in a conciliatory spirit, suggesting that both departments work more closely and consult each other concerning future press releases. When, early in 1928, the reports of the Commerce Department concerning the chemical cartel proved

56. Reports of the American Consulate in London (Alfred Nutting, Clerk), Aug. 25, 1927, NA, RG 59:840.659; *New York Times*, Oct. 16, 19, and Dec. 8, 1927; NA, RG 59:840.659/1-6 (consular reports).

57. Memorandum of Julius Klein to Wilbur J. Carr, Dec. 17, 1927, NA, RG 59:840.659/8.

58. *Ibid.*

to be correct, the Department's prestige increased still more, probably reaching its historic peak just before Hoover's nomination for President that year.[59]

59. Reply from Carr, Dec. 31, 1927, *ibid.* For a discussion of the decline in power of the Commerce Department after 1932, see: Wallace J. Parks, *United States Administration of Its International Economic Affairs* (Baltimore, 1951), pp. 106-107; in chapter V, Parks refers to the gradual renewal of the Commerce Department's prestige in the prosperous 1940's and 1950's. For the "rehabilitation" of Herbert Hoover in the conservative climate following World War II see: Foreword to James W. Prothro's *The Dollar Decade* and Eugene Lyons' *Our Unknown Ex-President, passim.* In a letter to the author, May 26, 1961, Dr. Julius Klein maintains that American business has suffered from the loss of invaluable "commercial intelligence" since the transfer of commercial attachés to the State Department. The direct contacts and "swiftness of communication" in the Hoover days are "far from possible under the present regime of State Department procedure," says Dr. Klein.

SECTION TWO

HOOVER SLAYS THE DRAGON
OF FOREIGN MONOPOLY

CHAPTER IV

EXPOSING FOREIGN MONOPOLY
AS A
THREAT TO AMERICA

General Principles

In the second volume of his *Memoirs* Hoover explains how the European economic disturbances of the 1920's forced him to divert "attention from national development and needed reforms to the defense of our economic and social life." This "European economic hurricane," wrote Hoover, not only brought depression to the United States, but also "opened our flesh deeply to collectivist infections from Europe." Herein lay Hoover's *raison d'être* for his *Memoirs*, for they were written "to support the American people in their own true philosophy of life — and to present the consequences of turning away from it."[1] While he was Secretary of Commerce, Hoover did not hesitate to act forcefully in defense of principles he considered representative of the American way of life, especially in the face of European "collectivist" tendencies.

Some of these "undesirable" currents from the Old World first became apparent, according to Hoover, after World War I, when foreign producers of essential raw materials not produced in the United States formed government-sponsored cartels or combinations. Hoover considered such "monopolies" incompatible with America's traditional practices and a threat to the

1. Herbert Hoover, *Memoirs*, II, vi.

nation's economic well-being. He attributed to these agreements the two-fold increase in cost of the essential raw materials which the United States needed to import. Concluding that American consumers were being victimized by foreign controls which forced them to pay two billions in 1925 for the same quantity of raw materials which had cost only one billion in 1922, Hoover mobilized a campaign in defense of America's interests.[2]

In his *Memoirs* Hoover credits their inevitable downfall to the "fallacious" principles on which the foreign combinations were based, as well as the bold counter-measures initiated against them by the Department of Commerce. He wrote proudly of this object lesson, one which he considered a victory for American ideals of free enterprise. Furthermore, he recalled, successful American resistance "demonstrated [that] the United States could protect itself."[3]

While campaigning for President in 1928, Hoover was wont to remind his audience how "soon after the war certain foreign governments possessing [a] practical monopoly of . . . raw materials . . . began the organization of controls designed to establish prices to the rest of the world, and especially to us, the largest purchaser." He described how these controls grew in number and effectiveness so that their "undue tax upon our consumers reached hundreds of millions of dollars." Hoover then enumerated the ways in which "our government used its influence to meet the situation [one which it] regarded . . . to be in the long run uneconomic and disastrous."[4]

The Department of Commerce alerted the American public to the dangers "of foreign government controls of price and distribution of our import raw materials" as early as 1922, when it published an "exhaustive investigation" of the problem. The public was informed of "governmentally controlled foreign combinations in nine raw materials: long staple cotton, camphor, coffee, iodine, nitrates, potash, mercury, rubber and sisal." The

---

2. *Ibid.*, II, 81. The comparison is none too valid because 1922 was a depression year, particularly anent raw materials in international trade.
3. *Ibid.*, II, 84.
4. Hoover address in Boston, October 15, 1928, *The New Day*, pp. 123-124.

most important of these products, rubber, represented the most serious problem. It took the form of British Government regulations known as the Stevenson Plan. The Department believed that many other foreign restrictions could be "retarded by the demonstration of practicable defense action [by the United States] in the case of rubber."[5]

Speaking before the Erie (Pennsylvania) Chamber of Commerce in 1925, Hoover pressed a spirited attack on the foreign "controls of production and price [which] amount practically to trade war." Citing the "international monopolies" of rubber and coffee as prime examples of "combinations in restraint of trade [in which] the [American] consumer has no voice at all," Hoover maintained that in those two commodities alone the United States was being overcharged by as much as $300 million annually. If foreign governments want "trade war," Hoover warned repeatedly, "the time has arrived when we require either disarmament or defense"; America must take immediate and specific steps to "retaliate" or to choose her "defense measures."[6]

Of the possible "defense" alternatives, Hoover preferred those which would not involve government intervention in "the free flow of supply and demand." His Department already had noted declines in the consumption of rubber and coffee and increases in the use of substitutes, in part the result of the educational campaign launched by Commerce publications. But there was an impressive reserve of more rigorous actions also to which the American government could resort.

Some of these measures, Hoover admitted, would arouse overseas antagonism against American foreign policy. "We could," he speculated reluctantly, "prohibit the extension of credit to countries where such controls are maintained . . . [and] establish rival production" under the American flag. American farmers had long been clamoring for government aid to stimulate synthetic nitrates production at home; other imported raw mate-

5. *Fourteenth Annual Report of the Secretary of Commerce*, pp. 35-36.
6. Hoover, *Foreign Combinations Now Fixing Prices of Raw Materials Imported Into the United States* (Washington, 1925), pp. 2, 4, 7. Commerce Library pamphlet (address of Oct. 31, 1925).

rials could also be produced in the United States or its possessions. Although Hoover declared, "I have no liking for any actions of this sort," necessity made him champion all of them.[7]

Carrying his public campaign into the pages of *Current History*, Hoover, in an article entitled, "America Solemnly Warns Foreign Monopolists of Raw Materials," summarized the nation's need. The article began by denying any intention to criticize foreign governments or their nationals, but proceeded to outline the extent and seriousness of the "combinations which have been set up either directly by legislation of foreign Governments or indirectly by Government patronage." As a foremost purchaser of raw materials, the United States had the right, continued Hoover, to object even to friendly nations whose governments fixed the price of essential commodities through export restrictions or producers' agreements.[8]

As an important official in the American Government, the Secretary of Commerce could speak authoritatively of the United States' tradition-rooted opposition to international monopoly and of its fears concerning "the spread of these ideas" to other commodities in international commerce. If this should occur, Hoover predicted, each government would be forced to come to the aid of its nationals, and "government patronage" would exacerbate existing international hostilities. In a thinly veiled threat, Hoover declared, "We are, of course, a large producing as well as consuming nation in raw materials, and we have it in our powers to retaliate [by controlling such commodities as American copper or wheat, for example]." Repeating his estimate that the United States was paying $300 million in overcharges on imported raw materials, Hoover saw even darker possibilities, for, he concluded, "no unregulated monopoly is ever content with the reasonable."[9]

Hoover warned these "combinations" that their attempt to ignore the law of supply and demand by maintaining artificially

7. *Ibid.*, pp. 8, 9, 10, 11.
8. Hoover, "America Solemnly Warns Foreign Monopolists of Raw Materials," *Current History*, XXIII (Dec. 1925), 307-308.
9. *Ibid.*, p. 309.

inflated profits would not only injure American consumers. It would boomerang against the foreign producers as well. Manufacturers in the United States increasingly would turn to conservation and the use of substitutes, such as synthetic rubber. (At the time, synthetic rubber was little more than a dream, still this illustrates Hoover's intimate knowledge of latest developments in applied technology.) To previous threats of retaliation, Hoover now added the possibility of creating American Government-approved buying pools, as another means to deal with foreign sales monopolies. America could defend itself readily under conditions of commercial anarchy, warned the Commerce Secretary, but what of international amity and "trade peace"? In the name of the latter, he appealed for "abandonment of all . . . Government controlled production and prices."[10]

What was the reaction of the American public to Hoover's campaign to defend their economic freedom? One indication of America's diverse views is the editorial opinion of the American press. *The New York Times,* for example, at first took a rather moderate stand; later it turned clearly against the Hoover program.

The *Times'* editors complimented Mr. Hoover for preferring to exert pressure against foreign controls by conserving the stockpiles of raw materials and by encouraging the use of substitutes rather than resort to outright retaliation. At the same time they accused Hoover also of using "inflammatory" language which stimulated talk of American "reprisals." Did not the Department of Commerce, the *Times* asked, advise American farmers to cut down on their wheat production because of world trade conditions? "The whole conduct of the agitation thus far is, unfortunately, such as to make the judicious grieve," concluded New York's most influential newspaper.[11]

On another occasion, the *Times* began its criticism by quoting Hoover's favorite rhetorical question: "Is it not a national

10. *Ibid.,* pp. 310-311; Hoover, *The Future of Our Foreign Trade* (address of March 16, 1926), *passim.*
11. *The New York Times,* Jan. 8, 1926.

obligation to secure a free flow of raw materials upon which national life is much dependent?" The editors' rejoinder came in the form of their own query: "How can we condemn a foreign ·government for raising prices by legislation, when our own Government sets out to do the very same thing . . . ?" Even some Republicans, the *Times* found, were of the opinion that Hoover's campaign was at least inappropriate, as long as the American protective tariff encouraged combination at home.[12]

Liberal opposition to the anti-foreign-monopoly campaign was centered in *The Nation*, which criticized the "Republican tariff" as a worse evil than the rubber controls proposed by the Stevenson Plan. Unlike "Republican" protectionism, the Plan was at least "born of dire necessity." It was an effort to save the British growers from ruin. Continuing in this vein, *The Nation* accused Hoover of threatening to retaliate with American export and price restrictions on cotton, wheat, and oil, commodities which Europe required for her very existence. These editorialists saw in the campaign of the Secretary of Commerce an apparent case "of the pot calling the kettle black — in which Mr. Hoover is obviously the pot."[13]

The struggle against foreign combinations aroused wide national interest. Aware of this, the *Literary Digest* published a useful summary of pertinent contemporary press comment. This synopsis also presented rather interesting indications of division of opinion along sectional lines, even though the whole conveyed a picture of apparently overwhelming approval for Hoover's campaign. For example, the Democratic, New Orleans *Times-Picayune,* as quoted by the *Literary Digest,* spoke out in favor of retaliation against the foreign combinations. Raising the price of Southern cotton was one of the measures advocated by this paper. On the other hand, the St. Paul *Pioneer Press* — in the heart of the Spring Wheat belt — proposed that American *wheat* controls be used to bring Europe to her knees. Reminiscing

12. *Ibid.,* Jan. 10, 1926.
13. "Rubber and Mr. Hoover" (editorial), *The Nation,* CXXII (Jan. 20, 1926), 50.

fondly of World War I days, the Kansas City *Star* recalled how the American threat to raise copper prices brought successful results in the form of lower prices on British wool.[14]

The automobile-conscious Detroit *Free Press,* of course, was worried about the adverse effects of the rise in crude rubber prices following the British adoption of the Stevenson Plan. "Certainly," it wrote, "the American people cannot afford to be held up indefinitely by get-rich-quick foreign monopolies."[15] Joining in the chorus against "the growing evil of international profiteering," the Washington *Post* admonished "certain foreign governments . . . [to] heed the warning" of Secretary Hoover. The Charleston (W. Va.) *Mail* was certain that resort to retaliation was inevitable, if American industry was to obtain imported raw materials at reasonable prices. Writing in an area where credit was scarce, the Minneapolis *Tribune* supported the "withholding of [American] credit from nations which use monopolistic control for squeezing purposes."[16]

It appears from the *Literary Digest's* survey that at least some of the press did not neglect the patriotic motives behind the compaign of the Secretary of Commerce. The Memphis *Commercial Appeal* ("a Democratic daily") promised that, "He [Hoover] will have the backing of every true American, irrespective of political affiliations." Other newspapers also commented favorably on the need to cooperate with the promising program of a man of Hoover's national and international stature. The opposition to Hoover, however, accused him of expediency in espousing free trade only when it suited his purposes. This "sort of quackery . . . is unworthy of our Secretary of Commerce," complained the St. Louis *Post-Dispatch.* This paper was joined by the other ones who criticized also American protectionism and efforts "to soak the foreigner." The assertion that the British were simply taking "a leaf out of the American note-book,"

14. "Mr. Hoover's Warning to Foreign Trade Gougers," *The Literary Digest,* LXXXVII (Nov. 21, 1925), 12-13.
15. Quoted *ibid.,* p. 12.
16. Quoted *ibid.,* p. 12-13.

which appeared in the Baltimore *Evening Sun,* seemed a typical anti-Hoover commentary.[17]

Hoover was not unaware of the charges of "hypocrisy" hurled against him in the United States and abroad for his opposition to foreign controls while favoring the protective tariff. He denied, however, the imputation that his program sought to deprive foreign producers of a "fair price" for their goods. He maintained that American tariff protection was required to make up "the difference in the cost of production at home and abroad," because of lower foreign wages. Hoover was convinced that even the Democratic South would recognize the stimulating effects of protection.[18]

There was, indeed, some justification for Hoover's analysis that politics and emotion had exaggerated the tariff controversy in the 1920's, even if he himself grossly oversimplified the picture by stressing that there was no duty at all on 63 per cent of American imports.[19] As for government assistance to the American farmer, Hoover felt that in most cases it was amply justified, since farm prices had fallen "below the cost of production." This, Hoover maintained, was a far cry from the contrasting "highly profitable . . . unreasonable . . . and extortionate price levels" of the foreign combinations.[20] Explaining his opposition to American loans for the Franco-German potash monopoly, Hoover said:

We, as a government, have set up no such controls, and through the Sherman Act we prevent our citizens from doing it [for] we have clung tenaciously to the belief that economic progress must depend upon the driving force of competition.[21]

The basis for Hoover's ideological attack on the foreign monopolies seemed to be not so much "monopoly" *per se* as the fact of government intervention on behalf of the producers of raw materials. It was "the increasing practice of *foreign govern-*

17. Quoted *ibid.,* p. 13.
18. Wilbur and Hyde, *The Hoover Policies,* p. 181.
19. Hoover, *Memoirs,* II, 291.
20. Hoover, *The Future of Our Foreign Trade,* pp. 10-11.
21. Hoover quoted in Emerson, *Hoover and His Times,* pp. 249-250.

ments directly or indirectly to create controls of raw materials for price-fixing purposes, where such nations dominate the production of a commodity . . . [the] suspension of the law of supply and demand by *governments"* — these were Hoover's main objections.[22]

Continued government intervention in the international economy would inevitably force the American Government to "negotiate the terms, and thus fix prices on behalf of the consumer, or to authorize the trades or banks to do so," Hoover warned. He considered such a development to be undesirable economically. Moreover, it clashed with American traditions of free enterprise. Perhaps the most deplorable consequence of foreign price-fixing which Hoover feared was, as he stated: "our Government, which we wish to keep out of business, is forced into the worst kind of it — dealing with commodities on behalf of whole nations of consumers." Hope was held forth, however, by two major efforts of the Department of Commerce which could obviate the need for more drastic government intervention: its conservation campaign seemingly bore fruit by 1926 in lower prices on imported rubber; its search for independent sources of supply also was proceeding satisfactorily.[23]

Officials of the Department of Commerce worked actively in support of the anti-monopoly campaign. They elaborated and detailed further Hoover's theme that the foreign monopoly problem was aggravated by the degree of *government* sanction and participation. Dr. E. Dana Durand (Chief, Division of Statistical Research) found these government-sponsored monopolies to be particularly objectionable because "governments work more ponderously and awkwardly and usually more unintelligently." Being unreasonable, he continued, foreign governments could not be convinced that their restrictions would only encourage speculation, violent price fluctuations, threats of retaliation, and

22. Hoover, *The Future of Our Foreign Trade*, p. 8. Italics mine.
23. *Ibid.*, pp. 9-10; for a favorable analysis of Hoover's watch-word that in conservation "the consumer possesses a potent weapon even against the formidable character of government price-fixing," see: *The Rubber Age*, XVIII (March 25, 1926), 421.

an actual shrinking of demand for the products which they were attempting to protect.[24]

When Dr. Durand wrote this (January, 1927) he could concentrate effectively on two factors which bolstered his conclusions. First, the upward speculative price spiral of controlled commodities had furnished "a powerful incentive to the development of competitive production in other countries [mainly the Dutch East Indies]" which did not join any control scheme. Secondly, the demand for such products as rubber and coffee actually decreased, as the consumer was "encouraged by exhortations and suggestions . . . from the Department of Commerce," not to mention the natural reaction against high prices. Durand, however, gave substantial credit for the resulting decline in rubber prices to his Department's "active agitation."[25]

Neither did Dr. Durand shrink from the controversy aroused by those who criticized Hoover on the grounds that he was being inconsistent in championing free trade in tropical commodities while supporting United States tariff protection. A "clear distinction may be drawn," Durand maintained, respecting "ethical and economic aspects, between [foreign] government controls of exportation and [American] protective tariffs restricting importation." The latter, he explained, were intended to make the United States prosperous, thus helping to create an even better market for raw materials from abroad.[26] He failed to mention that the reverse of his argument could be used just as readily by a *European* economic nationalist favoring protection of commodities sold to the United States.

Turning to another aspect of the controversy — "widespread injection of government into business [and the] renewal of old pre-war price-fixing devices" — Dr. Julius Klein (Director, Bureau of Foreign and Domestic Commerce) also joined in the

24. Dr. E. Dana Durand, "Economic and Political Effects of Governmental Interference with the Free International Movement of Raw Materials," *International Conciliation*, no. 226 (Jan. 1927), pp. 29, 31.
25. *Ibid.*, pp. 28, 32-33; Hoover, *Memoirs*, II, 84.
26. Durand, *op. cit.*, p. 30.

public crusade led by Secretary Hoover.[27] He, too, warned the public of the unsound business practices and tactics of "aggressive competition" which commodity monopolies abroad represented. He described the new European cartels as a potentially serious threat to America, for they combined "all the usual faults of monopolies" with the trappings of government sponsorship and protection; they involved, moreover, "such essentials as rubber, coffee, nitrate, sisal, potash, quinine," etc.[28]

In another article, Dr. Klein continued his attack on the foreign cartel problem, confining his attention this time mainly to the chemicals and manufactures. For the moment, he concluded, these cartels seemed to be intended mainly to stabilize European economic conditions. "Quite conceivably," however, they could "develop ultimately [into] a weapon for an offensive against America."[29] He concluded hopefully that "the industrial and commercial world is still a long way from abandoning its belief in individualism and competition," even though the evidence his article presented seemed to indicate an opposite trend for Europe.[30]

A distinctively moderate note in the opposition to raw material combinations was sounded in a book by William S. Culbertson, a member of the U. S. Tariff Commission (1917-25). He, too, agreed with Hoover "that international monopoly . . . should not be permitted to exact unreasonable prices from consumers in other countries." Culbertson, however, suggested that the problem be solved cooperatively, through the formation of an international agency to regulate world trade in raw materials. The purpose of this agency would be to assure, by peaceful means, the delivery of essential raw materials "at equitable prices and in equitable quantities to consumers in nations not holding political control over the raw materials in question."[31]

27. Dr. Julius Klein, "Business," *loc. cit.*, p. 106.
28. *Ibid.*, pp. 107-108.
29. Klein, "International Cartels," *Foreign Affairs*, VI (April, 1928), 448.
30. *Ibid.*, p. 458.
31. William S. Culbertson, *International Economic Policies* (New York, 1925), p. 334.

Congress Investigates "Foreign Government Controls"

In the years immediately following the end of World War I many Americans came to believe that their sacrifices in that conflict had not been worthwhile. The United States, after having been inveigled by European intrigues into a war from which it had gained little or nothing, was now faced by former friends turned economic enemies. Related closely to this line of reasoning was the feeling among some Americans that Europe would continue to seek her selfish ends at the expense of the United States, especially in economic matters. Some pessimists went so far as to predict that wartime and post-Armistice debts would not be repaid. Others regarded suspiciously foreign price-fixing of essential raw materials as an attempt to finance European recovery at the American consumer's expense.[32]

Prodded by numerous complaints made against controls on imported raw materials, the Sixty-Seventh Congress in February, 1923 "authorized and made appropriations for an investigation by the Department of Commerce of the growth and extent of foreign government controls of the production and exportation and the prices of crude rubber, coffee, nitrates, and other raw materials essential to our need." The Commerce Department was also asked to ascertain "whether these controls were being used to the detriment of the American consumer."[33] This was precisely the type of mandate which the Commerce Department had been seeking and for which Hoover had prepared so well the Department's information and publicity machinery.

In March, 1923 Congress instructed the Department of Commerce to organize a project which was even more challenging — "to investigate and report on the possibilities of developing the rubber-plantation industry in the Philippines and Latin America

32. Benjamin H. Williams, *Economic Foreign Policy of the United States* (New York, 1929), pp. 3, 219-220, 224-225; Benjamin B. Wallace and Lynn R. Edminster, *International Control of Raw Materials* (Washington, 1930), pp. 4, 275-277.
33. House Committee on Interstate and Foreign Commerce, *Preliminary Report on Crude Rubber, Coffee, Etc.* (Washington, 1926), p. 1. This work will hereafter be cited as *Preliminary Report*.

[as well as] the conditions of production and marketing of other essential raw materials for American industries."[34] Hoover had himself suggested such a survey to encourage the production of essential raw materials under American ownership. As part of his anti-monopoly program, he proposed "measures [such as this one] by which our consumers may set up such counter-action as will protect them."[35] With characteristic efficiency, Hoover proceeded to expand the Crude Rubber Section of his Department and recruited specialists from the business and academic fields to participate in the search for independent sources of rubber and other essential raw materials.[36]

While the search for alternate sources of raw materials continued, Hoover corresponded with such prominent political leaders as Senator Arthur Capper (Kansas), calling attention to "measures which can be taken in protection of the American consumer." In a letter to Capper (March, 1924), Hoover deplored the effects on the American farmer of controls in potash, coffee, sisal, etc., and proposed a new and controversial tactic — the legalization of American buyers' monopolies to combat the foreign combinations.[37]

By the end of 1925 rubber prices rose to record heights; Congress now heard even "louder" complaints from American importers. House majority floor leader John Q. Tilson (Connecticut) successfully engineered a new resolution, proposing that Congress, in full-scale hearings, should "investigate the control of production and exportation of certain essential raw materials and the effect of such control upon the commerce of the United States."[38]

34. Quoted by Hoover in Foreword to Special Agent David M. Figart's *The Plantation Rubber Industry in the Middle East* (Washington, 1925), p. vii.

35. *Ibid.*

36. Special File, "Investigation of Production of Crude Rubber," NA, RG 151:621.2; Hoover, *Memoirs*, II, 83.

37. Hoover letters quoted in Charles R. Whittlesey, *Governmental Control of Crude Rubber* (Princeton, 1931), Appendix "D", pp. 215-216; James C. Lawrence, *The World's Struggle With Rubber* (New York, 1931), p. 120; *The New York Times*, Dec. 15, 1925.

38. *Preliminary Report*, p. 1.

The conclusions reached by this investigation, conducted early in 1926 by the House Committee on Interstate and Foreign Commerce, reflected clearly the influence of its star witnesses, Secretary Hoover, Director Klein, and other members of the Department of Commerce. In twenty-three pages of almost uninterrupted testimony, Hoover painted the problem not only in terms of high prices for certain essential commodity imports, but also as a grave national issue involving "the whole policy that our country shall pursue toward a comparatively new and growing menace in international commerce and relations." Using even stronger language than had appeared in his previous statements, he condemned the government-sponsored combinations as a revival of "medievalism" and "war-time expediency." Citing nine imported commodities as being under such controls, Hoover estimated the annual value of these imports as $1,200,000,000, and warned that the movement easily could spread to many other products.[39]

Following his usual pattern of presenting the problem, Hoover's testimony denounced the "artificially created shortages and unreasonable prices" which placed an added burden of $500 to $800 million on the American consumer. Such overcharges, he inferred, were the characteristic result of monopolistic greed and speculation. Not only was "every family budget penalized," Hoover admonished, but the entire economy also was threatened by the inability of the American manufacturer "to rely upon his own judgment as to the conduct of his business when the policies of government officials in some foreign land dictate his destinies."[40]

Public and Congressional incriminations of this type tended to evoke an emotional response from many an American worker and consumer, who envisioned factory production cut-backs because of exorbitant rubber prices. Presumably, this affected also the American entrepreneur, who during the 1920's would not

---

39. House Committee on Interstate and Foreign Commerce, *Hearings on Crude Rubber, Coffee, etc.* (Washington, 1926), p. 2, *passim*.
40. *Ibid.*, pp. 3, 4, 6.

tolerate interference from Washington. How would he respond to interference by a foreign government? In a decade of reaction against European methods and motives, it was by no means incongruous that a nationally prominent Secretary of Commerce should attack boldly foreign restraints and serve "notice upon these controls that our people will resist." Furthermore, as Hoover warned, the United States Government's "defensive" powers could go far beyond merely an educational program advising conservation of imported raw materials.[41]

One of the more potent weapons in Hoover's arsenal was the plan for withholding American credit from the offending combinations. Everett G. Holt, Chief of the Rubber Division under Hoover, noted that various foreign control schemes had involved some unsuccessful efforts to obtain funds in the United States. As a matter of fact, Holt explained, public protests against the "attempt of other controls to borrow money in the American market with which to strengthen their position against the American consumer [led to the] investigation by the Committee on Interstate and Foreign Commerce . . . resulting in a unanimous report entirely confirming the views of the [Commerce] department."[42]

Hoover himself testified frankly concerning his explicit policy of opposing the extension of American credits to any foreign control scheme. "We have asked our banking houses in their own interest," he revealed, "not to arouse against themselves that criticism of the American consuming public that would inevitably follow if they were to engage in the financing of these monopolies, and thus become parties to mulcting of the American consumer." Hoover could report with satisfaction "that our bankers have cooperated in such a policy."[43]

41. *Ibid.*, p. 7.
42. Everett G. Holt in the *Fourteenth Annual Report of the Secretary of Commerce,* pp. 37-38; for British criticism of Holt's memorandum of Oct. 25, 1926 opposing the use of American capital to finance foreign controls see the report of William R. Castle (State Department, Division of Western European Affairs), Nov. 3, 1926, NA, RG 59:841.6176/123.
43. *Hearings on Crude Rubber, Coffee, etc.,* p. 4; Grosvenor M. Jones to Hoover, Nov. 30, 1925, NA, RG 151:235.1.

One of the valuable results of the Congressional hearings of 1926 was to suggest that the Hoover-directed campaign against "monopolies" in nine commodities and the prospects of others in as many as twenty or thirty was somewhat exaggerated and overly apprehensive. The evidence available indicates that only the controls in rubber, coffee, and potash were a significant hazard for the American economy, although no such limitation would have satisfied the Department of Commerce or the Republican majority among Congressional investigators. For example, the investigation brought out that the restrictions regulating the export of Egyptian long-staple cotton were infrequently enforced and appeared to be more a water conservation scheme than an insidious "monopoly."[44] Moreover, efforts by the U. S. Department of Agriculture to encourage production of longer staple cotton in Arizona and California mitigated substantially American dependence on foreign producers.[45]

Silk from Japan represented another product which ostensibly was under the control of the "menacing" monopoly headed by the Imperial Raw Silk Company, a combination using Japanese government subsidies to curtail exports. In this case, however, the Japanese controls reflected the dislocations caused by the 1922 depression and the successful competition of American rayon, rather than any overt Japanese attempt at monopoly.[46] Although Japan produced 75 per cent of the world's silk supply, her stabilization efforts at this time represented no real threat to American industry.[47] The effect of Japanese controls on camphor in this period was soon to be offset by American synthetics. The same was true of quinine too, at least in part. As for Chilean nitrates, the Commerce Department admitted that in spite of government price fixing and quotas the rates charged by this "natural monopoly," partly because of the competition of syn-

44. Edward T. Pickard (Chief, Textile Division), *Hearings on Crude Rubber, Coffee, etc.,* p. 27.

45. Hoover, *Memoirs,* II, 84.

46. Wallace and Edminster, *International Control of Raw Materials,* pp. 13, 362; *Hearings on Crude Rubber, Coffee, etc.,* p. 28.

47. *Preliminary Report,* p. 12.

thetic supplies, were no higher than before World War I. Fearing a future crisis, however, the Department demanded "a prompt solution of [the] Muscle Shoals [power development] to greatly facilitate [sic] our home production of nitrogen."[48]

Solicitous concern for the American farmer was never omitted from the official evidence presented against the cooperative society formed by the Mexican Government to control the production and marketing of sisal hemp (hennequin). Mexico supplied 90 per cent of the American demand for this important fiber, needed to make cordage and sacks. Its import value, though substantially lower than the value of other commodities under Congressional investigation was about $18 millions in 1925. A Commerce Department official (Edward T. Pickard) emphasized the fact that there was only a single sales agency for Mexican sisal in the United States which, he estimated, overcharged American agriculturists $8 to $10 million annually. The investigating Committee agreed with these accusations of "exorbitant prices exacted from the American farmer."[49]

Actually, sisal prices in 1926 had dropped to 9 cents a pound from the post-war high of 19 cents, when Mexican controls ostensibly had "cost the American farmer an extra $35-$40 millions." The House Committee on Interstate and Foreign Commerce recognized this fact, but concluded that "the present form of control" (1926) was still robbing the American farmer. Although the Mexican scheme proved incapable of maintaining prices in the face of competition from India and the Philippines, the Committee still indicted it as only "less iniquitous than some previous forms."[50] Secretary Hoover and his Department saw both the need and the opportunity for international economic action in this area. "In order to relieve the oppression

---

48. Charles C. Concannon (Chief, Chemical Division), *Hearings on Crude Rubber, Coffee, etc.*, p. 30. Hoover relates how his Department encouraged American companies to develop the production of synthetic camphor and nitrates to break the hold of foreign "monopolists" in Japan and Chile respectively, *Memoirs*, II, 83.

49. *Hearings on Crude Rubber, Coffee, etc.*, p. 28.

50. *Preliminary Report*, p. 12.

of the Mexican sisal control," Hoover wrote later, "we persuaded Cuba to begin producing that commodity."[51]

The recommendations resulting from the Committee hearings on foreign combinations approved the conservation program of the Department of Commerce and repeated the major conclusions of Secretary Hoover with regard to other "defensive" measures. Using the language of Commerce Department publications, the Committee's report criticized raw material controls as violating basic economic principles by stifling production and encouraging speculation. The report also termed these monopoly efforts a threat to international relations, since they exposed the American consumer to the whims of foreign politicians. The Committee demanded action on Hoover's suggestions concerning the development of Muscle Shoals as a means to aid the synthetic nitrates industry. More funds were requested to permit the Department of Commerce to explore for potash in Texas and New Mexico. The report praised the Commerce Department's surveys aimed to promote the development of American sources of essential raw materials, "either under its own flag or in suitable foreign countries."[52]

Paraphrasing Hoover's warning against loans to foreign control schemes, the Committee declared that "American citizens should refuse to aid or assist them by extending credit." If nothing else, the Committee counseled, "self-interest should prompt this action on the part of American financial interests, for the granting of loans of this character would create a just resentment against them on the part of the American public." Here, then, was a repetition of Hoover's inference that financial aid to foreign monopolies was inconsistent with national policy and at variance with the views of loyal Americans. The actual criteria established by Hoover for the approval or disapproval of foreign loans were correlative to the Committee's view that

51. Hoover, *Memoirs*, II, 83; for other aspects of this problem, see: Wallace and Edminster, *op. cit.*, pp. 277, 294-295.
52. *Preliminary Report*, pp. 13-14; compare to the Commerce Department's *Foreign Combinations To Control Prices of Raw Materials (Trade Information Bulletin)*, no. 385, 1926, *passim*.

it was the Government's duty to act as the executive arm of the "American public," by seeing that "requests for loans [by 'monopolies'] should be discouraged, and if made should be refused."[53]

Shortly after the conclusion of the hearings on raw material monopolies, it became apparent that the "American people" were by no means unanimous in their support of the Committee's recommendations. George O. May, a bank official and director of the Council on Foreign Relations, characterized the report as merely an "echo" of the views proclaimed by the Secretary of Commerce. In a feature article published in the *Atlantic Monthly,* May accused Hoover of a "strongly nationalistic approach [and] an overstatement of the case in specific instances." Reviewing the record of the hearings, he noted that in some cases the conclusions reached were "quite unsupported by testimony presented on behalf of the Department of Commerce . . . ; in the case of [Chilean] nitrates [for example] the evidence negatives any suggestion of restricted output or unreasonable profits."[54]

May's charges that the hearings were "mainly partisan and wholly inadequate" centered around the personality of Secretary Hoover, whose campaign against foreign combinations made him quite unpopular with the "liberals" and "internationalists." (In 1926 these two groups were a futile minority.) In a flight of ironic praise, May asserted that Hoover's "undeniably great gifts lie rather in the field of organization of [administrative] effort and of public opinion than in the fields of economics and the dispassionate analysis of controversial facts." This view was shared by others who felt that the investigation was both biased and partisan, and that the evidence failed to produce proof of a serious threat to the American consumer.[55]

Even some of the trade periodicals which opposed strongly

---

53. *Preliminary Report,* p. 15.
54. George O. May, "Rubber: The Inquiry and the Facts," *The Atlantic Monthly,* CXXVII (June, 1926), 805-806, 812.
55. *Ibid.,* pp. 807, 812; *The Nation,* CXXII (Jan. 20, 1926), 50; *The New York Times,* Jan. 8, 10, 12, Feb. 19, March 16, 20, 1926.

foreign price fixing of raw materials found fault with the Congressional investigation. The object of their censure was the Democratic minority which ostensibly made a political football of the hearings by raising the issue of profits earned by American tire manufacturers, a fact which the trade regarded as a dangerous drift toward interference with business.[56] In spite of this criticism, the American tire manufacturers had been given ample opportunity to testify, as were their major representatives, such as the Rubber Association of America, the American Automobile Association, and others. Not one witness, however, represented officially the views of the groups on trial, namely, the foreign combinations.

The accusations of partisanship in the Congressional battle on the raw material controls are borne out by the political claims and counter-claims concerning the relevance of American tariff policy to the area under investigation. Hoover and the Republican majority on the Committee repeatedly denied the opposition's allegation that foreign controls represented a justifiable reaction against American protectionism. They pointed out how Brazil attempted to control coffee prices; how the British made plans to control rubber, even before the passage of the Fordney-McCumber Act's high rates in 1922. This argument failed, however, to admit that protectionism in American tariff policy had become an expected phenomenon long before 1922. The Republicans were on somewhat safer ground when they pointed to the absence of American duties on imports of tropical raw materials and the favorable balance of trade which some producers of these commodities possessed in relation to the United States.[57]

Finally, Democratic representatives Sam Rayburn, George Huddlestone, and others on the investigating Committee framed their own minority report, charging the Republican Administration with having itself set the "precedents for the regulation of

56. *India Rubber and Tire Review* (Akron), XXVI (Jan. 1926), 16, 18.
57. *Preliminary Report*, p. 4; Rufus S. Tucker (Finance and Investment Division), *The Balance of International Payments of the United States In 1924* (*Trade Information Bulletin*, no. 340, 1925), Foreword by Hoover, *passim*.

prices . . . [for] trade restrictions, discriminations, and obstructions." In the minority's opinion, the British Stevenson Plan became "a price hold-up agency" only after they felt the effects of Republican tariff policies. Objecting to "boycott and retaliation" which might alienate America's friends abroad, the Democrats called instead for "fair trade agreements," unhampered by American credit controls or other forms of pressure.[58]

The minority, by publicizing their doubts, questioned "whether a country [the United States] which was enforcing a highly protective flexible tariff could with any grace criticize control of raw materials by countries whose prosperity was dependent on exports of raw materials rather than on manufacture."[59] In the course of the hearings Representative Huddlestone so belabored the moral issues involved as to wring an admission from Director Klein that the British controls on rubber were not necessarily "unethical," since they affected British manufacturers of rubber goods also.[60] Huddlestone then proceeded to expostulate on the "unethical" nature of Hoover's attempt to restrict American demand by encouraging conservation of imported raw materials.[61]

In analyzing the campaign against foreign monopolies organized by Secretary Hoover it is important to note the wide sea of reaction which his proposals aroused. At its simplest level, Hoover's campaign held forth the appeal of a resistance movement against efforts abroad "to soak Uncle Sam." The Commerce Department's effective use of publicity media and its influence with legislators and business augmented national interest in the anti-monopoly campaign. Sectional groups, trade associations, "liberals," Democrats, Republicans, and "internationalists," at one time or another, all participated in the controversy.[62]

58. Appendix to the *Preliminary Report*, pp. 17-18.

59. George O. May, *op. cit.*, p. 805.

60. *Hearings on Crude Rubber, Coffee, etc.*, pp. 326-327.

61. *Ibid.*, p. 328.

62. "Hooverism," lead editorial in the *Yorkshire Post*, Jan. 6, 1926, quoted by U. S. Consul Stillman W. Eels, Jan. 6, 1926, NA, RG 59:841.6176/68.

CHAPTER V

RUBBER IN THE POLITICAL ECONOMY OF BRITAIN AND AMERICA

Conflict Over The Stevenson Plan

At the end of World War I the prospects for a continued growth of Anglo-American friendship appeared bright. The democratic institutions of the two war-time Allies and the bonds of Anglo-Saxon culture and tradition had long transcended the Atlantic barrier. But in the world setting created by the Peace of Versailles, even nations sharing a common heritage were confronted by economic rivalries and tensions which pervaded the whole sphere of international relations. During the controversy over crude rubber prices in the 1920's the interests of England, the producer, appeared to be unalterably opposed to those of America, the consumer.

The demands of war and of the expanding automobile trade stimulated the relatively young plantation rubber industry of the Far East. With the end of the post-Armistice boom, however, lack of shipping and prevailing international economic uncertainties resulted in the accumulation of rubber surpluses. Faced with the threat of overproduction, the British Rubber Growers' Association adopted, in November 1920, a voluntary scheme for lowering output by 25 per cent. British-owned plantations in Malaya and Ceylon produced at the time about 75 per cent of the world's rubber supply, but the voluntary re-

striction plan failed because of the opposition of the smaller
producers who were not represented in the Rubber Growers'
Association. As a result, rubber prices fell to a new low in August, 1922.[1]

Winston Churchill, who at that time in his brilliant career
made a stormy Secretary of State for the Colonies, appointed
an investigating committee to save the rubber "industry, in which
quite £100,000,000 of British capital had been sunk, [from]
falling into ruin."[2] The committee, headed by Sir James Stevenson — "Churchill's personal financial adviser" — found that
voluntary restrictions had failed to stabilize rubber production. Its report, delivered in November 1922, recommended
compulsory restriction enforced by government machinery to
prevent widespread bankruptcy among the British growers.
Churchill agreed with the committee's conclusions and proceeded immediately to put them into effect, since he believed
"it was impossible for the Colonial Office to witness the financial ruin of the rubber-producing colonies owing to the continual
sale of their products below the cost of production."[3]

Subsequently, British legislation, formalized as the Stevenson Act, was denounced by Secretary of Commerce Hoover for
placing a "supercharge upon the American consumer of from
$625 to $675 millions per annum."[4] Looking back on the 1920's
through the medium of the *Memoirs*, Hoover upbraided Winston Churchill for the part he played, when, as Secretary of
State for the Colonies, he initiated this "worst example" of foreign price controls. The Stevenson Act, Hoover recalled, "forced
up" rubber prices from a "highly profitable" 20 cents per pound
(in 1922) to a $1.21 by 1925, "and the extra dollar was mulct-

1. Sir Andrew McFadyean, ed., *The History of Rubber Regulation 1934-
1943* (London, 1944), pp. 27-28. The first three chapters provide a useful
background for the Stevenson Plan and its consequences, from World War I
to 1928.

2. *Ibid.*, p. 29; Churchill is quoted in Howard and Ralph Wolf's *Rubber;
A Story of Glory and Greed* (New York, 1936), pp. 220-221.

3. Churchill, quoted in *ibid.;* Harold R. G. Greaves, *Raw Materials and
International Control* (London, 1936), p. 124.

4. *Fourteenth Annual Report of the Secretary of Commerce*, p. 39.

ing the United States at the rate of $900,000,000 per annum. . . ."[5] (The damage estimate, in Hoover's mind, apparently had grown with the passage of time.)

Under the terms of the Stevenson Act or "Plan," which was enforced by colonial legislation in British Malaya and Ceylon, the actual production of each rubber plantation for the year ending October 31, 1920, was fixed as the "standard output." When the Plan went into effect, in November 1922, rubber exports were limited to only 60 per cent of "standard." If a planter chose to ship 65 per cent of his "standard output" the usual duty of 1 penny per pound was raised to 4 pence on the entire shipment, not merely on the excess. Beyond 65 per cent of "standard," each 5 per cent increase added a penny's tax to the total shipment. In a none-too-successful attempt to adjust the Plan to changing market conditions, a cumbersome system was set up whereby the permitted percentage of "standard" production could be raised or lowered.[6]

Even British authorities on the Stevenson Plan — Sir Andrew McFadyean and Harold R. G. Greaves, for example — have agreed, since its demise in 1928, with some of the accusations made against it by Hoover. Undoubtedly, the Plan was too awkward and one-sided to permit elasticity in production and price; the Colonial Secretary's Advisory Committee and the local administrative committees were far too subservient to the vested interests of the growers. The latter had been "spoiled" by profits which in some cases were said to average 117-125 per cent.[7] Sir Andrew McFadyean, writing for the International Rubber Regulation Committee, recalled that the Stevenson Plan had permitted 100 per cent of "standard" production only in 1926, in spite of the vast new demand for rubber.[8] Although

5. Hoover, *Memoirs,* II, 82.

6. A factual report on the operations of the Stevenson Plan was presented by Representative Walter H. Newton (Minnesota) during the Congressional debate on his bill to legalize American pools for the purchase of rubber and other raw materials, *Congressional Record,* 70 Cong., 1 Sess., pp. 5974-5980 (April 5, 1928); Howard and Ralph Wolf, *op. cit.,* p. 223.

7. Greaves, *op. cit.,* p. 125.

8. McFadyean, *op. cit.,* pp. 33, 35.

rubber prices soared by July 1925, to $1.03 per pound, legal exports from the British colonies were still fixed at only 65 per cent of "standard."[9]

This type of inelasticity opened the Stevenson Plan to American charges of greedy profiteering and stifling of industry. "There is no question but what 36 cents [per pound] brings an ample return to the producer," calculated the (1926) Congressional investigators of foreign raw material controls. They also recalled that Sir James Stevenson and other "Britishers" had at least implied that their goal was a "fair" price of only 36 cents per pound, which the Americans estimated to represent a 15 to 25 per cent return for the planters. Worst of all, Department of Commerce statistics seemed to bear out the conclusion that the "exportation of potential [rubber] production [had] been restricted about one-half," depriving the world economy of an invaluable "146,126 long tons."[10]

Hoover Mobilizes the Machinery of Diplomacy

Only one month after the Stevenson Plan was adopted by the British Government, an American manufacturers' delegation headed by officials of the Firestone Tire and Rubber Company visited the Washington headquarters of the Department of Commerce. Received by Dr. Julius Klein, Director of the Bureau of Foreign and Domestic Commerce, they expressed their concern over the rising prices of crude rubber. Subsequently, taking note of Assistant Commerce Secretary (Claudius H.) Huston's impending visit to London, the delegation requested the use of his "good offices" to determine the outlook for a more flexible approach in the British Government's attitude on the Stevenson Plan. Soon, indeed, Huston was notified by Klein to place this matter on the agenda for the London trip. In the following years the Commerce Department's Foreign Service maintained

9. House Committee on Interstate and Foreign Commerce, *Preliminary Report*, p. 6.
10. *Ibid.*, pp. 6, 7-8.

a steady flow of reports concerning the rubber "monopoly" situation.[11]

The Department of Commerce under Hoover came to regard the Stevenson Plan as a crucial test in "the battle waged against foreign monopolies in raw materials." Its defeat, according to Dr. Klein, could be hoped to bring broader beneficial results

[by discouraging] foreign controls of other raw materials . . . [which] were stimulated originally by the flagrant purposes of the British so-called Stevenson law, the object of which was a deliberate campaign of raising the price of rubber from around 35 cents a pound, ultimately to about $1.25 a pound.[12]

As manifested in the Congressional hearings of 1926, the Department of Commerce, and most of the American rubber manufacturers, suspected the Stevenson Plan of legalizing extortionate prices, in spite of assurances by a British delegation of growers that there would be no runaway market.[13]

The Commerce Department's efforts to mediate a private-level agreement between British growers and American manufacturers bore little fruit. A group of visiting British representatives, organized to witness the vast productive potential of American rubber goods manufacturing plants, were not convinced that the United States could absorb the unregulated output of plantation rubber. No more successful were the informal representations of the Department of Commerce which were conducted "through official channels."[14]

Meanwhile, the Rubber Association of America, consisting of major importers and manufacturers, conducted a well-organized campaign against the Stevenson Plan. In this, they were helped by "Secretary Hoover . . . who was working jointly with the Secretary of State [Frank B. Kellogg]." Kellogg was finally

11. Klein to Huston, Dec. 4, 1922, NA, RG 151:254 (Straits Settlements).
12. Quotations from a letter to the author written by Dr. Julius Klein, Washington, Nov. 26, 1957. Dr. Klein left the Commerce Department in 1933. Since then, he has been active as a business consultant and writer on economic foreign policy problems.
13. *Preliminary Report,* p. 7.
14. *Ibid.*

prevailed upon to transmit to the British Government the protests of American rubber manufacturers, and to make "further
representations" which may have led to the slight increase in
the permitted percentage of "standard output" early in 1926.[15]
Although rubber prices remained high, A. L. Viles (General
Manager, the Rubber Association of America) could testify
that "the interests of the American public and the rubber
manufacturing industry have been admirably supported by our
Government, particularly by the Secretary of Commerce, Mr.
Herbert Hoover."[16]

The fact that the Secretary of Commerce was thus singled
out for praise was not without significance. It was an additional
reminder of Hoover's sanguine program at home and abroad
for the defeat of foreign combinations which he considered a
threat to American enterprise; moreover, it reflected the intimate cooperation which Hoover achieved with Viles and the
leading rubber manufacturers. By contrast, Secretary of State
Kellogg was restrained in the matter of foreign controls by the
diplomatist's prudence. His actions in this area appear to stem
largely from the initiative and pressure of Hoover and of the
rubber industry.

The exchange of confidential telegrams between Kellogg and
Ambassador Alanson B. Houghton in London sheds some light
on the diplomatic problems raised by the Stevenson Plan. In
July, 1925, after "consulting fully with Rutherford, Vice President of [the] Goodyear Company," Houghton conferred with
Foreign Secretary Sir Austen Chamberlain regarding the gravity
of the rubber situation. He warned Chamberlain that the United
States was fully prepared to encourage the use of rubber substitutes, and to seek independent sources of supply.[17]

If American manufacturers were forced out of business because of high rubber prices, with consequent unemployment in
the United States, Houghton continued, the "effect on public

15. A. L. Viles (General Manager, the Rubber Association of America),
Hearings on Crude Rubber, Coffee, Etc., pp. 35-36; *Preliminary Report*, p. 3.
16. A. L. Viles, *Hearings, supra.*, p. 44.
17. Houghton to Kellogg, July 23, 1925, NA, RG 59:841.6176/6.

opinion at home would be unfavorable, and [would] tend to bring up our position on free exports." There was no telling then what counter-measures might be considered by an aroused Congress.[18] This was a rather thinly veiled threat of retaliatory American controls on cotton and wheat, which probably did not surprise Chamberlain. Previously, on several occasions, Hoover and the Congressional investigators of raw material "monopolies" had commented bluntly on the availability of this weapon and pointedly reminded the British that the value of their exports to the United States had increased by 74 per cent between 1913 and 1925.[19]

Houghton finally explained his lack of success with the Foreign Ministry by affirming to Kellogg that "relief can be obtained" only through a broad settlement of differences between the two countries, "on general grounds of high policy."[20] Kellogg's telegraphed response repeated the demands of the Rubber Association of America, urging the State Department "to make further representations to the British Government . . . that the restriction plan should be entirely suspended November first [1925]." Both Kellogg and Houghton always kept "Secretary Hoover's views" under consideration. Kellogg feared, however, that the virulence of the American anti-Stevenson campaign "might make it more difficult for the British Government to modify its policy," especially if the news of State Department pressure on the British were to "leak out into the press."[21]

These misgivings were strengthened by Houghton's confidential warnings against extreme propaganda or pressure tactics by the American Rubber Association. In a tone reminiscent of the rivalry abroad between Commerce and State, Houghton complained that the Commercial Attaché's Office in London was acting on its own to discover the plans of the British Colonial

18. *Ibid.*
19. *Preliminary Report*, p. 5. Part of this increase was the result of an intensified demand for rubber in the United States, and inflated prices.
20. Houghton to Kellog, July 23, 1925, *loc. cit.*
21. *Ibid.;* Kellogg to Houghton, July 27, and October 10, 1925, *ibid.,* 841:6176/26, 27.

Office concerning rubber controls.[22] Somewhat later, Houghton telegraphed the results of a meeting, held without his prior knowledge or participation, between Colonial Secretary Churchill and representatives of American rubber manufacturers. Presumably arranged by the Commercial Attaché's Office, the meeting ended with a British promise to raise export quotas of rubber to 100 per cent of "standard output" in 1926. (Even this figure was considered by Hoover to be far below "potential" production.)[23]

Meanwhile, other State Department officials were hard put to keep up with their reports to Washington on the anti-Hoover and anti-American campaign in the British press. Consul Henry P. Starrett in Belfast reported widespread hostility toward the United States on the "rubber question." Noting that the issue was exacerbated by its relationship to the American attitudes on tariff protection and the payment of interallied war debts, he concluded that the "composite view . . . wears an ugly aspect." Part of Starrett's evidence were such editorials as the one in the Belfast *Northern Whig* (December 24, 1925) defending the policies of "Great Britain, Brazil, and other Powers [which] are simply retaliating now . . . on account of the nonsensical, outrageous and damnable rates of the [American] Fordney-McCumber Tariff Law."[24]

The American Embassy in London also collected clippings of "ill natured comment" aroused by what *The Outlook* called Hoover's "diatribe" against the Stevenson Plan. The latter, according to this London periodical, had saved the rubber industry and had even increased the world's production. Consequently, maintained the editorial, Hoover's "assumption of moral superiority" was unjustified, especially in view of American tariff policies and attempts to raise prices on cotton, copper, corn, and the products of "infant industries." Now that the United States had almost achieved a "corner" on gold, British-American

22. Houghton to Kellogg, Oct. 12, 1925, *ibid.*
23. Houghton to Kellogg, Dec. 4, 1925, *ibid.*, 841:6176/45.
24. Henry P. Starrett (U. S. Consul, Belfast), Jan. 4, 1926, NA, RG 59:841.6176/69.

friendship was being endangered by "the energetic measures undertaken . . . against the export of American capital," warned *The Outlook*. The kind of "laissez-faire which Mr. Hoover advocates," added the *New Leader*, "can only mean . . . the triumph of the Trust."[25]

Even the staid London *Times*, quoted by the United States embassy in "strictly confidential" dispatches, considered the attack on British rubber controls to be "inaccurate, unwise, and calculated to arouse ill feeling on the part of Americans imperfectly familiar with the facts." Its editors feared that "Hoover's laments may . . . serve to check a world-wide movement for the amicable adjustment of difficulties between the nations by mutual concession and agreement."[26]

Along with a sheaf of similar press reports, the London Embassy anxiously informed the State Department that Prime Minister Stanley Baldwin (Conservative) intended to make political capital out of American threats to retaliate with the controls on cotton and wheat. Baldwin, it was feared, would use these threats to obtain government subsidies for the expansion of cotton and wheat resources within the Empire, thus decreasing the need for American supplies. In effect, the Stevenson Plan controversy, as the London *Times* predicted, clearly involved the danger of full-scale trade war and autarchy.[27]

Other segments of the British press concentrated on invidious estimates of American wealth, coupled with more personal attacks on Secretary Hoover. The *Manchester Guardian* expounded on the prosperity of the typical American motorist and the high profits of the tire manufacturers. It concluded that "Mr. Hoover . . . has been making himself a little ridiculous" in fighting the Stevenson Plan at a time when American "monop-

25. *The Outlook* (London), Nov. 7, 1925, the *New Leader* (London), Nov. 6, 1925, and other clippings contained in the reports of Ray Atherton (First Secretary, U. S. Embassy, London), Nov. 13, 1925, NA, RG 59:841.6176/37.

26. U. S. Embassy (London) to the State Department, "Strictly Confidential" Dispatch #681, Jan. 6, 1926, NA, RG 59:841.6176/67, including editorial from the London *Times*, Jan. 5, 1926.

27. *Ibid.*

olies" operated as they pleased. In support of its contention, the newspaper quoted Congressman Loring M. Black's (D., N. Y.) statement that it made no sense "to legislate for the British when we cannot legislate for ourselves."[28]

The London *Daily Telegraph* also advised Hoover to look to the American rubber manufacturers if he honestly wished to find those who "fleeced" the American motorist. In spite of their wealth, continued the editorial, American companies, though previously unwilling to participate in the risks of developing plantation rubber were now finding fault with the justifiable profits of British capital. How could Hoover charge the Stevenson Plan with monopoly, asked the *Telegraph,* when Harvey S. Firestone (pioneer of mass production in rubber manufacturing) possessed the resources to start his own 100,000 acre rubber-growing project in Liberia?[29]

In a similar lead editorial titled "Hooverism," the *Yorkshire Post* censured the Department of Commerce for having replaced "the Anglo-American sentimental attachment" of World War I days with a crude debtor-creditor relationship. Attacking the Hoover letters to Senator Arthur Capper regarding the inequities of the Stevenson Plan, the *Post* concluded bitterly that "in the United States abuse of Great Britain is always a good political move."[30]

Understandably, these sentiments were amplified in the *Rangoon Gazette,* a journal described by Consul Charles J. Pisar (Burma) as closely connected with the (British) Colonial Office. The *Gazette* saw in "Mr. Hoover . . . one of those political economists who would like [to see his country] . . . prosperous while all others are either poverty stricken or struggling with second rate conditions." Its editorial, captioned, "America versus Europe," predicted a combination of aggrieved European

28. U. S. Embassy (London) to the State Department, Jan. 21, 1926, NA, RG 59:841.6176/72, including editorials from the *Manchester Guardian,* Jan. 12, 1926, and the *Daily Telegraph,* Jan. 9, 1926.

29. *Ibid.*

30. *Yorkshire Post,* Jan. 6, 1926, quoted by Stillman W. Eels (U. S. Consul, Leeds), Jan. 6, 1926, NA, RG 59:841.6176/68.

debtors and raw material producers united in "an economic Pact of Locarno directed against America."[31]

In November, 1926, British opinion was inflamed further as the result of an article by Everett G. Holt (Acting Chief, Rubber Division) entitled, "Foreign Government Price Fixing of Our Import Raw Materials." Holt blamed the "unreasonable prices" of rubber and other raw materials on "governments whose whole course is in disregard of the economics of production and trade and whose policies are . . . determined by matters entirely foreign to the industry."[32]

As a result of these published comments, a British protest delegation descended upon the State Department, consisting of Envoy Extra-ordinary and Minister Plenipotentiary Sir Henry G. Chilton (who remained in Washington through the years of the Stevenson Plan crisis 1924-28), and Sir John Broderick, Commercial Counselor of the British Embassy. The two Englishmen demanded that the American Government should "either permit them to put their own views forward [to the American public] or . . . stop the Department of Commerce from making its attacks on the policies of the British Government." They declared it "inconceivable" for a corresponding official of the British Board of Trade to ever make similar accusations in public against official trade policies of another government.[33]

Undaunted, the Department of Commerce urged its commercial agents and "Special Representatives" in London to continue their struggle for "assurances of protection in the case of runaway prices." Paul L. Palmerton (Chief, Rubber Division) extended the Department's regrets to the Commercial Attaché in London for having to bear the brunt of British resentment, reassuring him, however, "that Mr. Hoover has been interested

31. Clippings from the *Rangoon Gazette,* dispatch of Consul Charles J. Pisar (Burma), Feb. 1, 1926, NA, RG 59:841.6176/77.

32. Holt article attached to a memorandum by William R. Castle (Assistant Secretary of State), Nov. 3, 1926, NA, RG 59:841.6176/123. The same article, in slightly altered form, may be found in the *Fourteenth Annual Report of the Secretary of Commerce,* pp. 35-41.

33. Castle memorandum, *loc. cit.*

in rubber only because it was one of the foreign trade monopolies claiming public attention at the time."[34] This was, perhaps,
an oblique recognition that British public opinion believed
Hoover was playing the political game of "twisting the lion's
tail" to further his own presidential ambitions.[35] Congressman
Black was much more explicit in suggesting that the campaign
against the Stevenson Plan's rubber restrictions was launched
by "Hoover . . . when he got ideas of being President and when
he [subsequently] became anti-British."[36]

The trans-Atlantic controversy over the Stevenson Plan
aroused so much passion, claimed Edwin Emerson in *Hoover
and His Times,* that "some American admirers of the League of
Nations wanted to have the quarrel about rubber submitted to
the League of Nations' proposed international economic conference [1927]." This was not done, according to Emerson,
only because "the officials of the League at Geneva had misgivings [as to] whether President Coolidge would agree to such
a proposal."[37] A more reliable authority, Ervin Hexner (in his
scholarly study of *International Cartels*), asserted that the "great
political and economic repercussions aroused [by] the Stevenson
scheme . . . [were] still mentioned even in 1945 . . . as a reason
why the United States public should resist all kinds of international marketing controls."[38]

Hoover and the Import Pool Idea: the Newton Bill

The defeat of the Stevenson Plan was, in the final analysis,
almost as much the result of its own inherent weaknesses as of
the campaign organized against it by Secretary Hoover. His
mobilization in this struggle of the available American weapons
— both economic and political — does represent, however, a

34. Paul L. Palmerton, instructions to Commerce Attaché O. M. Butler
(London), Feb. 3 and 8, 1926, NA, RG 151:254 (Straits Settlements).
35. Howard and Ralph Wolf, *Rubber,* pp. 227, 229.
36. Representative Loring M. Black (New York), *Congressional Record,*
70 Cong., 1 Sess., p. 5996 (April 5, 1928).
37. Emerson, *op. cit.,* p. 276.
38. Ervin Hexner, *International Cartels* (Chapel Hill, 1945), p. 284.

significant phase in the economic foreign policy of the United States. One of the counter-measures of "defense" which Secretary Hoover pressed was the idea of creating a legalized American buying pool whenever an imported commodity came under the control of foreign "price-fixing" schemes.

The legislative record already contained a similar law, namely the Webb-Pomerene Act of 1918, which permitted American combinations in the export trade. It was only logical that Hoover and other opponents of foreign raw material controls should seek an amendment of this Act to allow, under certain conditions, American *import* pools. Suggestions of this type were made only months after the initiation of the Stevenson Plan. By the Spring of 1923, Harvey S. Firestone excoriated members of the American Rubber Association for failing to cooperate promptly with "Secretary Hoover's suggestions of a buying organization to combat the British monopoly of rubber production."[39]

Throughout this campaign Hoover made good use of his connections with American business and with Congressional legislators. He was aided all along by "the best organized press contacts in Washington."[40] In a widely publicized letter to Senator Capper, Hoover argued that "if by an extension of . . . the Webb Pomerene Act . . . our consumers were allowed to set up common purchasing agencies for these imported raw materials where there is positive combination in control, I am confident that our people could hold their own." He specified that in such cases pooled buying would be quite feasible because of the "limited numbers of primary purchasers of these raw materials." As a result of impending American "counter activities," Hoover noted that the foreign combinations already had

39. Harvey S. Firestone to the Rubber Association of America, May 8, 1923, quoted in James C. Lawrence, *The World's Struggle With Rubber* (New York, 1931), p. 120. Lawrence was Dean of the University of Minnesota, president of a rubber manufacturing company, and a top executive of the B. F. Goodrich Co. See also: Whittlesey, *op. cit.*, p. 159n.

40. Lawrence, *supra*, p. 102.

been forced to concede somewhat to United States economic interests.[41]

Writing in *Foreign Affairs,* Harry N. Whitford (Chief, Crude Rubber Section), expounded further on Hoover's proposition that "centralized control [of raw materials] . . . is a factor which American industry cannot afford to neglect." Whitford indicated his concern over the altered geopolitical standing of the United States and pointed out that during "the course of a few years America's dependence on rubber shifted from the American continent to Asia," where the bulk of world production was controlled under a "scheme of government intervention [developed by] the British Colonial Office."[42] Referring to his chief's proposals for strengthening America's international position in the face of the Stevenson Plan, Whitford explained that "it was just such a danger . . . that the Secretary of Commerce foresaw when he advocated an amendment to grant legislative sanction to a combination of buyers of foreign-controlled commodities."[43]

Professor Edward M. Earle of Columbia, writing in *International Conciliation* (1927), also backed "Mr. Hoover [when he] urged upon Congress the desirability of permitting American manufacturers to enter into combinations, anti-trust legislation to the contrary notwithstanding, for the purchase of raw materials from abroad."[44] A rubber industry expert and former "Special Agent" of the Department of Commerce, David M. Figart, distributed his own privately printed pamphlet which also supported the idea of American buying monopolies, on the grounds that United States appeals for additional supplies of urgently required rubber were falling on deaf ears. Figart dismissed as unreasonably hostile the "agitation in the British press when

41. Hoover to Capper, March 6, 1924, quoted fully in Whittlesey, *op. cit.,* p. 216 (Appendix "D").

42. Harry N. Whitford, "The Crude Rubber Supply: An International Problem," *Foreign Affairs,* II (June 15, 1924), 613, 617.

43. *Ibid.,* p. 619; Eugene W. Staley, *Raw Materials in Peace and War* (New York, 1937), pp. 130-131.

44. Edward M. Earle, "International Financial Control of Raw Materials," *International Conciliation,* no. 226 (Jan. 1927), p. 49.

Mr. Hoover proposed that Congress should give manufacturers the power to combine."[45]

Authorities like Whittlesey, Staley, and Robert F. Martin agree that the rubber industry actually had formed a buying pool by the end of 1926, but wished to obtain legislation to remove any doubts as to the legality of such a combination. The pool was formed with a capital of $50,000,000 "to centralize purchases as far as legally possible," operating "with the encouragement of Secretary of Commerce Hoover, through 1927 and part of 1928.[46] Long before this, the influential *India Rubber World* had announced to the trade Hoover's approval, in principle, of a rubber buying pool as part of an inevitable "trend toward consolidation."[47]

A. L. Vile's plea of The Rubber Association of America for legalized "cooperative" buying of rubber, made at the hearings on raw materials held by the House Committee on Interstate and foreign Commerce (1926), was also recalled by the *India Rubber World*.[48] Subsequently, the legislative Committee's official recommendations recognized the demand for a "law permitting combinations of American purchasers to buy cooperatively," but no specific bills were brought forward at that time.[49] Although Speaker Nicholas Longworth had castigated the British rubber controls at the end of 1925 as a gross "international swindle," Congress did not proceed to consider the legalization of buying pools until 1928.[50] This action took the form of a bill introduced by Representative Walter H. Newton (R., Minn.) to amend the Webb-Pomerene Act by permitting import combinations in those commodity areas which, according to the

45. David M. Figart, *America and Rubber Restriction* (New York, 1926), p. 17.

46. Robert F. Martin, *International Raw Commodity Price Control* (New York, 1937), p. 96; Staley, *op. cit.*, p. 131; Whittlesey, *op. cit.*, p. 159n.

47. Editorial, including Hoover's statement to the editors, *The India Rubber World, LXXIII* (Nov. 1, 1925), 63.

48. *Ibid.*, LXXIII (Feb. 1, 1926), 254.

49. *Preliminary Report*, p. 15.

50. Article by Sir Robert Horne, *The New York Times*, Jan. 3, 1926; Martin, *op. cit.*, p. 97.

Secretary of Commerce, were threatened by foreign "price fixing."

The evidence available in 1928 to the House Judiciary Committee considering the Newton Bill appeared to present the rubber buying pool as a *fait accompli*. With Hoover's assistance, the Rubber Association of America (U. S. Rubber, Goodyear, *et al.*) joined with the National Automobile Chamber of Commerce (General Motors, Chrysler, *et al.*) "for the purpose of preventing wide price swings in the crude rubber market [through] cooperative buying."[51] John J. Raskob of General Motors reportedly told the House Judiciary Committee that "the pool was buying and selling rubber all during 1927 and was controlling a large tonnage . . . as much as 50,000 tons."[52] In March, 1928, the "American Rubber Pool" was said to have received a new credit of $60,000,000 from American banks in addition to previous allocations.[53]

While Congress was sifting this type of evidence, Dr. Klein publicly predicted the "likelihood" of recognized "buyers' combinations" to combat foreign raw material "cartels," as proposed in the Newton Bill. The latter, he claimed, "has had the strong support of large groups of consumers of raw materials, notably rubber, potash, and sisal, and is intended to afford some measure of defense against possible exploitation by foreign combinations operating in the American market." Under the pending legislation "consumer combines" were to be "exempted from the anti-trust law."[54] Klein's description of the Newton Bill was essentially correct, but the Congressional debate raised substantial doubts as to whom the Bill was intended to benefit — the small consumer and farmer, or the large rubber manufacturers.

51. "Cooperative Buying and Restriction," *The India Rubber World*, LXXV (Jan. 1, 1927), 193; *The New York Times*, Jan. 13, 1926, reported on Hoover's first conferences with the Rubber Association of America and the National Automobile Chamber of Commerce concerning plans "to produce, purchase and deal in raw rubber."
52. *The Rubber Age*, XXII (March 25, 1928), 655.
53. *Ibid.*
54. Klein, "International Cartels," *Foreign Affairs*, VI (April, 1928), 457.

This issue was seized promptly by the fiery Fiorello H. La Guardia, then a Republican Representative of New York, who especially denounced the Bill's provisions permitting import associations for rubber or any other commodity "certified by the Secretary of Commerce" as controlled by foreign combinations. Not the consumer, but only a few huge corporations would be benefited by such a law, insisted the eloquent New Yorker. La Guardia went so far as to demand that Congressmen owning rubber company stocks be disqualified from voting on the Newton Bill, only to be overruled promptly by Speaker Longworth.[55]

Veteran Representative Hatton W. Sumners of Texas added his powerful voice to the opposition sparked by La Guardia, as did Representatives Lozier and Black. Sumners thundered that the Newton Bill flew in the face of established anti-trust legislation, and that it endowed the Secretary of Commerce (Hoover) with undemocratic prerogatives. "The effect of this bill," warned Sumners, "would be to . . . send the individual not to the public statutes but to the Secretary of Commerce as the permissive or prohibitive power of the land." Black accused Hoover and the Congressional sponsors of the Newton Bill of creating a potentially worse evil than the foreign rubber controls by encouraging "price-gouging" activities on the part of an "illegally" formed domestic buying pool.[56]

Quoting the Department of Commerce and the *India Rubber World*, Black hammered also at such statistics as the "tripling" of cash dividends supposedly paid by the rubber manufacturers, even in the years when the British Stevenson Plan had been most effective (1922-25). He declared that an American buying pool was unjustifiable because of the great strides taken by American companies in acquiring their own plantations, in addition to the increased supplies from the Dutch East Indies.[57] Lozier and other Farm bloc representatives likewise cited these arguments in attacking the unnecessary "creation of a monop-

55. *Congressional Record,* 70 Cong., 1 Sess., p. 5971 (April 5, 1928); *The New York Times,* April 6, 1928.
56. *Congressional Record, supra,* pp. 5983-84, 5996.
57. *Ibid.,* pp. 5995-5996.

oly" which might involve the United States in international trade retaliation. They chided Hoover for being inconsistent by favoring the Newton Bill in spite of his previous warnings against America's entanglement "in a thousand frictions in international relations."[58]

Congressman Newton replied in defense of his own bill with detailed analyses of the "unfair" and "oppressive" effects of the Stevenson Plan, repeating the charges made against it in the Congressional investigation of 1926. Citing evidence prepared by the Department of Commerce to support the need for American buying pools, Newton and Republican floor leader John Q. Tilson congratulated Hoover on his consistent struggle against the foreign "monopolies."[59] Their efforts failed, however, to move the hostile Democratic-Farm area coalition which doomed the Newton Bill to defeat. *The New York Times* headline presented its usual succinct summary: "Buying Pools Lose in House, 181-120; Democratic and Farm Bloc Kill Import Measure Urged by Hoover."[60]

Significantly, commented the *Times,* "a political tinge was given the debate on the Newton proposal by the frequent references to Secretary Hoover," both favorable and unfavorable. Representatives from the farm states, many of them Republicans, were not appeased by the inclusion of potash and sisal in the list of foreign controls to be combatted by the proposed legislation. Furthermore, the much-abused Stevenson Plan no longer could be a very live issue, for two days before Congress voted on the Newton Bill, Prime Minister Baldwin announced his intention to discontinue the rubber controls by the end of the year (1928).[61]

What became the center of controversy in the Congressional debates instead was the role of the Secretary of Commerce in a campaign which, some legislators believed, encouraged profiteering by American companies that were previously represented

58. *Ibid.,* pp. 5980, 5984, 5994.
59. *Ibid.,* pp. 5974-5980, 5985-5987, 5997.
60. *The New York Times,* April 7, 1928.
61. *Ibid.;* Martin, *op. cit.,* p. 97.

as hapless victims of foreign controls. Some farm-state Congressmen claimed, even in the course of the 1926 hearings, that the anti-monopoly campaign was nothing but a hoax. For example, Nebraska's Representative, Ashton C. Shallenberger, quoted the *Wall Street Journal* to the effect that profits of the Fisk Rubber Company rose more than 100 per cent between 1924 and 1925, and that the other major manufacturers of rubber products benefited similarly from a rise in tire prices which was quadruple the rise in crude rubber costs.[62]

Automobile and Rubber industry spokesmen questioned concerning these allegations generally confirmed the view that net profits from their manufactures had actually increased, in spite of the Stevenson Plan. Alvin Macauley, President, Packard Motor Company, testified in 1926, "we are glad to associate ourselves today with the distinguished Secretary of Commerce, Mr. Herbert Hoover, in his effort to secure relief from an arbitrary addition to the cost of rubber." Almost in the same breath, he admitted that "these charges [resulting from the Stevenson Plan], like all other manufacturing charges of whatever nature, are ultimately passed on to the consuming public."[63] A. L. Viles of the American Rubber Association admitted, furthermore, that prices of crude rubber had fallen substantially "since the American consumer began to protest and to take measures in his own protection with the assistance of Secretary Hoover."[64]

A document of which Congress took note in considering "defense" measures for the American consumer was an article by Sir Robert Horne, former British Chancellor of the Exchequer, featured in *The New York Times* (January 3, 1926). Horne blamed the rise in rubber prices on American speculators who hoarded crude rubber stocks against further price rises. Noting that British manufacturers paid the same price as American manufacturers, he found the anti-Stevenson Plan agitation unjustifiable at a time when the Firestone Company, for

62. *Hearings on Crude Rubber, Coffee, Etc.*, pp. 55-56; Staley, *op. cit.*, p. 131.
63. *Hearings on Crude Rubber, Coffee, Etc.*, p. 273.
64. *Ibid.*, p. 43.

example, increased its net profits by over 40 per cent between 1922 and 1925. (Horne's figures were later substantiated in the course of a lengthy exchange between Harvey S. Firestone and Congressman Shallenberger).[65]

Congressman Black and Milton C. Garber (R., Okla.) also pointed out that American tires had gone up in price far more than the comparable European product. In the wake of this criticism Hoover was directed by Representative John G. Cooper (R., Ohio) to investigate this price differential, for otherwise "the impression might go out to the American people that our tire manufacturers are making an exorbitant profit at this time."[66]

It is probable that the Department of Commerce under Hoover was not so much concerned with the high price of crude rubber, which could be passed on by the American manufacturer, as with the lack of price and supply stability resulting from the Stevenson Plan. The Department's *Fourteenth Annual Report* denounced the "criticism directed at the rubber manufacturers over profits earned during the last half of 1925," explaining that a part of these profits was cancelled out by the depreciation of rubber inventories during the precipitate drop in the 1926 spot prices of crude rubber.

The goal of price stability alone, even if on a higher plateau, may have served the interests of the major manufacturers of rubber products who took advantage of their capacity for long-range planning, stockpiling of raw materials, and mass production and marketing. However, the smaller producers were in a different position, their business activities more flexible and competitive, more responsive to price changes. Represented by the Bowring Company (New York), they protested to Hoover that "the big tire factories don't care if the [crude rubber] prices are high; all they want is stability . . . as they have to carry

65. *Ibid.*, pp. 45-46, 264, 266.
66. *Ibid.*, pp. 279, 302. The British press welcomed statements of this type, as shown in the London *Daily Telegraph* (Jan. 9, 1926) and the *Manchester Guardian* (Jan. 12, 1926), NA, RG 59:841.6176/72.

four to five months' supply, and they don't want their competitors to buy cheaper and be enabled to cut prices for tires."[67]

Hoover's reply to these arguments against the major producers' desire for stability, even at the cost of more expensive rubber, recognized that "in a certain sense this situation may be true." He warned, in addition, that "the market for products manufactured out of high-priced rubber is considerably more restricted than the market for such products at lower rubber prices."[68] Thus, he attempted to placate the lesser manufacturers who stood to benefit from sharp, if sudden, declines in crude rubber prices.

Although Hoover opposed "exorbitant" charges for rubber and other raw materials, his efforts were, in a large measure, devoted to assisting the leading American producers to reach a "fair price" compromise with the Stevenson Plan authorities in order to establish relatively stable conditions. This was reflected in the buying pool proposal (to strengthen the bargaining position of organized American manufacturers), as well as in the testimony of Hoover and A. L. Viles in 1926. Evidence such as this consistently emphasized Hoover's contention that high prices could be tolerated "under a free flow of the law of supply and demand" but not under a system of foreign government controls.[69]

For his work on behalf of a stronger and well-organized American business community, Hoover gained the gratitude and admiration of its leaders. Magnus W. Alexander, President of the Industrial Conference Board, praised him specifically for his valiant efforts to foster trade associations and other forms of "business cooperation" in spite of obstructionism by lesser souls who considered this a violation of the anti-trust laws.

---

67. Bowring Co. press release addressed to Hoover, April 26, 1926; letter to Hoover from J. E. Stone, Kleistone Rubber Co., April 27, 1926, NA, RG 151:254 (Straits Settlements).

68. Hoover to J. E. Stone, April 30, 1926, *ibid.*

69. *Hearings on Crude Rubber, Coffee, Etc.*, pp. 43-44; *Foreign Combinations to Control Prices of Raw Materials (Trade Information Bulletin, no. 385)*, p. 13.

From Elbert H. Gary, Chairman of the Board, U. S. Steel Corporation, came the flattering verdict that the "Honorable Herbert Hoover has filled the position as Secretary of Commerce with consummate skill . . . and with great advantage to the industries of the United States."[70]

70. Quoted in *Industrial Management*, LXXI (April, 1926), 200, 204.

CHAPTER VI

ECONOMIC NATIONALISM
AND THE
SEARCH FOR RUBBER

The National Need

Hoover's conception of the government's role in private enterprise caused him to refuse to limit the struggle against foreign monopolies solely to the type of legislative relief which finally crystallized into the abortive Newton Bill. In the case of raw material controls, Hoover believed that the American Government was obliged to intervene in behalf of its nationals because of the "undesirable" interference by foreign governments in the "free flow of supply and demand." This, however, did not shake his basic conviction that America's economic progress was the product of free initiative and self-help. "The Government," he said in 1926, "must at times act for those who cannot find solutions, but the Government can best serve by determination of fact, and by the stimulation and cooperation with the voluntary forces in our national life."[1]

In the same address, presented to the National Automobile Chamber of Commerce when controversy still flared around the British Stevenson Plan, Hoover reviewed his own two-pronged program of "defense" — conservation of raw materials and the search for new import sources. He warned that the "duty to

1. Quoted in "Herbert Hoover Praises Plan for American-Owned Rubber Plantations" (address of Jan. 12, 1926), *The Rubber Age,* XVIII (Jan. 25, 1926), 271.

provide . . . independent supplies [of rubber] . . . must rest largely upon our industries concerned . . . in the formation of some plan to assure rubber . . . from additional sources which cannot be controlled [by schemes such as the Stevenson Plan]." Cooperative business action of this nature, assisted by the Commerce Department's Rubber Survey, would be, Hoover concluded, "a contribution to [America's] national independence from many economic and political difficulties."[2]

Even when the legal production under the Stevenson Plan was raised in 1926 to 100 per cent of "standard output," the Department of Commerce continued its "energetic campaign" for augmenting the rubber supply, cooperating with the Rubber Association of America, the National Automobile Chamber of Commerce, the American Automobile Association, and the trade press.[3] In public appeals for conservation, reminiscent of World War I days, Hoover urged lower consumption of rubber to foil the "London speculators." To keep track of available supplies, the Commerce Department compiled "a special confidential summary of the forward commitments of all American rubber goods manufacturers."[4]

In addition to holding frequent strategy conferences with representatives of the rubber industry, Hoover issued periodic press releases "calling upon all of the people of the nation to assist in meeting the menace of the British monopoly."[5] The continuance of this campaign through 1926 was justified by the Commerce Department on the grounds that 100 per cent "standard output" still amounted to a restriction of 15 to 20 per cent below "full potential production." In 1927, an official Department publication estimated that the Stevenson Plan limited rubber production to as little as 60 per cent of capacity. Accordingly, as a proper answer to the British controls, the publication

2. *Ibid.,* 272.
3. *Fourteenth Annual Report of the Secretary of Commerce,* p. 39; "Hoover Calls on Public to Save Rubber in Every Possible Way," *The Rubber Age,* XVIII (Jan. 10, 1926), 219.
4. Lawrence, *The World's Struggle with Rubber,* p. 70.
5. *Ibid.,* p. 71; *The New York Times,* Dec. 23, 1925.

praised the tripled use of *reclaimed* rubber in the United States during 1925-26.[6]

When rubber prices dropped precipitately in 1926, Hoover issued a public victory statement summarizing his own role in this development: "I asked," he recalled, "for the cooperation of the manufacturers and consumers in a drive against the exorbitant price of rubber by conservation and the provision of American supplies. We have had that cooperation. . . ." To make specific the extent of this triumph, he noted: "If we . . . had continued to pay the price demanded last December . . . our rubber bill for 1926 would have been $350,000,000 more than it will be at the present level of prices."[7]

The British Colonial Office counter-attacked with an announcement (April, 1926) of lower rubber export quotas and a higher "pivotal price" (basic minimum) to aid the worried rubber growers.[8] This irritated still further the American trade press, which had never ceased its strident editorial attacks on the "speculative manipulation" and "uncertainty" resulting from the Stevenson Plan. *The Rubber Age* threatened that "if the British will not provide the world with rubber at something less than twice its cost, someone else will," referring to the Commerce Department's Rubber Survey and various plans to make the United States independent of foreign supplies.[9]

Actually, the campaign to give the United States control over its supplies of strategic raw materials dated back beyond World War I. The United States had, at least in the twentieth century, consistently opposed any serious restrictions on international access to vital resources, always championing "freedom in the

6. Everett G. Holt, *Marketing of Crude Rubber (Trade Promotion Series,* no. 55, 1927), pp. 54-55; *India Rubber and Tire Review,* XXVI (Feb. 1926), 16; *The India Rubber World,* LXXV (Jan. 1, 1927), 194.

7. Quoted in *The New York Times,* Feb. 15, 1926; *The Rubber Age,* XVIII (March 25, 1926), 421, noted Hoover's comment that the decline in rubber prices should discourage "other price-fixing controls."

8. Lawrence, *op. cit.,* p. 73.

9. *The India Rubber World,* LXXIII (Feb. 1, 1926), 253, and "Minimum Prices vs. Promises," LXXV (Nov. 1, 1926), 63; *The Rubber Age,* XXII (Oct. 10, 1927), 25; (Nov. 10, 1927), 141; (Dec. 25, 1927), 295-296.

commerce of raw materials." For example, the United States objected, even before 1914, to Germany's unilateral control of the world's potash supply. Later, minor international friction occurred when American-owned tin smelters in Malaya were subjected to "discriminatory" British export taxes. All of these problems resulted in specific relief proposals, ranging from simple forms of private American control to outright subsidies and the liberal application of other powers possessed by the Federal government.[10]

Writing at the end of the post-war decade, Benjamin H. Williams waxed somewhat over-dramatic — even for a contemporary observer — when he remarked how "the squirmings of little Liberia under the hand of a great rubber manufacturer [Harvey S. Firestone] remind us that the self-determination of small nationalities is sometimes a secondary matter to security in raw material supplies."[11] On the other hand, Williams clearly recognized — as was brought out in his excellent analysis of the *Economic Foreign Policy of the United States* — that economic motives have often played a most significant part in international relations. He justly deprecated the notion fostered by glib politicians that the totality of national policy can be "based [solely] on pure sympathy for the oppressed."[12]

Professor Earle narrowed the issue further in 1927 with a somewhat simplified historical analogy between Britain and the United States. Just as the American Civil War forced the British to seek alternate and secure sources of cotton, so the aftermath of World War I impelled the United States to develop its own independent supplies of rubber. In a world economy fraught with speculation and politically-inspired controls, the American government, he concluded, could not fail to recognize the "close correlation between industrial welfare and national defense."[13]

10. Williams, *Economic Foreign Policy of the United States*, p. 404 ff.; Wallace and Edminster, *op. cit., passim.*, NA, RG 151:272.6B (Tin) and 235.1 (Potash).
11. Williams, *op. cit.*, p. 358.
12. *Ibid.*, p. 3.
13. Earle, *op. cit.*, pp. 47-48.

The Democratic platform of 1920 pledged to secure for Americans equal access to petroleum and other overseas natural resources. Although the Democrats lost the election that year, Earle found that this plank was executed most satisfactorily by the Republicans. "It is with the name of Mr. Hoover," Mr. Earle concludes, "that . . . the active promotion of American foreign investments in raw materials is principally associated."[14]

Hoover's struggle against foreign raw material "monopolists" was intertwined with two distinct and laudable objectives: to secure for the United States its equitable share of strategic materials abroad and to channel surplus American capital into profitable and nationally beneficial investments. These twin goals represented ideally Hoover's belief in the close relationship between the stimulation of business opportunity and private initiative on the one hand, and the welfare of the whole American people on the other.

By attacking the overseas combinations, Hoover did not damage, to any significant degree, the position of existing American economic interests abroad. "It is true that American capital was involved in the production of some of these staples . . ." wrote Dr. Klein, "but the controls that were set up were . . . in countries where American capital was not at all concerned . . . [or where] U. S. investments were distinctly . . . minor. . . ."[15] As a counter-measure against these foreign "monopolies," Hoover encouraged American industry and finance to promote new and ambitious investment programs abroad — in the Philippines, the Dutch East Indies, and in Latin America — thus developing "safe" sources of raw materials. The Firestone Company's rubber plantations in Liberia and the Ford Company's similar grand-scale projects in Brazil demonstrated how American enterprise could rise to the challenge and the opportunity.[16]

Among those who favored Hoover's nationally oriented economic foreign policy was Henry Woodhouse, heir to the "Chester concession" in Turkey. This concession resulted from

14. *Ibid.*
15. Letter to the author from Dr. Klein, Nov. 26, 1957.
16. Irwin, *op. cit.*, p. 274; Lawrence, *op. cit.*, p. 47.

negotiations initiated by Admiral Colby M. Chester, assigned by President Theodore Roosevelt to secure the "Open Door" for American exporters and investors in Western Asia. The actual grant, made by the Government of Turkey in 1923, was issued to a syndicate, the Ottoman-American Development Company, founded by Woodhouse. This group undertook to build, in return for mineral concessions valued "at ten billion dollars," a vast network of railroads to the Mosul oil fields, modern harbor facilities, and a new capital city (Angora).[17]

This grandiose scheme inevitably clashed with the Anglo-French agreements to exploit the oil resources of the Middle East. Confronted with a tangle of conflicting claims and pressures, the United States did not intervene directly to save the "Chester concession," although, at the Lausanne Conference (1923), Secretary Hughes refused to recognize the extensive claims of the British controlled Turkish Petroleum Company.[18] Within this framework of international developments and as a result of his own personal involvement, Woodhouse wrote a barrage of articles in 1923 and 1924 — many of them in *Current History* — attacking the British policies, defending the "Chester concession as an aid to New Turkey," and demanding that the American government take energetic "measures for the protection of national industries."[19]

Woodhouse was particularly impressed with Hoover's program of investigating new rubber plantation areas abroad for

17. This estimate is given by Parker T. Moon, *Imperialism and World Politics* (New York, 1939), p. 264, a work which retains its value as a concise and readable authority on the "Chester concession" and similar topics.

18. *Ibid.*, pp. 263, 265-267; Pusey, *op. cit.*, II, 575, deals briefly with Hughes's role; for a broader treatment which is still valuable, see: Hans Kohn's *Nationalism and Imperialism in the Hither East* (London, 1932), pp. 118-119, 231-233; also, Foster R. Dulles, *The Imperial Years* (New York, 1956), pp. 203, 273, 306.

19. Henry Woodhouse, "America At The Mercy of British Rubber Monopoly," *Current History*, XVIII (April, 1923), 138; Benjamin Shwadran, *The Middle East, Oil and the Great Powers* (New York, 1955), p. 215, claims that the American oil companies agreed to back the Open Door policy in exploiting the Mesopotamian oil fields and the "Chester concession" only after "several conferences with Secretary of Commerce Herbert Hoover" (also pp. 194, 225).

America. He regretted that the United States did not acquire any suitable "equatorial lands" as a result of its role in World War I. Had it secured for itself some of these desirable territories, Woodhouse speculated, America might have been spared the critical situation presented by the British Stevenson Plan. As an adviser to the Navy and writer on military as well as diplomatic problems, Woodhouse preached ardently the strategic values of a basic raw material like rubber.[20]

Dr. Klein, too, in his official capacity as Assistant Secretary of Commerce (1930), recalled that the manufacture of tires and other rubber goods was "viewed as a key industry, to be carefully sustained as of basic importance in any well-balanced national economy [and] as essential to [national] security." This, he stressed,

was one of the major reasons for the determined stand by the American Government a few years ago, under the leadership of Herbert Hoover, as Secretary of Commerce, in the emphatic and ultimately effective protest against the attempted monopolistic exploitation of the world trade in crude rubber.

He noted, in addition, that several foreign governments had found it expedient in the 1920's to protect their own rubber industries by means of tariffs, patent laws, and special tax provisions.[21]

Suggestions for specific areas where American capital could be used to develop independent national sources of rubber varied in their emphasis, although well-nigh the same countries were discussed consistently. Woodhouse, for example, felt that American firms would be reluctant to risk their capital in developing South American rubber; he preferred the more readily controllable Caribbean island republics. Since labor costs there were

20. Woodhouse, *op. cit.*, pp. 134-137; for personal details concerning Woodhouse see *Who's Who In America*, XIII (1924/25), 3497.

21. Klein, "Migrating Machinery," *The Saturday Evening Post,* CCIII (July 5, 1930), 21. For a detailed analysis of America's relative position with regard to rubber and other strategic raw materials, including the possibilities of war, see: Brooks Emeny, *The Strategy of Raw Materials* (New York, 1934), especially pp. 20, 132, 138. Emeny predicted that "Russia alone [could] approach our advantage in this respect." (p. 20.)

higher than in the British Far East, American rubber interests would require Federal subsidies. Ending on a hopeful note, Woodhouse cited Secretary of Agriculture Henry C. Wallace's statement that "there was as much prospect of developing a [domestic] American [crude] rubber industry as there was of the sugar-beet industry a hundred years ago."[22]

Harry H. Whitford (Chief, Crude Rubber Section) also informed the public of the Commerce Department's findings that plantation labor costs were relatively high throughout Latin America and even in the Philippines. He advised the rubber interests to seek "an extension of America's present holdings in the East," especially through further investments in the Dutch East Indies. There were several possibilities available, but the overriding need, he urged, was "to consider . . . our national defense [and] not being dependent upon one geographical region."[23]

Negotiation and Exploration

The Rubber Survey, authorized by Congress in 1923, mobilized all the resources of the Department of Commerce, sending its agents to the tropical wilderness of Central America or Ecuador and to the bargaining tables of London and The Hague. Though less dramatic than the exploratory expeditions, and usually hidden from the glare of publicity, the Commerce Department's negotiations with the Netherlands government and the Dutch growers may have been the most influential factor in finally defeating the British rubber controls. In spite of official British pleas for cooperation with their restriction scheme, the Dutch producers did not join them in the 1920's, and their growing competition made the Stevenson Plan ineffectual. According to Professor John W. F. Rowe, the Cambridge University specialist on raw materials and author of *Markets and Men*, 1936,

22. Woodhouse, *op. cit.*, pp. 138, 140.
23. Whitford, "The Crude Rubber Supply: An International Problem," *Foreign Affairs*, II (June 15, 1924), 620-621.

"the British restriction scheme was benefiting Malaya not at all, but her chief competitor very much."[24]

Early in 1923, Hoover discussed with the Netherlands Minister in Washington (A. C. de Graeff) "the apprehensions of American capital" concerning the possibility that Holland might join forces with the British rubber control. This possibility was subsequently denied by an official telegram from The Hague Government which was transmitted to Hoover in the expectation that it would (according to de Graeff) "remove the apprehension which till now seems to have withheld American capital from investing on a larger scale in rubber plantations in . . . the Netherlands East Indies." Replying for Hoover, Dr. Klein agreed with this conclusion and expressed the Department's gratification.[25]

Hoover also reportedly played a significant part in encouraging American oil investments in the Middle East.[26] Much clearer evidence, however, exists in the Commerce Department's records to prove the extent of Hoover's interest in stimulating American investments in Far Eastern rubber plantations, especially in the Dutch possessions. At numerous conferences with representatives of the auto and rubber industries, Hoover appealed for such measures as large-scale purchasing of rubber plantation equities to bring more production under American ownership.[27] A stream of press releases from the Department of Commerce proclaimed widely also the doctrine of "American Controlled Rubber for American Industries."[28]

Negotiations with the Netherlands regarding potential American rubber investments were reported promptly to the Rubber

24. Quoted in Hexner, *op. cit.*, p. 285; Wolf, *op. cit.*, p. 231.
25. A. C. de Graeff to Hoover, Feb. 12, 1923; Klein to de Graeff, Feb. 21, 1923: NA, RG 151:254 (D. E. I.).
26. A. G. Veatch (Vice President, Sinclair Oil Corp.), *Report of the Federal Trade Commission on Foreign Ownership in the Petroleum Industry* (Washington, 1923), p. 127, quoted by Shwadran, *op. cit.*, pp. 90 n., 194, 215, 225.
27. Memorandum for the Cleveland auto and rubber conference of May 20, 1924. NA, RG 151:621.2.
28. Copy of press release of June 12, 1924, sent by Whitford to William Schall and Co., June 16, 1924, NA, RG 151:621.2.

Association of America "for guarded dissemination."[29] Firms not represented in this organization were advised also by the Commerce Department that the Dutch East Indies offered "advantages of labor supply and natural conditions coupled with the commendable attitude of their government in regard to artificial regulation of the rubber growing industry." Everett G. Holt (Acting Chief, Rubber Division) held up for the smaller firms the example of the U. S. Rubber and the Goodyear companies, "manufacturers who desire to control their crude rubber supplies" through investments in Dutch plantations.[30]

In March, 1926, Director Klein invited Emanuel Hertz, a New York attorney referred to him by Senator James W. Wadsworth, Jr. in connection with business efforts to expand rubber investments abroad, to come to Washington and "talk over the question of interesting Americans in rubber culture in the Dutch East Indies." Klein even promised that "we can undoubtedly arrange an interview with Mr. Hoover."[31] Significantly enough, Hoover at this time received an offer from private Dutch interests to lease a 130,000 acre tract in the East Indies to an American company desiring to develop its own rubber supply. The Dutch explained that "owing to the agitation caused by the British restrictions we take the liberty of transmitting the proposition to you" for referral to American companies. Paul L. Palmerton (Chief, Rubber Division) directed the prospective lessor to the Rubber Association of America and the National Automobile Chamber of Commerce.[32]

In mid-1926 the Commerce Department was gathering more information on Sumatran rubber concessions for the use of the proposed American rubber growing organization sponsored by the Rubber Association of America and the National Automobile Chamber of Commerce. But interest in this scheme was

29. Paul L. Palmerton (Chief, Rubber Division) to A. L. Viles, Feb. 19, 1923, NA, RG 151:254.
30. Everett G. Holt to the American Produce and Trading Co. (Chicago), April 9, 1923; *ibid.*
31. Klein to Hertz, March 17, 1926, *ibid.*
32. G. J. Kluyskens to Hoover, April 27, 1926; reply from Palmerton, April 30, 1926, *ibid.*

lagging, complained Holt, because "the manufacturers are disposed to assume a false security" as a result of declining rubber prices. Objections had also been raised on legal grounds, he added.[33]

That there was a temporary delay in large-scale American rubber investments abroad was certainly no fault of Secretary Hoover. He participated actively in the business conferences leading to the widely-touted $50,000,000 organization for growing rubber under American control.[34] In his highly significant address to the National Automobile Chamber of Commerce conference on January 12, 1926, he heartily "endorsed yesterday's decision of the chamber to launch a [separate] $10,000,000 corporation to give America its own rubber resources."[35] Emphasizing that "freedom in raw materials is the very life of industry and national progress," Hoover rose to "welcome these efforts on the part of our industries to themselves find solution to these problems."[36]

In another address, March 16, 1926, Hoover called again for developing "independent supplies" of rubber as a "potent weapon" to safeguard the interests of the American consumer.[37] Never losing command of this campaign, Hoover received from his subordinates periodic progress reports which kept him in constant touch with the profitable operations of the U. S. Rubber Company in Sumatra, the problems of Firestone's plant for milling Dutch native rubber, and other similar schemes.[38] Throughout the 1920's, Hoover was able to influence the Dutch from joining the Stevenson Plan, even though by June, 1927

33. Holt memorandum, June 16, 1926, NA, RG 151:621.2.

34. Wolf, *op. cit.,* pp. 227-228; Lawrence, *op. cit.,* p. 64; *India Rubber and Tire Review,* XXVI (Jan. 1926), 20.

35. *Ibid.; The New York Times,* Jan. 13, 1926.

36. Hoover quoted, *ibid.;* Edwin Emerson, *op. cit.,* p. 247, gives Hoover complete credit for the formation of the $10,000,000 rubber growing fund and claims that he persuaded also Henry Ford to start his own rubber development in Brazil.

37. *The New York Times,* March 17, 1926.

38. Memoranda from Holt, Aug. 6, 1926, and Klein, Jan. 6, 1927 in NA, RG 151:621.2.

they were reported to "fear the American rubber [buying] pool."[39]

In delicate negotiations, marked by the skill of Trade Commissioner Barringer (Java) and Commercial Attaché Jesse F. Van Wickle (The Hague), the Commerce Department sought to persuade the Dutch that the "American buying pool" was not "arbitrarily depressing prices." Klein and Holt recognized officially the existence of an "American Buying Pool" and exerted efforts in its behalf to arrange for negotiations with the Dutch growers aiming toward "a fair, stable price." Van Wickle, however, feared that the smaller American rubber manufacturers, pleased with the 1927-28 price declines, would be unwilling to join with the larger firms' program for stabilizing prices. Meanwhile, Holt faithfully kept the "Rubber Pool" informed. In this way the Commerce Department lent its invaluable assistance to the buying pool up until the demise of the Newton Bill, originally intended to legalize its activities.[40]

That American rubber interests did not limit their expansion to the Netherlands East Indies, where the most desirable locations were already pre-empted by the Dutch planters, is proved by the Firestone Tire and Rubber Company's successful development of its own vast rubber plantations in Liberia. Harvey S. Firestone, in 1922-23, launched his own personal anti-Stevenson Plan campaign. At first it threatened to eclipse Secretary Hoover's, in terms of national appeal. Immediately after the announcement of the British controls, Firestone proclaimed bellicosely that although "we are trapped by a maneuver for British imperial advantage . . . we can minimize the immediate cost to America . . . by meeting an invading nationalism with a defending nationalism." This could be achieved best, he maintained, by proving that "Americans can produce their own rubber."[41]

39. *Chargé d'Affaires* Henry Norweb (The Hague, June 29, 1927; report transmitted to Hoover by the State Department, *ibid.*
40. Reports from Trade Commissioner Barringer, Jan. 10, 1928; Commercial Attaché Van Wickle, Feb. 21 and March 22, 1928; Holt to the General Rubber Co. (N. Y.), Feb. 28, 1928, to Klein, March 17, 1928, to Van Wickle, March 23, 1928 in NA, RG 151:254 (D. E. I.).
41. Firestone quoted in Lawrence, *op. cit.*, p. 46.

Failing to convince the American Rubber Association and the American public "that when the British Empire, as an Empire, made a [hostile] move, it was time for the people of the United States to become aware of the threat," Firestone "urged Secretary Hoover to call [again] upon all American rubber manufacturers" to form a buying pool.[42] Quite probably Firestone's testimony before Congress (February, 1923) and his influence with Harding and Senator Joseph Medill McCormick (R., Ill.) were instrumental in obtaining the $500,000 appropriation for the Commerce Department's Rubber Survey. After this was accomplished, Firestone and representatives of other rubber and automobile firms met periodically with Commerce Department officials in Washington to plan further strategy.[43]

Firestone's nationalistic appeals and advertising campaigns urging that "Americans should produce their own rubber" may have been motivated partly by his concern over the competitive advantage then held by the rival U. S. Rubber Company. The latter firm, the world's largest rubber goods manufacturer at the time, obtained one-quarter of its crude rubber requirements from its own plantations in Dutch Sumatra. It could afford to overlook the high prices resulting from the Stevenson Plan. Consequently, U. S. Rubber officials snubbed the "sensationalism" of Firestone and, together with some smaller firms, looked askance at the proposals for an American buying pool.[44] Perhaps it was this kind of attitude which prompted Hoover to state later that "some of the rubber companies did not support the campaign by which we broke down the raid upon us, because of their desire to profit in stocks of raw rubber."[45]

Mutual cooperation seems to have governed the Firestone Company's relations with the Department of Commerce. When the Department prepared to send its exploratory mission to Liberia, the Rubber Survey Chief, Harry N. Whitford, first con-

42. Quoted, *ibid.*, pp. 47, 50.
43. *Ibid.*, pp. 50-51.
44. Henry S. Hotchkiss (Vice-president, U. S. Rubber), quoted in Wolf, *op. cit.*, pp. 225-226.
45. Hoover letter to Howard and Ralph Wolf, quoted *ibid.*, p. 227.

ferred with officials of the Firestone Company. On August 18, 1924, Whitford wrote that the Department's plans were carefully checked "with Messrs. Firestone and Ford and they both expressed themselves as being favorable to them . . . but [he added] I believe the Department would like a public statement from Mr. Firestone endorsing this [Liberian] project."[46]

Subsequently, the Commerce Department's official reports on Liberia mentioned such discouraging factors as the frequent destruction of rubber trees, largely the result of the natives' ignorance, but regarded the application of successful plantation methods as entirely feasible in that part of Africa.[47] By 1926, the newly formed Firestone Plantation Company received from the Republic of Liberia "a concession of a million acres" for the development of modern rubber plantations.[48] This project was praised lavishly in periodicals like *The Outlook* (New York), which in 1928 defended the Firestone Company against charges brought against it in the League of Nations by the International Society for the Protection of Natives.[49]

The Liberian project lent even more impetus to demands for similar developments elsewhere. Representing the Akron (Ohio) rubber manufacturing center, the *India Rubber and Tire Review* called on Americans "to submerge their petty differences and join hands in a leviathan rubber growing project." Its editors led the powerful chorus of those who favored the development

46. Whitford to Walker D. Hines (attorney for the Firestone Company), Aug. 18, 1924, NA, RG 151:621.2.

47. Whitford and Alfred Anthony, *Rubber Production in Africa (Trade Promotion Series,* no. 34, 1926), pp. 127-131.

48. Nicholas J. Spykman, *America's Strategy in World Politics* (New York, 1942), pp. 93 ff. This work was written for the Institute of International Studies, Yale University.

49. "No Rubber Peonage," *The Outlook,* CIL (Aug. 15, 1928), 607. For interesting accounts of the attempts to develop domestic rubber from the Texas and New Mexico guayule plant see: "Home-Grown Rubber," *ibid.* (July 4, 1928), pp. 367-368; for synthetic rubber prospects, see: "Artificial Rubber Again," *ibid.* (Aug. 8, 1928), p. 565. All of these articles looked forward to the day when America would no longer depend on British and Dutch producers of rubber.

of the Philippines and Latin America as secure sources of rubber.[50]

What the trade press demanded was not merely the "temporary palliative" of conservation and the use of substitute materials, but a bold campaign to acquire an "American rubber control." Toward this end Editor Ralph C. Busbey urged Federal subsidies for American rubber plantations. His conference with Coolidge, however, showed the President to be "deeply interested" in the general idea only, while opposing outright any use of government funds for this purpose.[51]

As a United States possession, the Philippines seemed to offer ideal conditions for fruitful American rubber investments. In addition to their geographical advantages, trade sources saw in the Philippines an opportunity for the "free use of public land."[52] Senator Simeon D. Fess (R., Ohio) fought also for governmental assistance to encourage American rubber plantations in the Philippines as the best solution to the challenge presented by foreign controls. With respect to both issues, Fess concluded, "too much credit cannot be given to our Commerce Department and especially to Secretary Hoover."[53]

The major difficulty presented by the Philippines as a potential supplier of American crude rubber needs was the local land law which limited holdings of individual plantations to 2,500 acres. According to the rubber interests and the Commerce Department, this placed an unjustifiable stumbling block in the path of potential developers already burdened with the costly task of clearing the islands' jungle areas. To relieve this situation, Dr. Klein (representing the Secretary of Commerce) conferred earnestly with Congressman Harold Knutson (R., Minn.) "on the possibility of an amendment to the Philippine land laws . . . to permit large rubber holdings." Klein also suggested

50. *India Rubber and Tire Review*, XXVI (June, 1926), 15.
51. *Ibid.* (Jan., 1926), pp. 16, 20; *Preliminary Report*, p. 15.
52. *The India Rubber World*, LXVIII (Sept. 1, 1923), 757-758; LXXII (Sept. 1, 1925), 709-712.
53. Senator Simeon D. Fess, "The Crude Rubber Monopoly — How It Can Be Met By America," *India Rubber and Tire Review*, XXVI (March, 1926), 18.

the feasibility of stimulating Philippine rubber production by means of a "large control plant to finance and direct small native growers . . . [like] the 'colono' operations in the exploitation of Cuban sugar."[54]

Knutson agreed to introduce an amendment modifying the restrictions contained in the Philippine land acts. Subsequently, the Commerce Department informed the major rubber manufacturers of this development, advising them to notify Knutson regarding the amount of land they might require in the Philippines.[55] In addition, Special Agents of the Department of Commerce in the Philippines were "requested by Secretary Hoover to stimulate interest among the Filipinos" in expanded rubber production and the influx of new American capital.[56]

These plans concerning the Philippines soon aroused the ire of the liberals, who attacked the Knutson amendment as a clear violation of the Jones Organic Act (1916) and as an attempt to strengthen American economic imperialism.[57] The Commerce Department, however, continued its open opposition to the Philippine land law restrictions. Furthermore, as stated by Whitford, the Department felt that the American investor was being hampered unduly by anxieties over the Philippines' future political status. This impediment to prospective investors in rubber plantations could be removed, according to Whitford, only by "definite [governmental] assurance that the sovereignty of the United States would be continued [in the Philippines]."[58]

Labor costs presented still another set of problems. In the Philippines, as in Latin America, the Commerce Department's

---

54. Klein to Knutson, July 22, 1926, NA, RG 151:621.2.
55. Holt to R. B. Bogardus (Goodyear Tire and Rubber Company) and other major manufacturers, April 18, 1927, NA, RG 151:621.2. In return, promises of cooperation were received from Harvey S. Firestone, Jr., and others, *ibid.*
56. Trade Commissioner O. M. Butler (Manila) to Holt, Feb. 3, 1927, *ibid.*
57. Vincente G. Bunuan, "Whose Land — Whose Rubber?" *The Nation,* CXXIV (Jan. 5, 1927), 22; Garel A. Grunder and William E. Livezey, *The Philippines and the United States* (Norman, Okla., 1951), pp. 151-156, 168.
58. Whitford, "Rubber and the Philippines," *Foreign Affairs,* IV (July, 1926), 678; "Rubber Industry's Outlook," *The India Rubber World,* LXXVII (Jan. 1, 1928), 53.

survey found that labor costs were higher than in the European-owned rubber plantations of Southeast Asia. Consequently, the Department seriously envisioned the need to import Chinese laborers if rubber was to be grown "under the American flag."[59] Recognizing early the crucial nature of this problem, the Commerce Department asked Carlton Jackson, the Trade Commissioner in Bogota, "to approach the Colombian Government with regard to labor importation," and, in addition, to supply "a collection of the latest immigration, colonizing, and land laws of Colombia."[60]

Still another possibility was suggested by Whitford. As a result of his Rubber Survey, he advocated, with the cooperation of the United Fruit Company (the main economic power in the Isthmus), the use of imported Haitian labor to develop rubber plantations in Panama.[61] As a means of exploring further the potential *native* rubber production throughout Latin America and the Philippines, the Department planned for additional Congressional appropriations, making possible a chain of "experimental plantations . . . to stimulate the production of crude rubber under American control."[62]

Highly significant in the American search for rubber was, of course, the vast amount of research data and specialized information supplied by the Commerce Department in its publications on rubber and in its detailed responses to individual queries from prospective investors.[63] It must be remembered, however,

59. Whitford, *supra*, pp. 678-679; "The Search for Rubber: New Prospects In South America," *Foreign Affairs*, IV (Jan. 1926), 334, 336; *Possibilities for Para Rubber Production in the Philippine Islands (Trade Promotion Series*, no. 17, 1925), *passim*; Figart, *The Plantation Rubber Industry in the Middle East* (Far East), *passim*.

60. J. R. McKey (Acting Chief, Latin American Division) to Carlton Jackson, August 31, 1923, NA, RG 151:621.2.

61. Whitford to Special Agent John C. Treadwell (Canal Zone), Aug. 8, 1923, and Jan. 15, 1925, *ibid*.

62. Memorandum by C. Reed Hill (Acting Chief, Rubber Division), Feb. 8, 1927, *ibid.;* Palmerton, Feb. 8, 1926, NA RG 151:254 (Straits Settlements).

63. For an outstanding illustration of the scholarly thoroughness and economic insights of these research efforts by the Commerce Department, see: Figart's excellent work, *The Plantation Rubber Industry in the Middle East* (with a foreword by Hoover).

that many of the Rubber Survey projects were possible only because of the great influence enjoyed by the United States in Latin America, enabling the agents of the Commerce Department to explore freely wherever they wished and to utilize the services of friendly local officials.[64]

Summarizing the Hoover Campaign: Economics and Politics

Was Hoover's struggle against the foreign "monopolies" — along with his "defensive counter-measures" — based on faulty economic reasoning and a narrow-minded interpretation of the national interest of the United States? Had the Department of Commerce become allied with "Big Business" to expand American economic influence abroad and to enforce the ideology of private enterprise? Questions such as these were asked not only by Hoover's political opponents, but also by independent and conservative analysts of international affairs during the "Prosperity Decade."

In 1926, John Foster Dulles — then a prominent attorney and bank director with substantial diplomatic experience — criticized unequivocally certain aspects of Hoover's anti-monopoly program. Dulles objected specifically to the Commerce Department's attempt to control the outflow of American capital in "cases where the control was sought . . . to promote what were believed to be the economic and financial interests of the American people." By denying the foreign combinations their rightful access to the capital markets of the United States, Dulles affirmed, the Secretary of Commerce practiced retaliatory measures much like the foreign controls he attacked so bitterly on ideological grounds. Dulles concluded by saying that the United States' use of its "monopolistic position [in surplus capital] for national purposes in effect pitted one monopoly against another . . . [in] a combat [which] cannot be justified on moral grounds."[65]

64. Acting Secretary of Commerce J. Walter Drake to Secretary of State Hughes, June 12, 1923, NA, RG 151:621.2.
65. John Foster Dulles, "Our Foreign Loan Policy," *Foreign Affairs*, V (Oct., 1926), 40-41.

Denying that the foreign controls were specially organized "to mulct the American people," Dulles pleaded that Europeans were entitled, if they so chose, to organize cartels in preference to free competition. After all, he pointed out, Federal legislation (the Webb-Pomerene Act) authorized also American firms "to combine for sales abroad." Dulles warned that it was futile — and damaging to international good will — for the United States to continue wielding the club of credit controls against the "continental conception of economic stabilization."[66]

Professor Jacob Viner, an authority in international trade, minimized the putative dangers stemming from the raw material combinations. The sharp rise in rubber prices (1922-25) was, he believed, less the result of the Stevenson Plan than of "the panicky rush for supplies [and] the alarmist interpretations of the situation issued by the Department of Commerce and by the American rubber industries."[67]

Explaining that no one country could hope to maintain an effective control over the world price of rubber, Viner proposed that Hoover exaggerated grossly the potential threat to the United States. As partial proof of this allegation, he noted the increasing share of Dutch producers in the world rubber market at the time of the Stevenson Plan, while the British percentage of the world's supply dropped from 72 to 53. Citing, on the other hand, various Federal Trade Commission decisions and the "objectionable" protective tariff as cases of governmental control in the United States, Viner concluded that they represented discriminatory American "suppression of the 'law of supply and demand' where foreigners were concerned."[68]

Judging by Viner's claim of a 20 per cent increase in the American consumption of rubber between 1924 and 1925 — in spite of the Commerce Department's conservation campaign — the British rubber controls fell far short of being a "stifling

---

66. *Ibid.*, 41-42.
67. Jacob Viner, "National Monopolies of Raw Materials," *Foreign Affairs*, IV (July, 1926), 592, 593.
68. *Ibid.*, pp. 593, 595, 598; Wolf, *op. cit.*, p. 224.

monopoly."[69] Dutch competition was probably the most influential factor in the spectacular decline in rubber prices during 1926 — even though Hoover's report claimed that this was rather a "remarkable result" of his Department's "countermeasures."[70] When Prime Minister Baldwin announced the end of the Stevenson Plan in 1928, the British press readily admitted that the Plan proved unworkable, primarily because it resulted in a 150 per cent increase in the Dutch East Indies production. At the same time the British continued, however, to be concerned over the threatened American wheat and cotton controls.[71]

Hoover's attack on the Stevenson Plan's interference with "the free flow of supply and demand" was based on economic theories which were largely obsolete after World War I. These theories, developed by "classical" economists such as John Stuart Mill, dealt with the mobility of capital and the need for free international exchange to provide the benefits of "comparative advantage" in world commerce. The wave of economic nationalism following Versailles Peace, however, made *laissez-faire* and "free trade" pathetically meaningless, long before John Maynard Keynes revolutionized economic theory. Hoover only weakened his stand further by fostering American buying combinations, while applying "free enterprise" principles to foreign producers.[72]

Undoubtedly, Anglo-American relations were damaged by the Stevenson Plan controversy. Burdened with a huge war debt and a series of economic crises, Britons were irked by reports

69. Viner, *supra*, 593; Whitford, "The Crude Rubber Supply: An International Problem," p. 619, admitted that the threat of foreign controls lay largely in future "abuses."

70. *Fourteenth Annual Report of the Secretary of Commerce*, p. 3; Paul Lamartine-Yates, *Commodity Control* (London, 1943), p. 120, and William Oualid, *International Raw Materials Cartels* (Paris, 1938), pp. 28, 44, 47, both deny the feasibility of "a geographical monopoly" and agree on the inevitable failure of the Stevenson Plan.

71. *Financial Times* and *The Times* (London), April 5, 1928, quoted in the American Embassy's reports, NA, RG 59:841.6176/142. See also: John W. F. Rowe, *Markets and Men: A Study of Artificial Control Schemes in some Primary Industries* (Cambridge, 1936), chapters V, VI; Wolf, *op. cit.*, p. 229.

72. May, *op. cit.*, p. 808.

that Hoover would not tolerate "exorbitant" rubber prices as an indirect means of enabling Britain to pay her debts.[73] The American drive for control of rubber was also regarded suspiciously as an attempt to expel British interests from their established economic and political positions abroad.[74] Less pleasant still were the revelations of direct pressure brought to bear on the British Government to abandon the Stevenson Plan.[75]

Being largely unfamiliar with American politics, foreigners were too credulous of Congressman Black's lurid portrayal of the "tire companies sicking the faithful Hoover on the British Lion just when they were about to inflate prices." Probably too many abroad agreed with Black's assertion that the anti-monopoly campaign presented the American rubber manufacturers with "an alibi to gouge the public."[76] This was, of course, an erroneous over-simplification of the Hoover program. Furthermore, wtih the exception of the Firestone Company, the profit rates of the five leading rubber manufacturing corporations in 1927 were below 10 per cent and also lower than their returns for 1925. In 1926, Firestone's profit rate — highest in the industry — was only 5.3 per cent.[77]

Contrary to Black's charge of a domestic "price-gouging" conspiracy, 1926 tire prices dropped, as a result of declining rubber prices. Although Hoover was popular with the tire industry as a whole, the *India Rubber and Tire Review* traced the declining tire prices to the "Hoover-Congressional probe and propaganda . . . to construct . . . political fences." Because of this "propaganda," complained the trade journal, falling tire prices were required "to appease the gullible American public . . . made to believe that tire costs are . . . influenced [primarily] by the spot crude rubber price."[78] At least for the moment, the

73. Whitford to Figart, June 16, 1925, NA, RG 151:621.2.
74. *Parliamentary Debates* (1925), quoted in Wolf, op. cit., p. 222.
75. *Hearings on Crude Rubber, Coffee, Etc.*, p. 33.
76. Quoted in *The New York Times,* Jan. 8, 1926.
77. *The Rubber Age, XXII* (March 25, 1928), 664, 666. Admittedly, profit analysis presents serious pitfalls, especially in this case, where one deals with relatively new industries and with changing inventory values, etc.
78. *India Rubber and Tire Review,* XXVI (Feb. 1926), 15.

anti-monopoly campaign seemed to backfire against the rubber manufacturers. As for Hoover, he had declared consistently that his struggle was on behalf of the American consumer.

Hoover's opponents repeatedly castigated him for his ostensible presidential ambitions and desire for personal power. These accusations were made even outside the halls of Congress and the partisan press. Leland L. Summers, an erstwhile official of the War Industries Board and an associate of J. P. Morgan, feared that Hoover's proposals "would place American industry under the thumb of the Secretary of Commerce." Citing his own personal knowledge of Winston Churchill's "fairness" (in drawing up the Stevenson Act), Summers, by contrast, "ridiculed Hoover's plaint on rubber."[79]

Undoubtedly, there was much truth in the oft-repeated comment — heard even abroad — that the zealous activities of the Secretary of Commerce were instrumental in his capture of the Presidency. The Radical Socialist Deputy Margaine told the French Chamber of Deputies that "Mr. Herbert Hoover, who has been selected as the Republican candidate for President, owes his popularity . . . to the active campaign he has carried on against foreign monopolies."[80]

Presidential aspirations are the traditional and quite honorable heritage of generations of American politicians and "public servants." Political ambition is, perhaps, the essential lubricant of most effective democratic organizations. According to James C. Lawrence, University of Minnesota Dean and rubber manufacturing executive, political ambitions motivated Winston Churchill, also, in initiating the Stevenson Plan. Churchill, wrote Lawrence, was convinced that the United States "could be made to pay" and "he saw political advantages to be gained from this action."[81]

When the furor over the Stevenson Plan subsided, influential groups in American society remembered the faithful struggle

79. *The New York Times,* Jan. 12, 1926.
80. *Ibid.,* June 17, 1928.
81. Lawrence, *op. cit.,* pp. 48, 74.

of their Secretary of Commerce. Thomas P. Henry (President, the American Automobile Association) expressed, in the name of "the country at large and particularly our twenty million owners of motor vehicles, the debt of gratitude due to Mr. Hoover for his leadership in the campaign just past." Hoover, continued the statement, "pivoted his position on a sound foundation, namely that artificial interference with economic laws is bound to end in disaster."[82] Congressman Tilson and other Hoover admirers also hailed the demise of the Stevenson Plan "as a direct result of the efforts of Mr. Hoover. . . ."[83]

82. Quoted in Emerson, *op. cit.,* p. 250.
83. *Congressional Record,* 70 Cong., 1 Sess., p. 5997 (April 5, 1928).

CHAPTER VII

BRAZIL, FRANCE, AND GERMANY IN THE ANTI-MONOPOLY WEB

Hoover's campaign against the British Stevenson Plan represented the most important phase of the anti-monopoly fight. After all, the rubber controversy affected American relations with the world's greatest empire. Moreover, imports of British rubber, in terms of its dollar value and strategic significance, represented a prime factor in the United States economy. Other commodities too, particularly coffee and potash, involved the Commerce Department in serious disputes with foreign government-sponsored combinations.

The Department's struggle against "price-fixing" of Brazilian coffee and Franco-German potash was marked by its own unique characteristics, although some of the tactics used were similar to those previously applied against the Stevenson Plan. A major distinction stemmed from the fact that Brazil, France, and Germany required American financing to a much greater degree than did the British. Taking advantage of this weakness, Hoover concentrated his attack on the coffee and potash "monopolies" by attempting, rather successfully, to exclude them from access to American funds. Another singular aspect of this campaign was the bold application of United States anti-trust laws to the Franco-German potash officials operating from New York.

129

Hoover and the "Coffee Defense"

A significant Commerce Department press release of 1928, quoted in the Washington *Herald*, made this proclamation:

Having smashed the foreign crude rubber monopoly, Uncle Sam turned his attention to the fight on foreign control of other essential raw material markets. Foremost among these was the monopoly on coffee held by the governments of Brazil and [the State of] São Paulo.[1]

Coffee was the recognized mainstay as well as the Achilles' heel of the Brazilian economy, at least since the turn of the twentieth century. Even before World War I, Brazil had developed a "valorization" system intended to maintain coffee prices. Under this scheme the principal coffee-producing State of São Paulo, backed by the central government, purchased coffee surpluses and retained them in government warehouses until such time as they could be sold profitably. This plan worked well through the boom and recession of the World War I era, in spite of the fact that the coffee barons refused to heed their own government's production restrictions. Brazil produced more coffee than the rest of the world, but its vastly expanded production in the 1920's was dangerously dependent on a parallel expansion of coffee consumption in the United States. Consuming no less than one-half of the world's supply, Americans, by 1924-25, imported annually $124,000,000 worth of Brazilian coffee.[2]

As early as 1922, the Commerce Department's Latin American and Foodstuffs divisions published a warning against "the valorization of coffee which signifies the entrance of the Brazilian Government . . . to control the price of that commodity." This bulletin objected most strongly to the attempt "to dominate the world market by restricting the movement of coffee from the interior *fazendas* to the seacoast ports."[3] The Department's

1. Contained in a memorandum from George S. McMillan (Managing Editor, the *Tea and Coffee Trade Journal)* to Director Julius Klein, Sept. 17, 1928, NA, RG 151:351.1 (Brazil).
2. *Hearings on Crude Rubber, Coffee, Etc.,* p. 9; Andrés Uribe C., *Brown Gold; The Amazing Story of Coffee* (New York, 1954), pp. 90-91, 174; Heinrich E. Jacob, *Coffee: The Epic of a Commodity* (translated from the German, New York, 1935), p. 258.
3. *Valorization of Brazilian Coffee (Trade Information Bulletin,* No. 73, Oct. 16, 1922), pp. 1-8.

fears were realized, in large measure, when Brazil formed a governmental Permanent Coffee Defense Institute, which built hundreds of interior warehouses and extended liberal loans secured by the planters' deposits of surplus coffee.[4] Generous financing in the London market made this scheme possible, but its continuance required the infusion of New York bank funds as well.[5]

One of the prime complaints of Americans against Brazil's Coffee Defense Institute was the allegation that it concealed the amount of coffee available in any given year and made secret sales to favored American distributors. Representatives of the Commerce Department in Brazil, especially Attaché William L. Schurz, worked faithfully to supply the correct information and to secure Brazilian pledges to discontinue the "unfair" practices. Their invaluable reports were transmitted promptly to the American trade associations, often in person, by Edward G. Montgomery (Chief, Foodstuffs Division) or other Commerce officials.[6]

Hoover, in a memorandum prepared for Congressman Edward C. Little (Chairman, Committee on Revision of Laws), complained that the Brazilian coffee controls were not trustworthy and that they fostered speculative excesses.[7] These accusations were amplified later. Although Hoover did not call clearly for a coffee buyers' strike, he noted that "the Brazilian authorities . . . are impressed with the success of our conservation campaign in breaking the monopoly price of rubber by more than 50 per cent." Similarly, he hoped, "vigilance on our part" would modify the coffee restrictions. As a part of his criticism of the Coffee Defense Institute's unsound fiscal measures, Hoover even proposed that Americans might overleap the re-

4. Vernon D. Wickizer, *The World Coffee Economy* (Stanford, 1943), p. 143; Martin, *op. cit.,* pp. 77-78.
    5. Rowe, *op. cit.,* pp. 34-35; Jacob, *loc. cit.*
    6. Cable from William L. Schurz, Oct. 6, 1922; reply from Ralph H. Ackerman (Chief, Latin American Division), Oct. 14, 1922 in NA, RG 151:351.1 (Brazil).
    7. Hoover to Little, April 3, 1924, *ibid.*

strictive governmental barriers by lending directly to the coffee planters.[8]

Meanwhile, Hoover received frequent appeals, such as Berent Friele's (the Atlantic and Pacific Company), to prevent a possible addition of $200,000,000 to the American consumer's food bill. Coffee prices, Friele noted, rose 100 per cent during 1923-24 alone.[9] In December, 1924, Hoover met with Friele and with representatives of the National Chain Store Grocers, the National Coffee Roasters, and other trade associations, to call for "a better understanding with Brazil as to the marketing of her coffee."[10] But disunity among the importers, chain retailers, and chain restaurants — not to mention their fear of coffee substitutes — hampered the Commerce Department's tentative proposals for a buyers' boycott.[11]

Nevertheless, Commercial Attaché Schurz (Rio de Janeiro) continued to advise the Department that press dispatches from the United States reporting a "buyers' strike and the increased use of substitutes would have a salutary effect on Brazil." He asked, furthermore, that his messages be transmitted to Felix Coste (National Coffee Roasters Association) for appropriate trade action.[12]

Hoover recognized soon that cooperative buying, or any of the other solutions he favored, would require a united American front to deal with the Brazilian control. With that goal in mind, Hoover assisted in the successful formation of the National Coffee Council, uniting American importers, roasters, jobbers, and distributors. The Council thus was able "to present to the Federal Government [of Brazil] the views of the entire [United States]

8. Hoover to E. H. Marsters (Boston chain restaurants), May 5, 1926, *ibid.*

9. Friele to Hoover, Nov. 10, 1924, *ibid.*

10. Friele to Richard F. O'Toole (Chief, Latin American Division), Nov. 22 and Dec. 12, 1924, *ibid.*

11. National Restaurant Association to Hoover, Dec. 8, 1924; memoranda by Edward G. Montgomery, Dec. 17, and O'Toole, Dec. 22, 1924, in *ibid.*

12. Schurz, Jan. 5, 1925, *ibid.*

coffee industry."[13] Representatives of the organized coffee industry now benefited even more from the close cooperation of the Commerce Department's staff. The latter exerted pressure on the Brazilian coffee interests to supply better quality at lower prices, relayed confidential marketing data, and interpreted the latest Brazilian legislation.[14]

Dr. Klein even suggested tactfully that Hoover be permitted to appoint two representatives to the new Coffee Council, in order to "help its prestige." Proposing a "thorough investigation of Brazil's coffee industry, along the lines . . . of the rubber investigation," Klein hoped that the Coffee Council would lend its support to "such an activity on the part of the Department of Commerce."[15]

In the 1926 Congressional hearings on raw materials, the House investigating committee agreed with Klein's complaint against the "arbitrary governmental controls over coffee production . . . and reservoirs of stocks . . . held over the heads of the [American] trade."[16] Congress, however, did not make the appropriations required for another series of projects comparable to those which resulted in the Rubber Survey.

The Commerce Department persisted, nevertheless, counseling the American trade to "show a united front [and] form some plan of defense." Its officials were consulted regarding proposals to join European and American trade associations in one gigantic coffee buying pool as a lever against Brazil.[17] Unlike the rubber industry, however, the less-organized coffee interests failed to form a pool, particularly when the legal complications were aggravated by the defeat of the Newton Bill (1928). The

13. A. A. Young (National Coffee Roasters Association) to the Commerce Department, Feb. 2, 1926; Klein to Coste, April 5, 1926; Leonard B. Gary (San Francisco District Manager, Commerce Department) to Klein, April 22, 1926, *ibid.* (351.1, General file).

14. Friele to Edward G. Montgomery, Nov. 12, 1926; Coste to R. S. Hollingshead (Foodstuffs Division), Jan. 30, 1925, *ibid.*

15. Klein to coffee industry leader F. E. Nortz (Nortz and Co.), March 19, 1926; Klein to Schurz, April 6, 1926, *ibid.*

16. *Hearings on Crude Rubber, Coffee, Etc.,* p. 27; *Preliminary Report,* p. 10.

17. Klein to Coste, March 3, 1928; Coste to Klein, March 6, 1928, *ibid.*

Commerce Department could do little more than arrange for conferences to discuss the remaining legal possibilities between the coffee trade and Assistant Attorney General William J. Donovan.[18]

At the same time, Hoover personally joined with representatives of the coffee trade in a session intended to convince Brazil's Coffee Defense "that when prices are too high . . . an unfavorable reaction sometimes sets in."[19] At the coffee interests' behest the prestige of the American government was carried even into the enemy's territory. Commercial Attachés Carlton Jackson and Walter McCreery maintained wearisome negotiations with the authorities in Rio de Janeiro. The two American officials acted on Washington orders, in spite of their own advice — arising partly from consultations with the American Ambassador in Rio — that "official intervention" was undesirable.[20]

Ironically, trade editor George S. McMillan directed the following question to Dr. Klein: "Will you tell us whether the employees of the Government, such as Mr. Carlton Jackson, will continue to act for the National Coffee Council and/or the National Coffee Roasters Association?"[21]

When the American coffee trade's "counter-activities" flagged somewhat, one of the Commerce Department's officials was bound to spur them on. Montgomery, for example, advised the National Coffee Roasters that "any venture to break the [coffee] monopoly" required a better "working cooperation within the industry." He was "surprised that more of the coffee trade has not been protesting through the press." Chidingly, he added that "perhaps a little sentiment created through the press might ease the situation." Montgomery concluded, that "the most effective thing would be to scare off some of the European bankers from continuing to finance Brazil's coffee control."[22]

18. Klein to Coste, March 23 and April 7, 1928, *ibid.*
19. Klein to Friele, March 19, 1928; Klein to Coste, April 2, 1928 (to approve limited publicity for this conference), *ibid.*
20. Friele to Klein, July 31, 1928; Jackson to Klein, Aug. 2, 1928; Klein to Jackson, Aug. 8, 1928; McCreery to M. L. Bynum (Tropical Products Specialist), Sept. 19, 1928, *ibid.*
21. McMillan to Klein, Sept. 17, 1928, NA, RG 151:351.1 (Brazil).
22. Montgomery to F. E. Norwine (President, National Coffee Roasters Association), May 22 and June 2, 1928, *ibid.*

Indeed, the American control of credit turned out to be a most potent weapon. Following the £9,000,000 Anglo-American loan to Brazil (1922), it was increasingly difficult for the Brazilian Coffee Defense to acquire new financing. English financiers, traditional lenders to the Brazilian coffee industry, were forced — in some cases — "to throw good money after bad," in order to save previous coffee investments.[23] When the Coffee Defense attempted, however, to float a loan in the United States, the American Government refused its approval.

"The opinion of the Department of Commerce," wrote Klein, "was no doubt a most influential factor in causing the State Department to disapprove the proposed financing." Citing a Hoover press release against loans to foreign "monopolies," Klein asserted that, "under the circumstances," no American banker would issue the coffee loan.[24]

When an American syndicate headed by Dillon, Read and Company proposed a new loan to Brazil, they had to assure "Mr. Hoover that the loan was not for speculative . . . but for strictly agricultural purposes."[25] The Commerce Department officially favored the establishment of American-owned agricultural credit banks in Brazil, only if "such a move were linked with the simultaneous abandonment of the valorization scheme."[26] In that respect, Hoover felt, the Dillon, Read loan would complement the Department's "sincerest sympathy for the unfortunate position of the Brazilian planter, who is required to pay extortionate interest rates [to British bankers]."[27]

But Hoover maintained "very strongly" that American funds must not be used for "coffee valorization and market manipulation." Such an eventuality, he warned, "would immediately arouse the objections of the American consumers since the whole

---

23. Jacob, *loc. cit.; Preliminary Report*, p. 10.
24. Klein to Schurz, Nov. 14, 1925, NA, RG 151:351.1 (Brazil); *The New York Times*, Nov. 14, 1925.
25. Friele to Klein, Nov. 13, 1925, NA, *supra*.
26. Klein to Schurz, April 6, 1926, *ibid*.
27. *Ibid.;* Klein to E. A. Kahl (San Francisco Chamber of Commerce), March 12, 1926; Washington *Star*, Jan. 31, 1926 (interview with Hoover), *ibid*.

principle at stake . . . is the problem of government price fixing." Throughout 1927 and 1928 American bankers were informed by the Commerce Department that its "position on valorization was unchanged." When relatively small loans to Brazil were finally approved, Hoover attached the proviso that the funds were not to be used "for price fixing purposes."[28]

Neither did the Commerce Department ever neglect that other scourge of "monopoly" — the search for alternate sources of supply. Commercial attachés and consuls were asked to report fully on such events as the 1924 Cartagena (Colombia) convention of the "mild-coffee producing countries" (Central America, the Caribbean, and Colombia).[29] Aside from supplying American coffee importers with information and business contacts for areas outside of Brazil, the Commerce Department considered also certain ambitious projects for expanding production in Colombia and Puerto Rico. By such means it hoped "to counteract the Brazilian activities."[30]

In December, 1925, Hoover conferred with representatives of the coffee trade concerning governmental encouragement of increased coffee production in Hawaii, the Philippines, Puerto Rico, and Cuba. A trade press editor (William H. Ukers) made much of a statement by an Agriculture Department official (William S. Lyon) "that the Philippine island of Mindanao alone had enough land to furnish all the world's coffee needs."[31] Some trade sources even spoke bravely of a campaign for Congressional appropriations to encourage coffee production under "the American Flag." Nothing came of this, however. On the contrary, American investors were discouraged by reports of

28. *Ibid.;* Grosvenor M. Jones to Klein, Aug. 29, 1927; Jones to Arthur N. Young (Economic Adviser, State Department), Aug. 31, 1927; Richard C. Long (Trade Commissioner, Brazil), to Louis Domeratzky, Jan. 2, 1928 in NA, RG 151:640 (Brazil).

29.   Montgomery to Coste, April 22, 1924, NA, RG 151:351.1 (Colombia).

30.   A. J. Barnaud (Manager, New York District, Commerce Department) to Klein, April 9, 1926; Bynum to Cairo (Ill.) Coffee, Tea and Spice Co., Oct. 31, 1927, *ibid.*

31.   William H. Ukers (Editor, *The Tea and Coffee Trade Journal*) to Hoover, Jan. 18, 1926; to Harold Phelps Stokes (Hoover's secretary), Jan. 29, 1926, *ibid.* (General File).

severe hurricane damage to Puerto Rico's coffee crop (1928), and Hoover received plaintive reports of low profits from American planters in Central America.[32]

By mid-1928, the Commerce Department realized that a collapse of coffee prices would cause most harm to Brazil's competitors, countries less ideally suited to coffee production.[33] Still "the most effective way of opposing the artificially maintained prices of coffee," advised Dr. Klein, was "for the coffee trade itself to take a strong stand and indicate that the [American] Government is spporting them," rather than dream of vast new alternate supplies.[34]

This advice was contained in Klein's reply to a letter sent by coffee trade leader Friele, expressing the "congratulations and best wishes of all friends of yours and of the Secretary," on Hoover's nomination for the Presidency. "Candidate Hoover has become the dread of Brazilian Coffee Interests," reported Friele's agent in Sào Paulo. Now that the National Coffee Council "has finally attained the prestige and position . . . to which [Dr. Klein] and the Secretary have greatly contributed," wrote Friele, Americans could afford to take a more moderate attitude toward Brazil. Consequently, he continued, "Candidate Hoover" would do well to issue a statement denying any hostility to Brazil's coffee industry as such, apart from its "excessive and artificially maintained prices."[35] In fact, Hoover did even better — he made a highly successful tour of friendship in Latin America following his election as President.

Brazilian sensibilities did require some conciliatory actions on the part of their North American "Good Neighbor." During the anti-monopoly campaign Brazilians were often angered by the Commerce Department's description of their coffee control as "futile exploitation by politicians . . . not remotely interested in

32. Hamberger-Polhemus Co. to Hoover, Aug. 24, 1925, *ibid.;* Bynum to W. H. Mahoney (Merchants Association, New York), Oct. 16, 1928, *ibid.* (Puerto Rico).
33. Grosvenor M. Jones to Klein, June 18, 1928, *ibid.* (Brazil).
34. Klein to Friele, July 6, 1928, *ibid.*
35. Friele to Klein, June 25, 1928, *ibid.*

the planters or . . . the consumers." The Department's refusals to approve American loans to Brazil were accompanied frequently by publicized attacks on government ownership of railroads and coffee warehouses in Sao Paulo and Brazil's use of government credit for political purposes. These charges, protested the Brazilian Ambassador, caused unjustifiable damage to his country's credit status. Moreover, he warned, they were prejudicial to the continuance of friendly relations between his Government and the United States.[36]

Hoover and the Franco-German Monopoly

It is a historical irony that Hoover's attack on the potash cartel formed by the governments of France and Germany actually interfered with one of the few cooperative ventures in the age-old rivalry of the two continental powers. Potash was one of the valuable minerals (such as iron and coal), which after Germany returned Alsace and Lorraine to France following World War I, enriched the French economy. In spite of this loss, German mines still produced most of the world's potash during the 1920's. Nevertheless, the governments of the two countries found it beneficial to form a "gentleman's agreement" for regulating sales abroad.

A formal Franco-German syndicate was hammered out at the Lugano (Switzerland) Conference (1926). It provided for joint selling in foreign areas — at the syndicate price — apportioning to France and Germany, respectively, about 30 and 70 per cent of the world's potash market.[37]

Doubting Thomases, who questioned the significance of pot-

36. Kellogg to Hoover, Feb. 17, 1926, a lengthy memorandum containing statements by Dr. Klein and the Brazilian ambassador's protests. Hoover's reply, Feb. 24, 1926, expressed his complete confidence in Dr. Klein, who drew up the Department's response; to the Klein memorandum Hoover simply appended his own view that it "explains the attitude of the Department of Commerce fully, and I do not think that I need add anything . . .", *ibid.* (General).

37. Oualid, *op. cit.,* pp. 32-33; *Potash: Significance of Foreign Control and Economic Need of Domestic Development (Trade Promotion Series,* no. 33, 1926), *passim.*

ash for America, needed but to heed the Commerce Department's warning that "any restrictions on the importation . . . of this essential raw material would result in the gravest consequences to the American public." Potash formed the basis of almost all commercial fertilizers, and was used also in the manufacture of glass, soap, chemicals, explosives, medicines, etc. "How vitally necessary it is," preached the Commerce Department, "will be appreciated from the fact that on abundant supplies of potash depend . . . our bread, meat, vegetables and fruits, the prime necessities of life."[38]

Before World War I, the United States imported 90 per cent of its potash requirements from Germany. During the war, when foreign supplies were cut off, about $50,000,000 was invested in developing the domestic potash industry, so that it was capable of satisfying about 50 per cent of the American demand. These gains were almost wiped out by the post-war Franco-German cartel agreement, controlling more than nine-tenths of the world's supply. This factor helps to explain why Hoover's anti-monopoly fight aroused the interest of the Florida phosphate industry and other domestic producers affected by foreign potash.[39]

Inadequate consideration for Germany's sharp currency fluctuations marred Hoover's initial potash campaign at the end of 1922. Replying to a query by Congressman Frank L. Greene (Vermont), who thought potash prices were rising steeply, Hoover reported a 250 per cent rise in one month. Greene used this data in a speech demanding governmental protection for American interests. Subsequently, Congressman Elijah C. Hutchinson (New Jersey) protested to Hoover that he personally, as the president of a "manufacturers' cooperative buying association," considered potash price levels to be the "lowest we have ever quoted." Hoover, in turn, apologized for the error con-

38. *Ibid.*, pp. 42-43.
39. *Ibid.*, p. 1; William F. Notz, *Representative International Cartels, Combines and Trusts (Trade Promotion Series*, No. 81, 1929), pp. 59, 65, 69.

tained in his report to Greene, which was calculated in terms of the badly inflated German *mark,* not in dollars.[40]

With the substantial recovery of Germany by 1924-25, however, the Commerce Department reported a further consolidation of the potash industry under governmental control. As early as March, 1924, Hoover notified Senator Capper that the world's "potash is controlled by combinations of German producers." *Commerce Reports* warned that this was "unquestionably the nearest approach to a monopoly." Although the French potash agency in the United States, *Société Commerciale des Potasses d'Alsace,* protested to Hoover that it still maintained competition with the German producers, the Commerce Department, on the basis of evidence it possessed even before the end of 1924, was convinced of the existence of a Franco-German syndicate.[41]

Pointing to the "leadership assumed by German industries" in initiating the European cartel movement, Director Klein attacked the "Franco-German potash entente," as well as "the Franco-German dyestuff cartel," as conspiracies to control the American market.[42] The Congressional investigators of 1926, following the testimony of Hoover and other Commerce officials, agreed with them regarding the threat presented by "France and Germany, operating as a monopolistic unit to control the potash business of the world." Somewhat enigmatically, the Congressmen's report concluded thus: "though the potash price is no higher than it was in 1913, the price is believed to be none the less exorbitant."[43]

40. Hoover to Greene, Dec. 13, 1922; Hutchinson to Hoover, Jan. 9, 1923; Hoover to Hutchinson, Jan. 25, 1923; NA, RG 151:235.1 (Germany). See also: Robert Liefmann, *Cartels, Concerns and Trusts* (London, 1932), pp. 67, 69.

41. Bureau of Foreign and Domestic Commerce, "Chemical Trade Bulletin" (no. 13e), Feb. 15, 1924; *Société Commerciale des Potasses d'Alsace* to Hoover, March 18, 1924; Trade Commissioner Fayette W. Allport (Berlin) to Klein, Aug. 16, 1924, *Ibid.* See also: *The New York Times,* March 17, 1924; *Commerce Reports,* II (April 6, 1925), 23.

42. Klein, "International Cartels," *Foreign Affairs,* VI (April, 1928), 452-453.

43. *Hearings on Crude Rubber, Coffee, Etc.,* p. 2; *Preliminary Report,* pp. 10-11; Staley, *op. cit.,* p. 128.

Meanwhile, the American potash industry, hoping to supply at least 20 per cent of domestic needs in 1926-27, appealed, along with its sympathizers, for Hoover's assistance against the "potash octopus . . . reborn through the [German] agreement with the French."[44] According to Isaac F. Marcosson, writing in *The Saturday Evening Post,* "the potash combine . . . touched the remotest Yankee home."[45]

Praising Hoover's request for a thorough governmental survey of domestic potash resources, *Time* magazine agreed fully with his angry opposition to "the German-French potash monopoly . . . about to mulct the U. S. farmers." Hoover "might threaten [also] some international trade retaliation," suggested *Time.*[46]

As in the case of other foreign combinations requiring United States "defense measures," the Commerce Department favored "the pooling of potash purchases" by the manufacturers of American commercial fertilizer. The Department worked, therefore, for the passage of the Capper Bill to permit "cooperative import purchasing of raw commodities" such as potash.[47] This attempt to modify the United States anti-trust laws met an abortive end, as did the similar Newton Bill of 1928. Yet, the selfsame laws which Hoover sought to amend for the benefit of American firms were eventually turned in full force against the foreign potash combine.

In August, 1926, the German "potash authorities" complained to the American Embassy in Berlin against the Commerce Department's charges of governmental monopoly. "Anxious to show their good will," wrote Dr. Klein, they even offered their records to disprove the Department's "conviction that this is a

---

44. Dr. John E. Teeple (U. S. potash industry consultant) to Hoover, Sept. 19, 1924, NA, RG 151:235.1 (Germany); Isaac F. Marcosson, "The Franco-German Economic Entente," *The Saturday Evening Post,* CXCVIII (Jan. 6, 1926), p. 127.

45. *Ibid.* The final text of the "confidential" Lugano agreement was delivered by Commercial Attaché Chester L. Jones (Paris), Jan. 14, 1927, NA, RG 151:235.1 (Germany).

46. *Time; The Weekly Newsmagazine,* VIII (July 19, 1926), 27-28. This periodical eulogized "Dr. Klein (who really is Ariel to Prospero Hoover." (Ariel assisted the potent wizard Prospero, in Shakespeare's *The Tempest.*)

47. Klein to Teeple, Oct. 14, 1924, NA, RG 151:235.1 (Germany).

dangerous government combine." Consequently, Klein outlined
for Charles C. Concannon (Chief, Chemical Division) a plan
for investigating the combine's operations in Europe and America "to see whether they are simply bluffing."[48]

The investigation, conducted mainly by Commerce agents in
Germany, was to concentrate on evidence of discrimination
against the United States. Aside from the difficulties inherent in
this type of study, special political and economic problems complicated the potash dispute still further. First, the potash cartel
operated under the direct control of the French and German
governments. As such, would it be subject to the anti-trust laws
of the United States? Second, if prices were lowered as a result
of anti-trust action, would this discourage unduly the domestic
potash industry?[49]

In spite of these obstacles, the Commerce Department
continued to compile evidence against the potash syndicate. For-
tified with this record, the Department of Justice instituted
injunction proceedings against the officers of the syndicate on
the grounds that it violated the anti-trust laws. The "highest
ranking officials of the French and German producers" were
presented with subpoenas "promptly after their arrival in New
York" for what they believed to be merely conciliatory talks.
This action "may have created some disturbance in certain
parts of Europe," admitted Concannon. In a *Hamlet*-like vein,
however, he envisioned "the Department of Justice as the means
by which we hope and expect to work our will on the Franco-
German potash monopoly." While still the "active and activating
influence," the Commerce Department was now "deliberately
keeping out of the [public] picture."[50]

Still, the Commerce Department asked its agents throughout
Europe to maintain their flow of information confirming that
the potash controls "contravene our anti-trust laws." According

48. Klein to Concannon, Aug. 19, 1926, *ibid.*
49. Concannon to William T. Daugherty (Trade Commissioner, Berlin),
Sept. 4, 1926; Concannon to Hoover, Dec. 23, 1926, *ibid.*
50. Concannon to William L. Cooper (Commercial Attaché, London),
detailed statement of the Department's position, April 14, 1927, *ibid.*

to Concannon, who, at Hoover's request, headed this clearing-house of evidence, "the Germans have even inhibited the development of potash mining in Poland and Spain" in order to monopolize the world's supply.[51]

When the Attaché in Berlin refused to take responsibility for assisting with the anti-trust suit, Concannon retorted that "the participation of the Bureau and of myself in this suit . . . was under instruction from and with full knowledge of Mr. Hoover and Dr. Klein." In this argument, he was backed by a speedy assertion of administrative authority on the part of Assistant Directors Hopkins and Thomas R. Taylor.[52] Hopkins later reminded the temporarily recalcitrant attaché that "the potash suit is considered a very important matter by people in Washington who decide things."[53]

Assistant Attorney General William J. Donovan, in charge of the anti-trust action, relied heavily on the aid of Commerce agents in obtaining copies of pertinent French legislation, marketing data, and the operational details of the potash syndicate. Donovan was especially enthusiastic concerning the cooperation of Hoover and his staff after conducting a personal investigation in Berlin with the aid of the Commercial attaché in that city. All this was regarded by Klein as a boon to the Commerce Department's prestige.[54]

Other official reports, however, showed a wave of *anti*-American "animosity" in France and Germany as a result of the *anti*-potash-monopoly proceedings. This was to be expected in the case of "the most 'political' of the existing international cartels," as recognized by the Department of Commerce.[55]

51. Concannon to Chester L. Jones (Commercial Attaché, Paris), April 25, 1927; to Allport (Commercial Attaché, Berlin), April 25, 1927; to Cooper, May 2, 1927, *ibid.*

52. Allport to Klein, May 27, 1927; Concannon to Taylor, May 31, 1927; Hopkins to Allport, June 2, 1927, *ibid.*

53. Hopkins to Allport, Sept. 13, 1927, *ibid.*

54. Concannon to Donovan, Jan. 23, 1928; Donovan to Concannon, April 11, 1928; Klein to Allport, June 12, 1928, *ibid.*

55. Concannon to Daniel Reagan (Commercial Attaché, Paris, Oct. 14, 1927, *ibid.;* Louis Domeratzky, *The International Cartel Movement (Trade Information Bulletin,* no. 556, 1928), p. 39.

By 1928, the German authorities were willing to accept a consent decree settling the potash controversy.[56] The French Ambassador, however, argued that an American court could not claim jurisdiction in the case, especially since many of the Alsatian mines were national property. These arguments were rejected by Judge William Bondy (U. S. District Court, New York), who ruled that no corporation, even if partly owned by a foreign government, could operate in the United States in violation of the anti-trust laws. In spite of Hoover's attack on the potash cartel as "a monopoly . . . in which the French Government is participating," Bondy decided that the suit did not actually involve the "Republic of France."[57]

By the time of Hoover's Presidential inauguration, both the French and Germans agreed to sign a consent decree restraining them from activities in violation of the anti-trust laws. The suit, wrote Concannon, was a triumph "for the American farmer." He predicted that "good will [on] both sides" would supersede the bitterness aroused by some of the European press.[58]

Most important, however, according to Concannon, was the fact that the United States Government could "practically dictate what the Potash Syndicate might or might not do in merchandising potash . . . in conformity with the consent decree." Consequently, the Commerce Department now saw "no objection" to American loan flotations on behalf of the Syndicate,[59] thus reversing its policy of the previous years.

Undoubtedly, the exclusion of the potash syndicate from American loan markets was the most powerful factor causing the Franco-German surrender.[60] Because of the Commerce De-

56. Allport to Klein, "confidential" cable, June 10, 1928, NA, *supra.*

57. Horace R. Lamb (Attorney-General's office) to Klein, report including photostatic copy of the Bondy decision, Jan. 9, 1929, *ibid.* See also: Wallace and Edminster, *op. cit.,* pp. 295-296.

58. Concannon to all Commercial Attachés in Europe, March 1, 1929; to Daugherty, March 13, 1929; to Commercial Attaché (London), March 13, 1929 in NA, RG 151:235.1.

59. Concannon to Ray O. Hall (Acting Chief, Finance and Investment Division), Jan. 2, 1930, *ibid.*

60. Allport to Klein, "confidential" cable, June 18, 1928; William D. Mitchell (Attorney-General) to Kellogg, March 18, 1929 (relayed to Concannon, April 1, 1929), *ibid.*

partment's anti-monopoly campaign, the Burbach Potash Company, "a [leading] member of the German Potash Syndicate," failed repeatedly to obtain dollar loans. The State Department, collaborating with Hoover, simply objected to all potash bonds "on the ground that the Syndicate maintains a monopoly inimical to the best interests of the United States."[61]

When American bankers considered a $40,000,000 potash loan in 1925, the Commerce Department's tentative "assent was conditioned upon the bankers giving assurances that the price of potash will not be boosted."[62] The Department kept a wary eye also on the J. Henry Schroeder Banking Corporation, a firm suspected of planning a loan for the "foreign potash interests."[63] In 1927 Director Klein warned Assistant Attorney-General Donovan of a new attempt to float a German potash loan with the editorial support of the *Journal of Commerce* (April 9, 1927). The "pro-German slant of that sheet" was ascribed by Klein to "its purchase by the Ridder-*Staats-Zeitung* crowd."[64]

Later pressure from the potash syndicate and the Dillon, Read financial interests failed also to sway the Commerce Department's opposition to a $25,000,000 potash loan.[65] Indeed, the Department even feared, on the basis of its Berlin agents' reports, that dollars borrowed by German banks might benefit indirectly the German potash interests. The Harding and Coolidge Cabinets supported these Hoover policies, particularly with regard to the American Government's disapproval of the proposed Dillon, Read loans.[66]

In view of the Department's belated admission that the potash

61. Discussion of proposed flotations in 1925, contained in a memorandum from Secretary of Commerce William F. Whiting to Kellogg, Feb. 7, 1929, NA, RG 151:640 (Germany).

62. Grosvenor M. Jones to Hoover, Nov. 30, 1925, NA, RG 151:235.1 (Germany).

63. A. J. Barnaud to Klein, Feb. 5, 1926; Concannon to Barnaud, Feb. 6, 1926, *ibid.*

64. Klein to Donovan, April 11, 1927, *ibid.*

65. Concannon to Cooper, April 14, 1927, *ibid.*

66. Concannon to Donovan, Nov. 4, 1927; Concannon and Grosvenor M. Jones, statement of Hoover's loan policy to brief the new Secretary of Commerce (Robert P. Lamont), April 4, 1929, *ibid.*

cartel was actually content with moderate price levels, and the lack of evidence for "price gouging," it appears that the syndicate was interested primarily in a more efficient sales organization. It desired also to increase the use of its product through world-wide advertising.[67] August Diehn, the Manager of the German Potash Syndicate, disavowed any intent to "gouge" the American farmer and blamed possible price increases on the unwillingness of United States importers to accept a "stabilization" agreement.[68]

Was it judicious to invite international friction over the operations of the potash cartel in the United States? The cartel did not represent a very serious threat, even if one should accept the Commerce Department's assertion that the "American potash bill has been increased by nearly $1,000,000" (1925-26). There are overtones of a superficial tempest in Hoover's reported anger at this "jugglery of the German-French potash monopoly," which caused him to order the $100,000 national geological survey of domestic potash (conducted by the Bureau of Mines).[69] This was, in turn, made part of a world-wide search which dealt the potash cartel its *coup de grace*.

In terms of popular appeal alone, the Commerce Department's program was based on an undeniably solid foundation. The Department stressed not only the "monopolistic and price-raising tendencies" of the cartel, but also the importance of agricultural self-sufficiency in case of war. Without ample potash sources the American farmer could not "adequately [sic] supply the food needs of a continuously growing population." Consequently, the Department pleaded, "independence of foreign sources and the development of national resources . . . should be a matter of national concern."[70] Thus, the Department set for itself the apparently unassailable goals of protecting the American farmer, consumer, and the domestic potash industry,

67. Domeratzky, *The International Cartel Movement*, p. 44.
68. Marcosson, "The Franco-German Economic Entente," p. 123.
69. *Time; The Weekly Newsmagazine, loc. cit.*
70. *Potash: Significance of Foreign Control and Economic Need of Domestic Development*, pp. iv, 1, 45, 85.

as well as upholding free enterprise and the security of the United States.

Even before the Franco-German cartel agreement was formalized, "Secretary Hoover called upon [his Department] to carry on a survey of potash production, either potential or in operation, in every corner of the world."[71] Subsequently, detailed analytical reports were compiled covering the potash trade from Spain to Palestine's Dead Sea. The survey's most significant success, however, was the discovery of rich potash deposits in New Mexico and Texas. "We ultimately relieved the American consumer," Hoover concluded, "from the oppression of the German potash cartel." Moreover, he boasted, "we not only destroyed German exports to the United States but exported to the cartel's previous markets."[72]

71. J. W. Delenhanty (Acting Chief, Chemical Division) to Chester L. Jones, Sept. 12, 1924, NA, RG 151:235.1.
72. Hoover, *Memoirs,* II, 83. On the domestic front the Commerce Department's Bureau of Standards mobilized the efforts of eminent scientists, including Thomas A. Edison, to produce a variety of synthetic substitutes for imported raw materials.

SECTION THREE

FEDERAL CONTROL OF
AMERICAN LOANS
AND INVESTMENTS ABROAD

CHAPTER VIII

FORMULATING
A
FOREIGN INVESTMENT POLICY

The Need and the Means

In the course of World War I the position of the United States changed drastically from that of a debtor nation to a net capital exporter. A ravaged Europe looked to a booming America for the funds required to repair the damages of war and to expand peacetime industries. Although investment opportunities were not lacking at home, American capital was attracted by the promise of high returns abroad. By 1924-25 foreign security issues offered publicly in the United States reached the impressive total of $1,382,000,000. Included in this figure were newly issued flotations amounting to $974,000,000, from which about $54,000,000 was deducted in bankers' commissions.[1]

These developments were, on the whole, favored and even stimulated by Secretary Hoover. Commerce Department publications hailed "the marked improvement" in the general economic situation of Europe resulting from the influx of dollars. While the London *Economist* (January 14, 1925) feared a too great reliance on the cooperation of the American Federal Reserve Board, bankers on both sides of the Atlantic were sanguine about the rapid return of sterling to parity and the revival

1. Hoover's Foreword to Franklin W. Ryan, *The Balance of International Payments of the United States in 1925 (Trade Information Bulletin,* no. 399, 1926), p. iv; *Fourteenth Annual Report of the Secretary of Commerce,* p. 50.

151

of the free gold market.[2] Hoover believed that by helping to
stabilize European currencies the United States could assure the
"free international exchange" essential to its own domestic
prosperity.[3]

In the midst of the brief post-war depression of 1920-1921
Hoover told the American Bankers' Association (December
1920) that "the vicious economic cycle can be broken . . . by
the establishment of credits abroad." Specifically, he amplified,
such investments would raise "the capacity of foreign people
to purchase American goods and to repay [their] obligations
to the United States."[4] Two major qualifications, however, were
added immediately by Hoover: the new loans were to be made
only for economically productive purposes and extended through
private channels. "The world," he said in 1920, "needs to get
away from the notion of governmental help . . . and get back
to work and to business."[5]

Hoover, "insisting that Europe must now rely on private
credits . . . on a business basis," opposed the American "propa-
gandists" who clamored for a huge postwar governmental loan
to America's erstwhile allies. He was willing, on the other hand,
to assist the American Bankers' Association program for "a
corporation through which credits could flow, with proper checks
against speculative, wasteful, and bad loans."[6] Herein was ex-
hibited once more Hoover's genius for organized enterprise, perhaps again as a bargaining point against foreign interests. This
plan failed to materialize, however, and Hoover determined to

2. Klein's Foreword to Charles E. Lyon (Trade Commissioner, London),
British Financial Conditions in 1924 (Trade Information Bulletin, no. 336,
1925); *ibid.,* pp. 8 and 20. See also: Charles E. Lyon, "Great Britain and the
Gold Standard," *Commerce Reports,* I (March 16, 1925), 612-613.
3. *Fourteenth Annual Report of the Secretary of Commerce,* p. 50.
4. Address of Dec. 10, 1920, quoted in Wilbur and Hyde, *op. cit.,* p. 349;
Hoover's Foreword to Ray O. Hall, *The Balance of International Payments of
the United States in 1927 (Trade Information Bulletin,* no. 552, 1928), p. iv.
Wilbur and Hyde p. 350, regard Hoover's encouragement of capital exports as
"the least expensive relief of unemployment and agriculture ever devised."
5. Hoover, *Memoirs,* II, 13.
6. Hoover, *Memoirs,* II, 13.

apply governmental supervision of credit exports when he was appointed Secretary of Commerce.

At Hoover's suggestion President Harding called a White House conference in 1921 to discuss the subject of foreign loans. Besides the President and Secretaries Hughes, Mellon, and Hoover, the conferees included representatives of J. P. Morgan and other leading investment groups. Recognizing the "interest of the Government in the public flotation of foreign bonds in the American market," the conference decided that the Administration should be informed of future flotations "so that it might express itself regarding them."[7]

There the agreement ended. Hoover stood out as favoring definite and firm standards to assure the "security and reproductive character" of each loan. With these goals in mind, his Department provided, "informally," the kind of factual business-like advice it considered useful to the financial promoters, even though the State Department preferred not to express the government's opinion regarding the business risks involved. Secretaries Hughes and Kellogg were concerned simply with those few transactions, such as loans to foreign governments not recognized by Washington, which conflicted with the major principles of American foreign policy.[8]

An explanation of the official attitude on foreign lending was finally made public on March 3, 1922. Under this mild formula, the issuers of foreign loans were asked to consult the State Department voluntarily before each flotation was offered to American investors. The State Department, in turn, sought the counsel of the Treasury and Commerce departments before rendering the verdict of "objection" or "no objection." Hoover was able to play a most prominent part in these decisions by virtue of his own interest and "unique experience in economic affairs throughout the world," not to mention his Department's superb informational facilities.[9]

7. *Ibid.,* 85-86; Grosvenor M. Jones to William F. Whiting, Feb. 8, 1929, NA, RG 151:640 (General). Hereafter, only the surname of Mr. Jones (above) will be used.
8. Feis, *op. cit.,* pp. 10-13; Hoover, *Memoirs,* II, *supra.*
9. Letter to author from Klein, Nov. 26, 1957.

Hoover, moreover, was forced to protect the loan approval system, limited as it was, from attacks arising out of both private and governmental circles. Many financiers felt hampered by the need to consult Washington before making a clear commitment. Although the loan approval program depended on voluntary cooperation alone, few bankers dared to incur the risk of not being able to call for their government's assistance in case of foreign default or confiscations. They were, nevertheless, apprehensive of official meddling, and frequently pressed the State Department for prompt and favorable replies.[10]

On the other hand, Senator Carter Glass thundered that even a statement of "no objection" on the part of the government gave the stamp of official approval to loans which were often highly speculative. This, he feared, would foster government "involvement and imperialism."[11] Even Governor Benjamin Strong of the New York Federal Reserve Bank asked the State Department to discontinue the controversial loan controls.[12]

Replying specifically to Strong's protest, Hoover maintained that a great "responsibility" devolved upon the Federal government to examine the merits of each loan, so that it would not be required to intervene on behalf of American citizens in case of default. Furthermore, as the "final reservoir of international capital," wrote Hoover, the United States was duty-bound to assure its use for "reproductive purposes" (mines, factories, and the like), not for rearmament or the maintenance of unbalanced budgets. Referring to American inexperience with investment abroad, Hoover pointed to the huge losses suffered already by speculators in inflated foreign currencies and by those ignorant of previous repudiations and indebtedness by overseas borrowers. "Our Federal authorities," Hoover concluded, "must . . . inform our citizens . . . that these nations will probably have to confess inability to meet their creditors."[13]

Although Hoover did not receive the full authority he desired

10. Jones to Whiting, *loc. cit.*
11. Feis, *op. cit.,* p. 13.
12. Hoover, *Memoirs,* II, 87-89.
13. *Ibid.*

to maintain his qualitative loan standards, he personally "sought to educate the public to look hard into the security and reproductive possibilities of the foreign bonds they were buying." Among the "uses for American capital that bless both the borrower and the lender" he listed such items as the "furnishing of raw materials, construction of transportation facilities, public utilities," and the like. In 1927, still steadfastly opposed to "any further lending by the Federal Government," Hoover continued to remind American finance of the responsibilities it shared with the government to maintain the quality of private loans to foreign countries.[14]

At the same time, he warned the Pan-American Commercial Conference that "the ability to repay the capital to the borrowing country must come out of the wealth and higher standards of living created from enterprise itself." Productivity, a free economy, and stability, Hoover advised the Latin Americans, would encourage the flow of additional United States capital and bring prosperity to the entire Western hemisphere. The *Wall Street Journal* editors and others who criticized his disapproval of loans to Brazil's Coffee Defense and similar "monopolies," were reminded by Hoover of the United States "cotton and truck farmers" (requiring cartelized potash) as well as the "numerical importance of the coffee consumers."[15]

Though hampered by the qualms of the State Department and the caution of Presidents Harding and Coolidge, Hoover proceeded to act according to his own conviction that American investors deserved their government's guidance. The Commerce Department announced, before the end of his Secretaryship, a "public warning that German municipal and other bond issues would rank after reparations and therefore were most doubtful of repayment."[16] Periodic questionnaires sent to all major investment houses dealing in foreign securities provided the Department with precise information concerning the value of

14. Wilbur and Hyde, *op. cit.,* p. 349.
15. Hoover, quoted, *ibid.,* pp. 355-356.
16. Hoover, *Memoirs,* II, 90; NA, RG 151:640 (Germany), *passim.*

proposed loan flotations, the interest rate, and other terms of the loan.[17]

The Department of Commerce offered to interested American investors data on the condition of specific foreign money markets, from Bolivia to Poland. Austria, Hungary, and Poland, for example, were classified as countries affording the highest interest rates; investors were taught also to distinguish among German national, provincial, and corporate securities. The Department's intimate knowledge of investment affairs included, for example, the fact that discounts as high as 12-1/2 per cent were earned in Dillon, Read's $20,000,000 loan (1925) to the French railroads, that Chase Securities Corporation was planning a $30,000,000 debenture issue of the International Hydro-Electric System and so on.[18] Hoover's staff improved its efficiency steadily in this type of financial-statistical work, from the first none-too-successful project for determining the unfunded foreign credit balances owed to American bankers and exporters.[19]

The Commerce Department's program was always limited, however, to aiding the export of capital by private sources. Hoover opposed consistently any efforts on the part of the Federal Reserve Bank to assist European finances through "easy money policies" and credit expansion. Regarding the "open market" operations of the Reserve System as an artificial stimulus to domestic inflation, Hoover joined Senator Irvine L. Lenroot (R., Wisc.) and other Senators in protesting the "pro-British" financial policies of Governor Daniel R. Crissinger (Federal Reserve Board).[20] Hoover felt that the average return of 6 per cent on American investments in foreign securities was

17. Klein to Senator Frank R. Gooding (R., Idaho), June 19, 1926, NA RG 151:640 (General).
18. Klein to Senator Frank R. Gooding (R., Idaho), June 19, 1926, NA, RG 151:640 (General). Jones to Chase Securities Corp., *et al.,* March 26, 1929, *ibid.* The French loan was approved during a lull in the war debts controversy.
19. Hoover to the Chase National Bank, *et al.,* Dec. 15, 1922; Benjamin M. Anderson, Jr. (Chase Economist) to Hoover, Jan. 9, 1923, *ibid.*
20. Hoover to Crissinger, quoted in Myers and Newton, *op. cit.,* pp. 9-10.

none too excessive, and he saw no need for the direct financial involvement of the Federal Government.[21]

Foreign Loans and American Economic Expansion

Commerce Department executives yearned to achieve for America the same type of loan policy which had secured for the British interests their economic dominance in so many areas of the world. For example, Walter H. Rastall (Chief, Industrial Machinery Division) admired "the ways in which British capital is induced to invest in a myriad of enterprises in a multitude of countries." American loans, "totaling many hundreds of millions of dollars" in 1921 alone, were not as well planned to serve the national interest. Rastall complained that little attempt was made to tie these loans with the sale of such American exports as machinery, unlike European financing which "frequently stipulates that machinery required for a given project must be purchased in the countries supplying funds."[22]

The proper solution, as seen by Commerce, was to publicize European credit practices among American bankers, and even help to organize "investment corporations along the lines of the British Trust Companies." Toward these goals, the Department launched a program of "educative publicity . . . to lead the American investor into different channels." Thus Hoover and his staff took the initiative in guiding the export of capital along lines consonant with their national policies.[23]

This task was facilitated by contacts with all members of the Investment Bankers' Association, the New York Stock Exchange, and the New York Curb Market. The Department followed the international securities market with the closest attention, thus being able to advise its financial correspondents, and Congressmen, of the latest details concerning specific loan

21. *Trade Information Bulletin,* no. 552, p. 21, quoted in George P. Auld, "Does High Protection Hamper the Repayment of Our Loans and Investments Abroad?" *The Annals,* CXLI (Jan. 1929), 201.

22. Rastall to Walter S. Tower (Commercial Attaché, London), Jan. 24, 1922, NA, RG 151:640 (General).

23. *Ibid.*

issues.[24] "Big Banking," furthermore, monopolized the bulk of foreign issues, making it easier to trace the course of capital exports. J. P. Morgan, for example, "offered or participated in the offering of $435,000,000 of foreign loans" in 1924 alone.[25]

The Commerce Department's agents abroad furnished not only reports on financial conditions in foreign countries, but also specific information on the credit standing of foreign enterprises and "important projects that . . . offer an excellent opportunity for the investment of American capital."[26] This data appeared in the Department's "Special Circulars," mailed to hundreds of American banks. Ultimately, Secretary of State Kellogg agreed that the Commerce Department is "the normal channel of inquiry for bankers," and urged his own staff to inform it of "particular credit situations requiring confidential dissemination."[27]

Although the Commerce Department did not intervene directly in the management of American financial institutions, it was quick to note alleged policy errors on their part. For example, in 1926, the Department was concerned over the fact that Chicago's Continental and Commercial National Bank had more money in German loans than any other mid-western bank. On hearing that it planned also a London branch, Jones noted that this was "quite a departure for an interior bank" and wondered "if it will pay."[28]

An interesting illustration of the cooperation rendered by the Commerce Department to organized financial enterprise is the case of the Federal International Investment Trust. This organization, incorporated by Franklin D. Roosevelt and others, was

24. Klein to Rep. Emanuel Celler (D., N. Y.), April 11, 1928; Jones to Rep. William W. Cohen (D., N. Y.), July 28, 1928; Klein to Cohen, Sept. 13, 1928, *ibid.*

25. Jones to Hoover, for the information of Sen. Lenroot, Nov. 30, 1925, *ibid.*

26. Jones to Klein, Jan. 12, 1928, *ibid.;* memorandum by Arthur S. Hillyer (Chief, Commercial Intelligence Division), Dec. 10, 1925 in NA, RG 151:602 (General).

27. Kellogg to Hoover, Jan. 9, 1928, NA, RG 151:640 (General).

28. Jones to F. L. Roberts (District Manager, Commerce Department, Chicago), March 26, 1926, *ibid.*

active in schemes to provide credit for foreign importers of American products. Its imposing letterhead bore the legend, "To Be Chartered By The Federal Reserve Board," and it hoped to have its stock approved as "a legal investment for national banks." These ambitious plans never materialized, although through no fault of Hoover's Commerce Department.[29]

At the request of Georges St. Jean, public relations counsel of the Federal International Investment Trust, the Department supplied relevant data on interest and discount conditions to be found in Poland, Latvia, Spain, Cuba, etc. Commercial attachés from Buenos Aires to Vienna were directed to negotiate with prominent financiers regarding the Trust's interests. The latter included plans "to purchase a minority stock interest in foreign banks with which . . . rediscount relations may be established [and to] secure representation on the board of such banks."[30]

Thus, the Commercial attaché in Santiago (Chile) was asked specifically by the Department to interview Chilean banker Walter Van Dusen, for the purpose of "ascertaining his willingness to act as correspondent [for the Trust], . . . [the] interest and discount rates proposed . . . the joint venture business . . . and the sole venture business. . . ."[31] Aided by the Commerce Office in Montevideo, the Trust received a commission for guaranteeing half the loans made by Supervielle and Company of that city, without having to invest its own funds.[32]

In the last-mentioned instance, the Department assured its Montevideo office that the "Federal International . . . is entirely reliable and has sufficient capital to carry through its present program."[33] Assurances of this type, as well as the availability of government employees' services for the purposes of the financial interests and even the official code to transmit private busi-

29. Freidel, *op. cit.*, II, 146; special file under the corporation's name, NA, RG 151:640-F.
30. Freidel, *op. cit., passim.,* especially St. Jean to Jones, Oct. 19, 1928; Jones to St. Jean, Oct. 24, 1928.
31. Jones to Santiago office, March 15, 1929, *ibid.*
32. Jones to Montevideo office, May 25, 1929, *supra.*
33. *Ibid.*

ness messages by cable — albeit charged to the firms concerned — emphasize the Department's extreme involvement in foreign loans. At times, its actions appeared to over-reach the bounds of proper government assistance, at least for a free enterprise economy.

Hoover was well aware, however, of the popular appeal implicit in a well-publicized program stressing loans for reconstruction and for the encouragement of American exports. During his 1928 presidential campaign he declared, "it is an essential part of the sound expansion of our foreign trade that we should interest ourselves in the development of backward or crippled countries by means of loans from our surplus capital."[34] Helping to rebuild the world's economy would also help keep American factories booming.

This attitude was characteristic of Hoover's delight in utilitarian actions clothed in the garments of humanitarian charity and vice versa. It is also an understandable part of that healthy reconciliation between his Quaker ethics and the engineer-businessman's pragmatism.

A corresponding responsibility, to discover practical means of implementing these policies, lay upon the shoulders of Hoover's subordinates. Consequently, the Department was engaged, for example, in investigating and publicizing European methods of restricting international purchases to the creditor countries.[35] When Brazil received a sizeable American loan in 1921, Commerce was keenly interested in assuring that the loan's proceeds should benefit United States industry and "should not be utilized for the purchase of materials from competitive nations." The Bethlehem Steel Company, for one, was anxious to supply the steel used in a proposed Brazilian arsenal, and hoped to be given preference by virtue of the American financial involvement in this and other projects.[36]

Meanwhile, the American Chamber of Commerce in Brazil

34. Hoover, *The New Day* (address of Oct. 15, 1928), p. 136.
35. B. C. Getsinger (West European Division) to Edward A. LeRoy (National Foreign Trade Council), Feb. 28, 1922, NA, RG 151:640 (General).
36. Schurz to Klein, "highly confidential," Oct. 18, 1921, *ibid.* (Brazil).

was angered by the diversion of these loans "into the pockets of our competitors." Claiming official favoritism in Brazil toward European suppliers, the American interests called for "restrictions on loans floated in the United States . . . requiring preference for American engineers and materials." This attitude was reported sympathetically by Attaché Schurz, who advised the Department to "ascertain from the house of Dillon, Read and Company just what understanding they had with the Federal Government [of Brazil] and the Municipal Government of Rio as to the uses to which the loans were to be put."[37]

In reply to these reports a cable from Washington informed Schurz that "Secretary Hoover [was] interested . . . and [would] act personally [and] immediately" to assist the aggrieved Americans.[38] Additional problems of this sort involved also United States steel interests "attempting to force the [Brazilian] Government's decision on its naval program before the end of the Washington Disarmament Conference," and a Dillon, Read scheme whereby the "bankrupt state of Amazonas" agreed to cede "an enormous territory north of the Rio Branco" in return for a new American loan.[39]

In the case of the 1924 prospective sterling loan to Brazil involving Dillon, Read again, the Department inquired anxiously whether the agreement "stipulates that all of the money available for purchases abroad must be spent in England."[40] As it was, the loan did not materialize.

In Asia and the Pacific the Department reported successful business loans to private and governmental interests of the Dutch East Indies, Australia, etc. Noting that American firms were no longer inclined to confine themselves to domestic investments, the Department's agents reported on such investment opportunities as the proposed Tokyo subway and other Japanese projects. They realized, however, that the use of American funds would be determined by Japan's own national policy, and that

37. *Ibid., loc. cit.*
38. Klein to Schurz, Nov. 23, 1921, *ibid.*
39. Schurz to Hoover, Dec. 30, 1921; to Klein, Aug. 9, 1922, *ibid.*
40. Jones to Chauncey L. Waddell (Dillon, Read), March 17, 1924, *ibid.*

resulting purchases of American products would be limited to those vital for Japan's industrial development.[41]

As for China, the Department found abundant evidence of European tying clauses requiring the purchase of materials in the lending country. The subtle British simply included a clause in their loan contracts requiring the employment of a British chief engineer to direct the Chinese projects made possible by their loans; the engineer could then be counted on to order from British suppliers, even if at much higher prices. Working with the National Foreign Trade Council, the Department hoped that similar arrangements would be made by American bankers to encourage the expansion of United States exports. This was, in a sense, a reflection of America's traditional desire for at least an economic "Open Door" in China.[42]

Relevant to these efforts were the several instances when the American government officially notified underwriters of foreign loans that it desired to see "a part of the proceeds of the loans . . . expended in the United States."[43] Similarly, Hoover upheld the advice of his Division of Finance and Investment to approve a $33,000,000 loan to Greece under an inter-allied agreement — "now that [she] is willing to have the entire sum spent for public works . . . constructed by American engineers with American capital."[44]

Likewise, precautions were taken in the case of a defeated and unstable postwar Germany. The Department's agents in

41. C. C. Batchelder (Acting Chief, Far East Division) to H. A. Butts (Acting Commercial Attaché, Tokyo), Jan. 16, 1922; Butts to Klein, May 12, 1922; Hoover to Hopkins, Nov. 1, 1922; Elwood G. Babbitt (Assistant Commercial Attaché, Tokyo) to Klein, Feb. 23, 1924 in NA, RG 151:640 (Japan).

42. Jones to Oscar K. Davis (National Foreign Trade Council), January 10 and February 29, 1924; Rufus S. Tucker (Acting Chief, Finance and Investment Division) to Davis, May 5, 1924, admiring the effect of the British Trade Facilities Act tying foreign loans to purchases in Britain; Davis to Tucker, May 8, 1924; Klein to all Attachés in Western Europe, February 13, 1926, ibid. (U. K.).

43. Senate Committee on Finance, Hearings to Investigate the Sale of Foreign Bonds or Securities in the United States (1932), pp. 959, 963, 1800; Madden, et al., op. cit., pp. 240-241.

44. Jones to Hoover, Feb. 16, 1925, with appended note, NA, RG 151:640 (U. K.).

Berlin were notified promptly of the 1922 decision to require governmental "approval for foreign loans made by American financial interests." Since "Mr. Hoover is called in, in every case, to give an opinion . . . ." the Department continued, its staff was asked to file detailed reports on specific German investment projects. These, it noted, should "encourage the purchase of American material with the money raised from American sources."[45]

The Branch Enterprise Problem

While the Commerce Department under Hoover encouraged, on general principles, the indirect or portfolio investment of American capital in foreign bonds or stocks, this was not true of direct investment in foreign manufacturing plants. The reasoning behind this policy reflects the traces of mercantilism which recur in American economic relations during the Hoover era. Portfolio investments or loans, it was felt, provided a suitable safety valve for surplus American capital and even for surplus American goods. On the other hand, the establishment of branch factories abroad gave employment to foreign labor and augmented the economies of foreign nations.[46]

Several factors help to explain American interest in foreign-based plants. The high costs of trans-oceanic shipping, discriminatory foreign tariffs and patent laws, lower wages abroad; these were some of the reasons discovered in the Commerce Department's surveys of this problem.[47] By 1929, $1,300,000,000 was invested by Americans in factories abroad which were wholly or partly under their control. Two hundred American manufacturing firms possessed 4,000 branches abroad (half of them in Canada).[48]

45. Alan G. Goldsmith (Chief, West European Division) to Attaché Charles E. Herring (Berlin), March 22, 1922, *ibid.* (Germany).
46. Klein, "Migrating Machinery," *passim.;* "Do Foreign Branch Plants Pay?" *The Business Week,* I (Oct. 19, 1929), 22-24.
47. NA, RG 151:623, *passim.* Frank A. Southard's *American Industry In Europe* (New York, 1931) is out-of-date, but still the best treatment of this subject.
48. "Do Foreign Branch Plants Pay?" *supra,* p. 22.

These results were achieved without the wholehearted cooperation of the Commerce Department. The latter feared that the nationalistic foreign drives for manufacturing self-sufficiency would make serious inroads in American export markets. One cause of its anxiety, for example, was the Brazilian Government's plan to develop a domestic iron and steel industry, financed by a British syndicate combining the Rothschild, Baring and Cassel interests.[49] Perhaps to make up for this threat, the Department sent a mission to explore the continental Amazon Valley in search of new markets for United States hardware, iron and steel, and even electrical goods.[50]

In a 1927 policy statement, the Department declared that it would provide assistance to direct American investments only if certain "conditions in a foreign country make it necessary for an American concern to establish a foreign plant." Normally, however, it chose to "encourage as far as possible the employment of American equipment and labor in the United States." The Department even warned American firms that in specific cases where branches were established abroad because of high foreign tariffs their subsequent reduction robbed the branch plants of any special advantage.[51]

Commercial agents were ordered to refrain from assisting American firms seeking a market for their products manufactured abroad. "It would be an unpatriotic act . . . to promote the sale of foreign products competing with those of the United States, even when such foreign products are the results of investment of American capital," warned the Department. Going even further, it concluded that albeit the manufactured article might bear the American trade name, "the labor employed is

49. William L. Schurz, *The Brazilian Iron and Steel Industry* (*Trade Information Bulletin,* no. 6, 1922), *passim.*

50. *Merchandising Methods and Trade Conditions in the Amazon Valley* (*Trade Information Bulletin,* no. 320, 1925), *passim.*

51. Louis Domeratzky (Assistant Director, Bureau of Foreign and Domestic Commerce) to the Detroit Board of Commerce, Nov. 22 and Dec. 10, 1927, NA, RG 151:623.

native and the product so manufactured cannot be regarded as a bona fide American product."[52]

In one instance the Commerce office in Washington refused to supply essential information to the China General Edison Company, on the grounds that it undersold its American competitors in the Far East. Finally, the Department's Trade Commissioner in Shanghai was moved to protest that China General Edison was a branch of the International General Electric Company (Schenectady, New York), that it "imports all metal parts from the United States and [operates] in a thoroughly American manner."[53]

In another case the Department refused to publicize the availability of a prime Belgian site suitable for an American branch plant. Subsequently, several reasons were given officially to explain why it generally opposed manufacturing abroad by American firms. One of these was the danger that such branch plants might be taken over by foreign financial interests or other groups "to the disadvantage of our own competing industries." In addition, taxes and various revenues would accrue to the foreign administration. "In other words," continued the Department's policy statement, "this government is practically obliged to extend to such [branch] companies the protection due them as Americans without securing any reciprocal advantages."[54]

Actually, there was much evidence to warrant the Commerce Department's conclusions. The economic nationalism prevalent during the 1920's presented grave problems, as well as incentives for the establishment of American branch factories. In the case of the automobile industry, for example, European tariffs on assembled autos and the need to cater to national tastes influenced both General Motors and Ford to invest heavily in European plants. The Ford Motor Company, Limited, a major

52. Domeratzky, draft for the "Foreign Service Manual," Jan. 23, 1925, *ibid.*
53. A. Viola Smith (Trade Commissioner, Shanghai) to Klein, June 13, 1928, *ibid.*
54. Oliver P. Hopkins (Acting Director, Bureau of Foreign and Domestic Commerce) to the Brussels office, June 28, 1928, *ibid.*

producer in Western Europe, was organized in England with assets of $35,000,000. On the other hand, General Motors was the American leader in Germany and Eastern Europe, especially after its acquisition of the vast Adam Opel, A. G., plants. Foreign lawsuits, labor problems, and nationalist opposition complicated, however, the functioning of these operations."[55]

In Poland, labor unrest in the new General Motors plant, coupled with the nationalist propaganda of competing Polish manufacturers, caused disturbances quelled only by police responding to the pleas of the American Legation.[56] Frenchmen considered American sales techniques "impudent" and ignorant "of the French temperament." More serious still was the French threat of customs charges and other legislative action against American-made auto parts. The Commerce Department reported also the forced sale of a Ford plant in Trieste and the effects of anti-foreign feeling in Japan.[57]

Even in the favorable industrial climate of England, warned the Department, the Westinghouse Electric Manufacturing Company was forced "to get out" because of "cheap reproductions and buyers who wave the flag and discriminate in favor of British goods." Its facilities and valuable designs were transferred to British owners who now "confronted the Westinghouse Company in all foreign markets." The same results occurred, according to the Department, after "a similar divorce" between Frazier and Chalmers, Limited, and its founder, Allis-Chalmers Company (Chicago).[58]

55. Southard, op. cit., pp. 10, 69-75; correspondence of General Motors counsels J. H. Fishback, John F. Smith, and Lee Warren, NA, RG 59:861.797, 660, etc.; James T. Adams, Big Business in a Democracy (New York, 1945), passim.; Arthur Pound, The Turning Wheel (New York, 1934), passim., Allan Nevins and Frank E. Hill, Ford; Expansion and Challenge; 1915-1933 (New York, 1957), Chaps. XIV, XXI.

56. J. Webb Benton (Chargé d'Affaires, Warsaw), July 1, 1929, NA, RG 59, supra.; for background, see the report of Clayton Lane (Commercial Attaché, Warsaw), July 11, 1928, NA, RG 151:623.

57. Southard, op. cit., p. 158, passim.; Perry J. Stevenson (Liaison Officer, Commerce) to Frederick T. F. Dumont (Liaison Officer, State), April 15, 1929, supra.

58. Ibid.

Dr. Klein pointedly brought out some of these illustrations, without mentioning the names of specific firms, in the hope, as he stated, that "repeated instances of disaster in recent years" would persuade businessmen to "look twice before you branch."[59] Hewing to the Department's adopted role as defender of American principles, the Assistant Secretary warned of the contrasting dangers of class struggle and socialism in Europe, the costly social insurance programs, and "the whims of political expediency . . . unheard of under a two-party government."[60]

When one considers the efforts devoted by both Hoover and Klein to fostering the standardization and increased efficiency of domestic American industry with the goal of steadily rising exports, it is not difficult to understand their opposition to competing branch production overseas. Hoover, moreover, was always apprehensive of the ideological "menace" presented by postwar European radical movements.[61]

On the whole, however, American enterprises abroad were by no means unprofitable. In that respect the Commerce Department's opposition represented considerations of broad national interest, as contrasted with an individual firm's limited quest for profitable expansion. American entrepreneurs were concerned largely with the financial success of their own foreign operations in the face of "antagonism aroused by the competition of their products [and] apprehension regarding their influence . . . on the labor markets of the countries involved."[62]

Consequently, Attaché Frederick Todd had to accept ruefully the "refusal of concerns that we know to be American to acknowledge" this fact. For fear of injuring native sensibilities, he reported, some American branches refused to be associated with the Commerce surveys and fact-finding missions. "Even the

---

59. Klein, "Migrating Machinery," p. 42.
60. *Ibid.*
61. Hoover, *Memoirs,* II 79, *passim.* Marcosson, "Commercial Exploration," p. 53, *loc. cit.*
62. Domeratzky, "American Industry Abroad," *Foreign Affairs,* VIII (July, 1930), 570.

Standard Oil of Cuba insisted that it was a purely Cuban enterprise."[63]

Some American firms, on the other hand, were turned down when they requested Commerce Department assistance because of their partnership within marketing agreements unfavorable to American-made products. For example, the Victor Talking Machine Company, a subsidiary of R.C.A., succeeded in purchasing the chief English producer of phonographs on condition that the American-made "machines" would be excluded from European markets. The Department objected that this scheme did not benefit the export or employment status of the United States and refused any assistance either to the American firm or to its English subsidiary.[64]

Similarly, National Cash Register's branch in Germany was treated as a foreign firm because it "imported only a limited number of special parts from the American parent factory." The same ruling applied to the Ford Motor Corporation of Canada, Limited, and other well-known enterprises. In all cases the Department advised American business not to be dazzled by supposed cheap labor costs abroad. Even in an "advanced" country like Germany, it pointed out, the labor productivity was lower than in America. Burdensome European taxation, possibly stemming from war debts and reparation requirements, was named as an additional deterrent.[65]

In spite of all these efforts — perhaps they came too late in the "Prosperity Decade" — economic expansion abroad grew until the Great Depression. For lack of the Commerce Department's policies, the speculative investments might have been even greater in volume. At any rate, the record provides evidence to contradict those who later criticized Hoover for neglecting, as

63. Todd to Rastall, July 20, 1928, NA, RG 151:623.
64. Van Wickel to Klein, Feb. 1, 1929; Eric J. King (Chief, Specialties Division) to Van Wickel, Feb. 21, 1929, ibid.; Southard, op. cit., p. 107.
65. Stevenson to Dumont, supra., loc. cit.; Rastall, memorandum on the "Desirability of Establishing American Branch Factories Abroad," June 7, 1929, NA, RG 151:623.

Secretary of Commerce, to warn Americans against direct foreign investments which involved appreciable losses during the Depression.[66]

66. Daniel C. Roper (Secretary of Commerce), *American Branch Factories Abroad*, (1934), 73 Cong., 2 Sess., Senate Document no. 120, *passim*.

CHAPTER IX

LOANS AND FOREIGN POLICY: "HE WHO PAYS THE PIPER"

War Debts and our Former Allies

The war debt issue, as well as the reparations question, cast a threatening shadow over America's financial and political relations with Europe in the era between Versailles and the Great Depression. It was during this period that the United States incurred the "Uncle Shylock" epithet. Although the controversy reached a climax in the mutual recriminations of the Depression itself, it was not forgotten until the holocaust of World War II.[1]

It was not so much America's withholding of postwar credit that caused bitterness among Europeans, as her willingness to dispense it on her own terms only. Some of these terms, as developed by the Commerce Department, were recapitulated by President Coolidge in 1924. The President favored "the export of such capital as is not required for domestic business, and which the American people feel can be profitably [invested], having in view the financial returns, [the] enlargement of our trade . . . [and] especially . . . a larger market for our agricultural production."[2] One of the most severe governmental qualifications for the approval of loans to Europe, however, was the

1.   F. Cyril James, "Benefits and Dangers of Foreign Investments," *The Annals,* CL (July, 1930), 79; Cleona Lewis, *America's Stake in International Investments* (Washington, 1938), chapter 19, *passim.*

2.   Calvin Coolidge, *The Mind of the President* (C. Bascomb Slemp, ed., New York, 1926), pp. 41-42.

170

requirement of concluding war debt agreements with the United States.

According to John Foster Dulles, "the most notable use of the control of foreign loans has been to exert pressure upon nations which are considered by our government as derelict [with] regards [to] their debts owing to the United States Treasury." This policy amounted also to a partial trade embargo, for Europeans needed dollar credits to buy American goods.[3]

Hoover exerted a dominant influence in implementing the American position on war debts, while he was Secretary of Commerce. Taking a surprisingly liberal attitude at first, he proposed that the United States follow the British example of cancelling the pre-Armistice obligations, even hoping for a student exchange program to be financed by part of the debt payments. Yet, as a member of the World War Foreign Debt Commission, Hoover agreed to recommend to Congress the repayment of the *total* inter-allied debt to the United States (amounting to $11,000,000,000).[4]

Thenceforth, Hoover censured "repeatedly . . . [those of] our inter-national bankers [who] agitated for cancellation night and day." He denied that war debt payments were hampered seriously by the lack of international exchange, or that the flow of gold into the United States impeded world recovery. Hoover pointed out, in statistical terms, that the American settlement plan actually granted "very great concessions," such as the provision for low-interest installment payments spread over 60 years.[5]

The connection between the signing of a war debt agreement with the United States and the approval of new American loans to the signatory nation was soon apparent. For example, Rumania's application for a substantial loan in 1922 was turned down because Washington objected to the absence of a debt funding agreement between the United States and this World

3. Dulles, "Our Foreign Loan Policy," pp. 35, 37.
4. Hoover, *Memoirs,* II, 178-179.
5. *Ibid.* The standard reference in this general area is: Harold G. Moulton and Leo Pasvolsky, *World War Debt Settlements* (New York, 1926).

War I ally. Once such an agreement was completed, Rumania received the desired loan.[6]

Much more serious problems were involved, however, in United States relations with the principal World War I allies, particularly with France. The latter country suffered immeasurable losses as a result of the war and was forced to liquidate most of her foreign securities and direct investments.[7] Frenchmen were overwhelmingly of the opinion that they had contributed more than their just share in the joint struggle against the Central Powers. They recalled warmly Senator Albert B. Cummins's wartime proposal that the United States assist its allies financially in the form of gifts, not loans, in order to avoid future embarrassment.[8]

Paris journals were incensed by what they considered American greed and ingratitude in demanding the payment of about three billion dollars in war debts. Their campaign, carried into the Chamber of Deputies, weighed rhetorically the value of dollars as against "the French blood poured out for the liberty of the world."[9]

Some in France went to far as to calculate that the unpaid principal and interest on the French loans granted to the American colonies during the Revolution amounted to as much as $80 billion. They insisted that if business-like considerations were to be enforced in the case of World War I debts, a similar policy should govern also the Revolutionary "obligation." This historical dunning caused no end of embarrassment to American representatives abroad, who pleaded for an authoritative retort from Washington. Some weeks later, the cooperative efforts of the Treasury and Commerce departments produced a lengthy, figure-studded document purporting to demonstrate that the young United States actually had overpaid its French creditors by $250,000. This memorandum was dispatched promptly to

6. Angell, *op. cit.*, p. 101.
7. Lewis, *op. cit.*, pp. 139 ff.
8. Sen. Cummins, quoted approvingly in Benjamin H. Williams, *op. cit.*, pp. 219-220.
9. Reports of Attaché Samuel H. Cross, June 10, 1922, NA, RG 151:640.

the aid of beleaguered Commerce offices in Paris, London, Rome, Brussels, elsewhere abroad, and in Washington.[10]

Before the end of 1925 debt funding agreements were concluded with twelve of America's wartime allies, but France was still recalcitrant. Consequently, Hoover launched a full-scale investigation of the French war debt problem to ascertain France's "capacity to pay" plus related economic and political considerations. Secretaries Hughes and Mellon promised Hoover their full cooperation in this effort. Subsequently, Treasury and State department personnel assisted in the war debts investigation under the leadership of the Commerce Department's Finance and Investment Division.[11]

The investigation involved such delicate questions as the status of the £53,000,000 sterling shipped from France to Britain in the darkest hours of World War I. Commerce Department officials abroad sought also to ascertain, without offending the French Government, the amounts owed to France by other countries and French obligations to such non-American creditors as Japan. The Commerce Department, moreover, studied anxiously the recurring French failure to balance the budget, stabilize the *franc,* and reduce the short term obligations of the Bank of France. In their conclusions, American attachés, as well as the Commerce publications, advised sounder financial policies and added taxes to enable France and other ex-allies to meet their debt obligations.[12]

This well-meant counsel received so unwelcome a reception in Europe that the Commerce Department was forced to deny any intention to "advise the French Government." Belgium joined France, furthermore, in asserting that American failure to guarantee the fulfillment of German reparations and other

10. Alan G. Goldsmith (Chief, West European Division) and S. Parker Gilbert, July 18, 1922, *ibid.*
11. Hughes to Hoover, Jan. 5, 1925; Mellon to Hoover, Jan. 8, 1925, *ibid.* (Interallied Debts).
12. Herter to Hoover, Dec. 10, 1923; Jones to the Japanese Consul General, New York, Jan. 18, 1924; Samuel H. Cross (Chief, European Division) to Attaché Mitchell (London), Sept. 17, 1925; Mitchell to Cross, Sept. 19, 1925; Chester L. Jones (Attaché, Paris) to Klein, Jan. 7, 1927, *ibid.*

financial obligations aggravated the international transfer of payments problem. Commerce agents abroad were confronted also with accusations that American banks, such as the Guaranty Trust Company, collaborated with the Germans during World War I and were still interested solely in their German contacts.[13]

Hoover continued, however, to emphasize, for the Administration, that "the keynote of our policy is not to tie up debts with reparations." The latter were to be regarded separately from a business-like treatment of the war debt issue. Hoover's European Division Chief asserted that "we need not be too much surprised at the unfavorable reaction of the uninformed section . . . of public opinion overseas or that of the extreme nationalists. They are an ungrateful bunch at best."[14] On the other hand, as the Department knew well, the French remained suspicious of the American Dawes Plan for Germany; consequently, they were unwilling to yield to Washington's pressure for a war debt agreement.[15]

No settlement resulted from the Franco-American Washington Debt Conference of 1925, even though Hoover strove valiantly to mollify the French delegates. The latter demanded unqualified provisos that "if there should be no reparation payments by Germany there would be no debt payments by France."[16] In 1926 the war debt agreement between Mellon and French Ambassador Victor H. Bérenger was rejected by the Chamber of Deputies. As a result, the Commerce Department's hostile attitude toward new loans to France hardened still further.[17]

The State Department agreed to withhold approval from proposed American loans to France so long as there was no debt settlement. Even American-controlled corporations in France

13. Chester L. Jones to Klein, June 21, 1923; Cross to Hoover, Sept. 1, 1925; Grosvenor M. Jones to Chester L. Jones (Paris), June 25, 1926, *ibid.* (France).

14. Cross to Allport, Sept. 12, 1925, *ibid.* (Interallied Debts).

15. Domeratzky to Hoover, Nov. 30, 1926, *ibid.* (France).

16. Cross to Hoover, Nov. 4, 1925, *ibid.* (Interallied Debts).

17. Angell, *op. cit.,* p. 102; Feis, *op. cit.,* pp. 19, 23.

were refused access to United States capital markets for fear "the door might be opened to other French loans."[18]

In August 1927, Dillon, Read pleaded the right to float a refunding issue of a previously approved dollar bond loan to French interests. Dillon, Read maintained that this did not represent a solicitation for new capital. Division Chief Jones (Finance and Investment) replied "that the French ought not to be allowed to get by indirection what they cannot have directly." According to Jones, American policy "refused to countries whose governments have not settled their war debts not merely the right to raise additional capital in this market but also the right to use the facilities of this market for any public offering."[19]

This American attitude became increasingly unpopular as French finances deteriorated. Even the Paris edition of the New York *Herald* criticized the United States severely for funding the total inter-allied war debt of $10.5 billions at levels expected to bring over $22 billions in repayments.[20] The Commerce Department's executive officers deplored this lack of "justification for the American side of the question . . . at a time when Americans are far from popular in Europe." Some in the Department attributed the newspaper's views to "fear that it might be suppressed by the French Government." Harold Phelps Stokes, then Hoover's secretary, explained that the *Herald* reflected "the attitude of the American colony in Paris which has been entirely out of contact with American public opinion."[21]

Lacking access to American capital, France applied to the credit markets of Holland for urgently needed financing. Dutch officials, in turn, now attacked the "discriminatory" American policy of "discouraging loans to France but not to Italy," which had signed its funding agreement in 1925.[22] The ac-

18. Jones to Hoover, Feb. 28, 1927, NA, RG 151:640 (France).
19. Jones to Hoover, Aug. 20, 1927, *ibid*.
20. Quoted by Attaché R. C. Miller (Paris), May 26, 1926, *ibid*. (Interallied Debts).
21. *Ibid.;* Klein to Hoover, June 11, 1926; Stokes to Klein, June 12, 1926, *ibid*.
22. Quoted in a memorandum by Leland Harrison (Assistant Secretary of State) to Hoover, Feb. 24, 1927, *ibid*. (France).

cumulation of various pressures, and a desire for a favorable commercial treaty with France, finally caused the American Government to permit, in 1928, the flotation of French industrial securities only.[23]

As an influential member of the Cabinet and of the Administration's Debt Commission, Hoover was in a position to utilize the potent resources at his command. His Department's representatives abroad carefully recorded and publicized Hoover's important addresses and acted as "trouble-shooters" for his war debt proposals.[24] Attaché Candler Cobb, for example, served Hoover well in London by restraining ex-Senator Theodore E. Burton from making potentially embarrassing statements concerning American war debt policies during the 1922 stage of the controversy. Cobb boasted of similar efforts with regard to Henry Morgenthau and James Cox, "volunteer statesmen and diplomats who are dangerous . . . because it is almost impossible to shut them up. . . . It is nervous work heading them off," he admitted.[25]

One of the main principles in Hoover's loan policy was to discourage further loans to debtor countries failing to strive for balanced budgets and economic stability even at the cost of higher taxes. His agents' reports were rarely optimistic concerning the adoption of these principles by France.[26] Much more encouraging, however, were their reports from Conservative-ruled Britain. London's "City" (banking and trade) opinion, moreover, favored a war debt settlement with the United States in the hope of resuming "normal" credit relations.[27]

23. Undersecretary of State Robert E. Olds to Hoover, Feb. 17, 1928, *ibid.* Probably, the State Department relented first, perhaps because of the French tariff threat to American automobiles and other products.

24. Goldsmith to all attachés in Western Europe, Nov. 8, 1922; William Ford Upson (Trade Commissioner, Vienna), Perry J. Stevenson (Trade Commissioner, Johannesburg), Dec. 13, 1922, *ibid.*

25. Cobb to Klein, Sept. 23 and 27, 1922, *ibid.*

26. Jones to Hoover, Aug. 29, 1924; Attaché Hugh D. Butler (Paris) to Jones, Jan. 10, 1925; Commerce press release, "Reform in Fiscal Policies Begun in Europe," June 8, 1926, *ibid.*

27. Attaché Walter S. Tower (London) to Klein, Dec. 8, 1921 and Jan. 30, 1923, *ibid.* (U. K.).

The United Kingdom, therefore, followed Finland by about one month in the first major debt funding pact after World War I (1923). Yet, in spite of the British agreement to make payments on a principal of over $4,600 million, the problem was not resolved.[28]

The Commerce Department was concerned especially with the terms Britain herself granted to the continental allies (France, Belgium, Poland, etc.). On one occasion, when Winston Churchill disputed some of the American debt claims, Hoover replied that "the terms of our settlements with the smaller countries were much more favorable to them than the settlement made by them with Great Britain."[29] Did the latter's terms offer also any "unfair" advantages to the creditor nation? wondered the Department. It assumed, for example, that the British gained valuable oil privileges in Rumania as a result of their own debt funding agreement with that country.[30]

Commerce publications carefully brought out the fact that while "John Bull" was expected to pay $4,600,000,000 to the United States, there was a corresponding total of about "ten billions owed abroad to Great Britain." These debts figured largely in the Department's assessment of the United Kingdom's "capacity to pay."[31] The London press, on the other hand, blamed the unyielding attitude of the United States for obstructing Britain's "natural inclination to give far more generous terms to France." This, in turn, claimed London circles, slowed the recovery of all Europe, especially France. Some of these problems were aired subsequently in the 1926 hearings of the Senate Finance Committee.[32]

The popular English press revived also such issues as the

28. Jones to Hoover, detailed report of all funding agreements, May 19, 1926, *ibid.* (Interallied Debts).
29. Hoover, cited in a memorandum from Jones to Charles E. Lyon (Trade Commissioner, London), Aug. 18, 1926, *ibid.*
30. *Supra., loc. cit.*
31. Ray O. Hall (Acting Chief, Finance and Investment Division), May 27, 1926, *ibid.* (U. K.).
32. Lyon to Cross, Aug. 27, 1925; Chester L. Jones to Klein, Nov. 9, 1926, *ibid.* (Interallied Debts).

defaults of American states on their own obligations to European creditors acquired in the nineteenth century. British taxes were now high, others claimed, because of the United States' harsh war debt terms. These arguments were a subject of heated debate in the House of Commons.[33] Only the London *Economist* could be cited appreciatively by Commerce officials. They brought to Hoover's attention its articles conceding that "the war was not America's war in the same sense it was Europe's war. . . . Europe must never cease to be grateful."[34]

On the whole, however, the Commerce Department's agents abroad continued to complain of press "propaganda" against the American debt settlements. Fearing that these "innumerable articles must damage good will and therefore make it difficult for American representatives to compete abroad," they appealed for a "concerted effort to present the facts."[35] Characteristically, the Commerce Department met the challenge by flooding its outposts throughout the world with "American side" memoranda, as well as such pamphlets as *The ABC's of the Foreign Debts* (published by the Bank of Manhattan Company, 1927). The latter, according to many attachés, was invaluable in their relations with foreign economists, bankers, and officials. It helped "to set them right . . . about the international debt problem."[36]

Those countries which signed debt funding pacts without excessive protestations were, of course, rewarded publicly with the Department's gratitude and praise. Among these fortunates was "sturdy and self-respecting" Czechoslovakia, which "made no appeal on the ground of poverty or currency weakness."[37]

The Department, consequently, continued to approve new

33. *Attaché* Hugh D. Butler (London) to Jones, July 27, 1926, *ibid.*

34. The *Economist*, July 17, 1926, p. 98, and July 24, 1926, p. 155; quoted in Jones's memoranda to Hoover, Aug. 6 and Aug. 14, 1926, *ibid.*

35. Lyon to Jones, Feb. 10, 1925 and April 7, 1926; Attaché Roger R. Townsend (London) to Klein, Oct. 16, 1930, *ibid.*

36. Jones to Hoover, Feb. 10, 1927; Attaché H. Sorensen (Copenhagen), April 20, 1927; Trade Commissioner Charles B. Spofford, Jr. (Calcutta), June 14, 1927, *ibid.*

37. Cross to Attaché James F. Hodgson (Prague), Oct. 13, 1925, *ibid.*

loans to Czechoslovakia, setting only its traditional conditions that the proceeds be used for "reproductive purposes" and spent, at least partly, in the United States.[38] Unfortunately for certain Czech borrowers, American Prohibition conflicted with their need for dollars. In at least one instance, the State Department disapproved loans to Czech breweries "on the ground that the administration could not consistently approve a loan for the manufacture of a beverage abroad considered illegal at home."[39]

The one major wartime ally presenting ever more doubtful prospects of debt settlement than France was Russia. In this case the problem was complicated by the Soviet Government's repudiation of both private and governmental debts incurred before its rise to power. A further difficulty was Washington's non-recognition of the Communist regime. On both these grounds, therefore, the American Government instituted its strictest loan embargo against the U.S.S.R. Even indirect credits, such as loans to German interests desiring to expand exports to the Soviet Union, were refused. "At the request of the State Department," reported Professor Harry T. Collings, "Mr. Averell Harriman abandoned his project to advance $35,000,000 to finance German exports to Russia."[40]

The American Government took a dim view also of proposals to sell Soviet railroad bonds in the United States privately by mail. It was opposed also to tentative schemes involving Dillon, Read and the Harriman interests in Soviet potash and transportation investments. As it was, Harriman and Company reportedly lost $3,000,000 in giving up their pre-war Caucasus mining concessions.[41]

38. Assistant Secretary of State Fred M. Dearing to Herter, March 14, 1922 (with attached letter to Kidder, Peabody and Co., March 15, 1922), *ibid.* (Czechoslovakia).

39. Edwards, "Government Control of Foreign Investments," p. 699.

40. Angell, *op. cit.,* p. 103; Harry T. Collings, "The Foreign Investment Policy of the United States," *The Annals,* CXXVI (July, 1926), 74.

41. Ambassador Jacob Schurman (Berlin) to the Secretary of State ("strictly confidential"), Dec. 9 and 16, 1926; Ogden Mills, Undersecretary of the Treasury, to the Secretary of State, Aug. 18, 1927 in NA, RG 59; see also, *The New York Times,* July 30, 1927. Soviet pressure made it impossible for the Harriman mines to operate successfully.

By 1929, Commerce Department officials abroad reported Soviet "overtures" for a debt settlement with the United States. These moves by members of Russian trade missions were attributed to Soviet "financial weakness" and a desire "to re-establish Russian credit in New York."[42] Hoover dreamed, throughout his term as Secretary, of the immense opportunity offered to American commerce and finance by a still underdeveloped Russia.[43] But this was impossible in the absence of an agreement on debts and other conflicting issues.

Reparations and German Loans

The victorious Allies of World War I, except the United States, presented the defeated Germany with a vast bill for damages caused by her war machine. The total sum of this reparations bill was scaled down by 1921 to $33 billion, to be paid annually. Transfer difficulties, "disastrous inflation" in Germany, and other factors, however, bore out John Maynard Keynes's prediction that the reparations plan would prove impracticable. The Dawes Plan of 1924 recognized this when it reduced drastically the required annual payments, but also when it extended a substantial gold loan to Germany. From then on the influx of American funds enabled Germany to meet her heretofore unfulfilled obligations, with an abundant additional margin for her own industrial expansion.[44]

Herbert Feis summarized this situation precisely in the following sentence: "American buyers of German securities financed the recovery of . . . Germany, the repair of the German monetary and banking system, and the payment of German

42. Attaché Daniel J. Reagan (Paris) to Domeratzky, May 29, 1929; E. C. Ropes (Chief, Russian Division) to Klein, September 10, 1929 in NA, RG 151:640 (Interallied Debts). See also: William A. Williams, *American-Russian Relations* (New York, 1952), *passim.*

43. *Ibid.,* pp. 201-202 ff.

44. Soule, *op. cit.,* pp. 263-264; Harold U. Faulkner, *American Economic History* (New York, 1954), pp. 689-690. For an excellent rebuttal to Keynes's *The Economic Consequences of the Peace* (New York, 1920), see: Étienne Mantoux, *The Carthaginian Peace; or, The Economic Consequences of Mr. Keynes* (New York, 1946).

reparations during the twenties."[45] By 1929, German banks, business houses, and government corporations owed $3 billion, mostly to American investors. This sum took on particular significance during the Depression, when Germany accounted for 32 per cent of defaults by all countries, with consequently heavy losses for Americans.[46]

Who was to blame for these investment excesses? Certainly, a breakdown of the Commerce Department's informational machinery was not the cause. It may be found, perhaps, among American investment bankers, the gullible public, and apathetic Congressional and Administration leaders. Commerce officials under Hoover and economists like Harold G. Moulton recognized early the need for cautious "appraisal of the character and terms of these [German] loans . . . in view of the fact that this is the first time in history that a highly industrial country has resorted to foreign loans on a vast scale."[47]

Soon after the Versailles Peace Conference, American businessmen consulted the Commerce Department regarding past and potential investments in Germany. Hoover was concerned with protecting the rights of American firms, like the United Shoe Machinery Corporation, whose existing stake in Germany could be influenced by decisions relative to reparations, German debts, and alien property confiscated in the United States during the war. The latter category, Hughes told Hoover, presented the possibility that unsatisfied American creditors might be compensated with the confiscated property of Germans in accord with the Versailles Treaty.[48]

The Senate of the United States, however, refused to ratify the Versailles pact. By 1924, a separate commercial treaty was negotiated with Germany, much to the delight of American interests concerned with re-establishing economic relations with

45. Feis, *op. cit.*, p. 39.
46. Lewis, *op. cit.*, p. 412.
47. Moulton, Preface to Robert R. Kuczynski, *American Loans to Germany* (New York, 1927), p. vii.
48. Hoover to Hughes, Sept. 22, 1921; Hughes to Hoover, Feb. 9, 1922 in NA, RG 151:046 (Germany).

the center of Europe. The Studebaker Corporation, for example, anxious to sell its cars in the German market, was informed officially that the commercial treaty provided equal treatment for American products. The Commerce Department even offered to "present your case to the proper officials" in Berlin, for the purpose of easing German auto import restrictions.[49] Consistently, during the 1920's the Department sought to maintain American "most-favored-nation" rights in Germany.[50] The commercial factor, no doubt, helps to explain the unimpeded flow of dollars into Germany.

In spite of the prevailing American interest in German investments, the Commerce Department could find few buyers for the German holdings delivered to the Reparations Commission by 1922. The Department did attempt, at Hughes's behest, to bring these holdings "to the attention of such Americans . . . as might be interested," but the poor results reflect, at least partly, official and popular American disaffection with Versailles and the reparations scheme.[51] Hoover informed Hughes in no uncertain terms that he considered utterly "preposterous" the French insistence on a $33 billion reparations figure.[52] The two men, moreover, were united in refusing to recognize any legitimate link connecting reparations, war debts, and the corresponding cancellation schemes. They agreed also that the economic up-building of Germany was essential to European peace.[53]

The first American postwar loans to Germany were negotiated before the 1922 system requiring official Washington approval became effective. In one case, where advance notice of a pro-

49. The Studebaker Corp. to Klein, Dec. 31, 1923; reply from Henry Chalmers (Chief, Division of Foreign Tariffs), Jan. 24, 1924, *ibid.*
50. State Department to Hoover, March 14, 1925; Chalmers to the U. S. Chamber of Commerce, April 28, 1925; Allport to Klein, July 3, 1926, *ibid.*
51. Hughes to Hoover, July 26, 1922; S. Bradshaw Jacobs (Raymond-White Corp.) to Klein, Aug. 4, 1922; District Managers (St. Louis and New York) to Klein, Sept. 29 and Oct. 3, 1922 in NA, RG 151:620 (Germany).
52. Hoover, *Memoirs,* II, 182.
53. *Ibid., passim.;* Hughes, *The Pathway of Peace* (New York, 1925), p. 54; Charles C. Hyde, "Charles Evans Hughes," in Samuel F. Bemis, ed., *American Secretaries of State and their Diplomacy* (10 vols., New York, 1929), X, 377-388.

posed loan was not supplied by the interested investment house, it was informed sternly by the State Department "that you are proceeding in this matter on your own responsibility, and that this Department reserves complete liberty of action in any contingency that may arise in this connection." In other words, the American Government "reserved the right to determine whether or not it will make representations in case of a default."[54] Both Commerce and State departments were, at the time, acutely aware of Germany's currency depreciation and economic instability.

The picture changed drastically by 1924. Hoover helped select Charles G. Dawes and other American representatives on the commission which revised the reparations plan in a manner much more favorable—even generous—toward Germany. "The Dawes Commission," according to Hoover, "succeeded beyond our hopes."[55] President Coolidge praised the Dawes Plan's proposal for "a considerable loan" to Germany and urged American capital to participate in financing German recovery.[56]

Subsequently, J. P. Morgan's $100,000,000 German loan was over-subscribed by ten times the amount. Prosperous Americans clamored for German securities. Largely ignored were reports to the State Department expressing doubts concerning "the actual desire for peace on the part of Germany . . . [and] the attitude of the Nationalists."[57]

The same year, 1924, Commerce executives Goldsmith and Jones warned Hoover about the uncertainties of Germany's international balance of payments. Reparation charges, they noted, represented the primary obligation of Germany, so that private lenders' risks would be abnormally compounded in the case of "excessive borrowing abroad." They concluded prophetically that in case "our Government passes these loans without some

54. Arthur N. Young to Hughes, April 7, 1922; Harrison to Farson and Co. (New York), April 15, 1922 in NA, RG 59:862.51 (with appended memoranda).

55. Hoover, *Memoirs*, II, 182.

56. Coolidge, quoted in Edwards, *op. cit.*, p. 696; Madden, *op. cit.*, p. 239.

57. Feis, *op. cit.*, p. 41.

indication of probable difficulties in the remittance of interest and amortization charges, it will be severely criticized if defaults occur." Their memorandum counseled against further loans to Germany for public utilities or fixed capital purposes.[58]

By the end of 1924, Hughes agreed that the Commerce Department should at least inform interested American bankers of these risks.[59] In practice, this policy had but slight effect. When Harris, Forbes and Company, for example, proposed a substantial loan to a German government-owned utility, the interdepartmental consultations resulted in a State Department reply offering "no objection." Approval was granted on the stated assumption that the bankers had considered the possible effects of the Versailles treaty's Article 248 concerning reparations.[60]

Meanwhile, Jones and Attaché Charles E. Herring (Berlin) agreed on the increasing "dangers of long-term loans to German industries." They recognized, however, that "the great problem is how to get the message to Garcia," the latter being "in Wall St. rather than Main St." Early in 1925, they predicted a financial "debacle" for American investors and wished Hoover to warn against German loans, even if only to protect the Department against future criticism. Jones wondered about the "political or other subtle motives behind the heavy, long-term dollar borrowing of German industries." He suspected that the prosperous German interests were "acting in some concerted manner" to sabotage the reparations program by claiming new debt obligations.[61]

In another significant memorandum Herring emphasized the tendency in Germany to exaggerate the need for American work-

58. Goldsmith and Jones to Stokes (for Hoover), Nov. 21, 1924, NA, RG 151:640 (Germany).

59. Hughes to Hoover, Dec. 30, 1924, *ibid.*

60. The issue was discussed with the Commerce Department and with Ambassador Myron T. Herrick (Paris), who cabled that the "exercise of authority under 248 is unlikely. . . ." See Hughes to Herrick, Jan. 26, and Herrick to Hughes, Jan. 30, 1925; Harrison to Sullivan and Cromwell (for Harris, Forbes), Feb. 5, 1925 in NA, RG 59:862.51.

61. Jones to Herring, Feb. 2 and Feb. 20, 1925, NA, RG 151:640 (Germany).

ing capital, "so long as there is no question of any kind of American financial control." He went on to expound:

"German efforts to obtain money from abroad under almost any conditions . . . their beggar psychology . . . the natural tendency of the race for self pity . . . the national desire to get something somehow without a too scrupulous regard to ways and means of obtaining or repaying it . . . to beg, borrow or steal something from Uncle Sam, the rich man of the neighborhood."[62]

American investment bankers, however, campaigned all the more vigorously for the profitable German flotations. Citing a case where representatives of Blair and Company "horned in" on the final day of an option belonging to another American firm, Herring deplored "reputable American banking houses actually bidding against each other for this doubtful [German] business."[63]

Jones, at one point, conceded that "there seems to be little we can do to discourage unwise loans to Germany." However, the Jones-Herring reports did begin to produce concrete results before the end of 1925. The State Department agreed to have the "gist" of these reports circulated, "in a quiet manner," among American bankers. Hoover was anxious to use more direct methods "but the Treasury frowned upon this."[64] Thus was laid the groundwork for at least a mild official attempt to dissuade Americans from sinking their savings into the German trough. The plan may have been successful if applied more directly to the average investor rather than his banking intermediary.

Hoover, like the good department head that he was, did not fail to perceive the validity of his experts' warnings. Consequently, he continued to demand closer governmental supervision of loans to Germany. Yet, neither he nor Hughes and Kellogg, certainly not Mellon, were willing to appear in the position of curbing American enterprise. Hoover, it is probable, hoped that American bankers would make the right choice voluntarily,

62. Herring to Jones, March 25, 1925, *ibid.*
63. Herring to Jones, Aug. 12, 1925, *ibid.*
64. Jones to Herring, Aug. 31, 1925, *ibid.*

if presented with the facts. His compromise formula, therefore, to be used in reply to investment houses asking approval of new German loans, was the following:

"While the Department of State raises no objection to this flotation . . . it feels that American bankers should know that the amount of German loans has become so large, and the control of exchange on behalf of the Allies is such, as to raise a question as to whether or not it may be very difficult for German borrowers to make the necessary transfers."[65]

Although the Hoover formula was applied jointly by the Commerce and State Departments, their kid glove approach and bureaucratic subtleties had little effect on the bankers. At the same time, Hoover had growing doubts about the German ability ever to repay the dollar loans, since "reparations constituted a first charge upon their resources and exchange." Writing to Kellogg, he protested that "it would not be fair for the American public . . . to remain in ignorance of . . . the situation."[66]

Even though almost all their German loan applications finally were awarded the "no objection" seal of the State Department, many American bankers felt that the government had no business telling them what factors they or their clients should consider. Personal conferences between Hoover and Kellogg on the one hand, and banker James Speyer on the other (accompanied by counsel Henry W. Taft, brother of the ex-President) did little good. Speyer, head of the influential Speyer and Company investment interests, interpreted literally the State Department's diplomatic explanation that it was "merely suggesting . . . consideration of certain factors . . . wholly within your own discretion." He and other financiers cited the opinion of "German authorities" who believed that the Allied Transfer Committee could not restrict German acquisition of foreign exchange "in the open market." To "even mention the possibility of future difficulty in German remittances," these bankers felt, would only "create unnecessary alarm" among American investors.[67]

65. Hoover to Harrison, Aug. 28, 1925, NA, RG 59:862.51.
66. Hoover to Kellogg, Oct. 8, 1925; George Akerson (Hoover's assistant) to Harrison, Nov. 23, 1926, *ibid.*
67. Memorandum of Arthur N. Young, Oct. 12, 1925; Speyer and Co. to Kellogg, Nov. 21, 1925, *ibid.*

Throughout 1926 the Commerce and State departments continued their largely futile reminders of Germany's prior obligations and the need to limit loans to "productive" purposes not in conflict with reparation payments. S. Parker Gilbert, American Agent General for Reparations, also reiterated that the Transfer Committee could offer "no assurances concerning the payment of . . . German loans floated abroad."[68]

But the New York Stock Exchange continued to receive additional listings of German stocks and bonds floated by leading investment houses.[69] This was in spite of new warnings by Commerce officials abroad that "the loans approved by American houses . . . and the whole credit position of the German municipalities . . . were lamentably weak."[70]

In 1927 Jones inquired hopefully of Lewis Strauss (Kuhn, Loeb and Company) whether "the New York Stock Exchange has considered excluding German loans from quotation, as a protest against the disregard of the State Department's warning letters to investment bankers." The reply was in the negative. When the Commerce Department, in the same year, found actual "misrepresentations in German loan prospectuses," Hoover was against revealing the issue to the glare of public opinion. "Publicity would involve the reputation and might incur the ill will of powerful financial houses," as well as panicking the bondholders, explained Ray O. Hall (Acting Chief, Finance and Investment Division).[71]

Perhaps under the pressure of these "powerful financial houses," the Commerce Department continued through 1929 to supply useful information advertising "prospective borrowers" in Germany, whether states, municipalities, or corporations. Especially prompt service was given to the Department's "im-

68. Harrison to Harris, Forbes and Co., Nov. 14, 1925; Harrison to Stokes, Dec. 1, 1925; Young to Hallgarten and Co., Jan. 13, 1926, *ibid.*

69. John Foster Dulles (representing Harris, Forbes and Co.) to Harrison (telephone conversation), Sept. 28, 1926; Harrison to Dulles (letter), Sept. 28, 1926, *ibid.*

70. Lyon to Jones, Aug. 5, 1925; Jones to Lyon, Sept. 10, 1925; Allport to Jones, June 1, 1926; Jones to Allport, June 2, 1926, *ibid.*

71. Hall to Klein, Jan. 20, 1927, *ibid.*

portant contacts" within financial circles.[72] Only occasional delays occurred in the approval of loans; for example, the proposed $30,000,000 loan to the State of Prussia (through Harris, Forbes) was postponed briefly when S. Parker Gilbert, fearing "excessive" lending, made "ready to use considerable publicity to support his views."[73]

American bankers, reported Jones, "bring out new German loans *ad infinitum* and the investing public is [still] . . . keen to buy."[74] During the second quarter of 1928 alone, German loans in the United States amounted to $153,300,000,[75] a record figure. By then, however, lesser officials of the Commerce and State departments were given the following precautionary instructions:

1. to avoid leaving an impression that the government undertook any responsibility in connection with foreign loans.

2. "carefully [to] avoid acting as intermediaries or participants in private business transactions."

3. to "discourage the transmission of private messages through official channels."

4. finally, advice to bankers "should be personal in tone, accompanied with some disclaimer of relieving the bankers of any part of the responsibility toward bond buyers which the ethics and practice of investment banking impose."[76]

Each of these instructions was obviously intended to ameliorate some existing abuse and to protect the government against accusations resulting from possible foreign defaults. Long before the crash of 1929 there were signs of the impending financial storm, although its magnitude was never anticipated fully. If some crisis were to arise, the only question, as the London *Economist* put it, was whether the claims of private investors would be given preference over the respective governmental ones

72. Jones to Allport, Sept. 21, 1927 (speaking of T. R. Goldsmith of W. A. Harriman & Co.); Jones to the Commerce Office in Berlin, April 19, 1928, *ibid.*

73. Jones to Hoover, Sept. 26, 1927, *ibid.*

74. Jones to Allport, June 2, 1926, *ibid.*

75. Jones to Klein, Sept. 27, 1928, *ibid.*

76. Kellogg to Hoover, Jan. 9, 1928, NA, RG 151:640 (General).

to reparations and war debts. This view, as summarized by Jones, was based "on the theory that in case of doubt as to whether the American investor or his Government came first, the former would win out."[77]

Hoover was not unsympathetic to this conclusion. When he first called for Federal guidance in the interest of American lenders abroad in 1922 he asserted that "unless some such action is taken, [these] citizens . . . would seem to have the moral right to insist that the Federal Government should not press its governmental claims to the prejudice of their investment."[78] Subsequently, the "business standards" Hoover wished to apply to American capital exports were never made truly effective. These factors may help to explain his Depression moratorium on intergovernmental debts, whereby the American Government deferred its own claims while private investors organized to press for continued recognition of their interests abroad.[79]

In view of the evidence relating to excessive loans . . . to Germany and the doubts raised as to their possible repayment, one wonders at the absence of a loan embargo policy in this case. Such a policy was applied on several occasions — against France and against the potash cartel, for example. According to Hoover himself, it was Harding, Coolidge, and Mellon who forced "a retreat from our original standards," with a consequent weakening of the loan control program.[80] While Hoover's loan policies aroused resentment among American bankers, the latter could indeed look to Mellon as an influential guardian of their interests.[81]

Diplomatic and strategic considerations, possibly a desire for a stable Germany as a bulwark against Bolshevism, figured also

77. *The Economist,* Oct. 22, 1927, quoted in a memorandum from Jones to Hoover, Nov. 5, 1927, *ibid.*
78. Hoover, *Memoirs,* II, 88.
79. *Ibid.,* III, *passim.;* Charlton Ogburn (for the "association of holders of German dollar bonds") to Jones, Dec. 9, 1931, NA, RG 151:640 (Germany).
80. Hoover, *Memoirs,* II, 88.
81. Harvey O'Connor, *Mellon's Millions* (New York, 1933) is biased but informative. See especially chapters 9-14 and the sections dealing with the Hoover-Mellon rivalry.

in the American government's reluctance to restrict the flow of credit to Germany.[82] In addition, the tactful Commerce and State department officials hoped that the controls established by Germany's own Finance Ministry and *Reichsbank* would help "protect American investors against the optimism or stupidity of some of our bankers."[83]

The German *Beratungsstelle,* a financial advisory council, optimistically was expected to disapprove "ill considered foreign loans . . . having a detrimental influence on foreign (capital) markets."[84] Subsequent to its formation, a German decree revalued past indebtness at only 15 per cent of the original gold value, and declared all pre-1924 government bonds as "non-redeemable until the Reich's reparations obligations have been discharged." These facts, as well as serious losses suffered even then by American investors, should have restrained the general enthusiasm for German loans.[85]

Such information, however, was not known widely outside of governmental and banking circles. Practically worthless 1922-issue German bonds, for example, were still being sold to Americans during the 1920's. In reporting these cases for possible prosecution, the Commerce Department could only attempt to prove actual fraud where the damage had already been done.[86] As for the loan control machinery in Germany proper, it was

82. Samuel F. Bemis, *A Diplomatic History of the United States* (New York, 1955), pp. 708-711; William Y. Elliott, *et al., The Political Economy of American Foreign Policy* (New York, 1955), *passim.;* Robert P. Browder, *The Origins of Soviet-American Diplomacy* (Princeton, New Jersey), pp. 39-43; James K. Pollock and Homer Thomas, *Germany in Power and Eclipse* (New York, 1952), *passim.*

83. Herring to Jones, Aug. 12, 1925, NA, RG 151:640 (Germany).

84. Joseph C. Grew (Under-Secretary of State) to Hoover, Nov. 14, 1924, *ibid.*

85. Klein to Rep. William A. Ayres (D., Kansas), Jan. 30, 1925; "Special Circular" no. 113, distributed by the Commerce Department, March 30, 1925; additional warnings in "Revaluation of Paper Mark Debts" ("Special Circular" no. 142), Sept. 15, 1925, *ibid.*

86. C. A. McQueen (Acting Chief, Finance and Investment Division) to H. J. Donnelly (Acting Solicitor), June 23, 1925; Harrison to Hoover, Aug. 4, 1925, *ibid.*

not until the fall of 1927 that the State Department's "representations" stirred the Weimar government "to recognize the vital
importance of exercising self-restraint." Even afterwards, few
loans were halted by the German authorities.[87]

87. Governor Strong (Federal Reserve Bank, New York) to William R.
Castle (Assistant Secretary of State), Oct. 1, 1927; Schurman to Kellogg, Oct.
4, 1927 in NA, RG 59:862.51.

CHAPTER X

LOANS AND FOREIGN POLICY (CONTINUED): PRESSURES AT HOME AND ABROAD

American Industry's Opposition to German Loans

There is now little dispute regarding the speculative excesses which marked American lending abroad during the 1920's, especially in the loans to Germany. An official Commerce publication, exercising the wisdom of hindsight in 1943, recalled critically the "high pressure salesmanship methods by which foreign issues were solicited and sold . . . without adequate regard to the growing burden of indebtedness."[1] That so little was done under the Harding and Coolidge administrations to curb this extravagant financing may be explained partly in terms of the economic optimism and *laissez-faire* attitude of the time.

One cannot fail, however, to note the clash of opposing economic interests in the determination of foreign loan policies: the investment and financial circles on one side, and the industrial firms on the other. The first favored the free flow of American funds abroad and profited from promoting this movement of capital. The latter, in significant instances, feared the competition of foreign enterprise, especially German, expanding in the 1920's with the aid of dollar financing. Hoover sympathized with these misgivings of American industry, which appealed so often for the Commerce Department's assistance against com-

1. Hal B. Lary, *The United States in the World Economy* (Economic Series, no. 23, 1943), p. 7.

petitors abroad. His inability to enforce tighter controls over loans to Germany reflects, to some degree, a limitation of his own influence in the Republican administrations.

The Commerce Department was quick to recognize that many "new German loans are frankly intended to develop foreign trade in competition against American firms." The latter, moreover, were justified in requesting Hoover's aid, for the threatened markets were ones "which this Department has done so much to open." Commerce, therefore, hoped to rally public opinion through the trade press, to exert pressure against "the liberal policy of bond brokers and financial promoters."[2]

This program was adopted soon by industrial groups, such as the Machine Tool Builders' Association, agitating against German loans. The Association protested that the influx of dollars enabled German machinery manufacturers to extend longer term credits than American manufacturers could afford. Senator William M. Butler (R., Mass.) criticized also the "wholesale" loans and investments abroad, while the New York *Commercial* suspected that German interests were buying up American chemical plants with borrowed dollars.[3] Such charges were accompanied by Commerce Department reports that "our American chemical industry is decidedly worried" by the threat of "German dominance."[4]

When the National City Company of New York proposed to float a loan for the I. G. Farben chemical and dye interests, official approval was delayed by several considerations. First, Mr. [Alfred I.] Dupont wrote to Hoover of his apprehensions concerning the use of this loan for added German dye manufacturing capacity in the United States. Hoover transmitted this letter to Kellogg, who dismissed the possible consequences it suggested. Consul General Hamilton C. Claiborne, moreover, reported from Frankfort that I. G. Farben had no designs on the American chemical industry. Arthur N. Young, Kellogg's Economic

2. Klein to Hoover, March 12, 1925, NA, RG 151:640 (Germany).
3. Jones to Herring, April 24, 1925, *ibid.*
4. Concannon to Herring, April 1, 1925, *ibid.*

Adviser, ridiculed as "hardly tenable," in this case, the notion presented by opponents of the German loans that American capital must not be permitted to stimulate "a potentially dangerous industry in a foreign country." The American chemical industry, he proposed, could always rely on protective Congressional legislation in the eventualities of unfair foreign competition.[5]

Hoover and his staff took a less optimistic view of the subject, especially in the light of warnings by Charles H. Herty of The Chemical Foundation that I. G. Farben threatened domestic production vital to American defense. In addition, the Commerce Department scanned anxiously the reports from its agents abroad concerning losses suffered by American exporters as a result of I. G. Farben's dumping and price-cutting. The German combine, however, had little difficulty in acquiring dollar credits, sometimes through its Norwegian branch or other subsidiaries.[6] By 1928 the Commerce Department's executives pleaded that they could do little to restrain such foreign loans, now partly because of Senator Glass's protests against Federal involvement in the export of capital.[7]

The Department still promoted actively the concept of tying agreements to specify that the proceeds of dollar flotations should be spent in the United States. But the investment houses would not accept this condition, causing an important Commerce official to comment, in 1927, on "their utter disregard for all interests outside their own." The German *Rentenbank,* he complained, held "$100,000,000 of our money for the development of agriculture . . . yet, no attempt is made to assure our manufacturers a fair share of the orders." At this time, it must

5. Young to Kellogg, Jan. 28, 1926; Kellogg to Hoover, March 22, 1926 in NA, RG 59:862.51D98/— Claiborne to Kellogg, Dec. 5, 1927, *ibid.,* 840.659/6.

6. Young memorandum (copy to Commerce), Dec. 15, 1927, *ibid.,* 862.-51D98/2; Attaché H. Lawrence Groves (Vienna) to Jones, Jan. 26, 1928, NA, RG 151:640 (General).

7. Jones to Groves, March 3, 1928, *ibid.*

be recalled, American farmers and American farm implement manufacturers were in the midst of a severe economic crisis.[8]

Just as they admired the British control of capital exports, so the Commerce staff recognized also the practical advantages held by German "combination and coordination" in the competition for world markets.[9] Dollars borrowed by the State of Bremen, Hoover was warned, subsidized three local automobile manufacturers, advertising mass-produced trucks and cars at prices which American industry could not match.[10]

It was, after all, quite consistent for the Department, which expended so much effort in encouraging the standardization and efficiency of American enterprise, to be concerned with the overseas markets for American products. Consequently, it is not surprising that the Department looked with something less than enthusiasm on the multi-million dollar loans to the Stinnes interests and other German firms[11]

Ineffectual as the loan controls often were, the supervisory machinery was also limited in scope by what turned out to be a most damaging loophole. Where official objection might be raised to a foreign loan issue in the form of bonds, prospective borrowers could, nevertheless, acquire the needed capital by floating an issue of stock. Neither State nor Commerce objected to this broad category. By this means Germany's United Steel Works, A. G., acquired needed financing.[12] So did the Hansa Steamship Line (Bremen), in spite of Hoover's zeal for shipping under the American flag and the bitter protests of "Congressional spokesmen for American merchant marine interests."[13]

The plain fact was that public opinion in the United States

8. Allport to Jones, Oct. 18, 1927, *ibid.*
9. *Ibid.*
10. Jones to Hoover, Dec. 10, 1925, *ibid.*
11. Jones to Herring, April 9, 1925, *ibid.* The Stinnes loans were negotiated by the United States and Foreign Securities Corp., organized by Kuhn, Loeb and Company and Dillon, Read.
12. William R. Castle to Dillon, Read, Dec. 15, 1928, NA, RG 59:862.51 (United Steel Works).
13. Hoover, *A Merchant Marine Policy* (address of Nov. 16, 1925), p. 4; Economic Adviser's Office to Castle, Sept. 24, 1929, *supra.*

did not regard loans to Germany as a hazardous investment or as a potential threat to American industry. Men like Henry M. Robinson, a nationally respected banker and member of the Dawes Plan committees, deprecated the concern in some quarters over Germany's ability to meet both reparation payments and debt obligations. His sanguine analysis proclaimed that "all evidence runs counter" to any fears that Germany would be unable to pay, emphasizing that the "reparations burden . . . is probably less" than German military expenditures before World War I. Robinson's optimism regarding the safety of loans to Germany extended to other dollar credits as well. "The dangers which our foreign loans now face," he concluded, "are more illusory than real."[14]

In this climate of financial optimism, the Commerce Department was reduced to occasional warnings, bolstered by faithful informational and statistical services. It published, for example, the details of the first large postwar loan to a German corporation — the $10,000,000 Krupp Iron Works Issue of 1924. This type of information was all the more useful because German government supervision was most lax regarding corporate, as contrasted with municipal issues. Between September, 1924 and June, 1929, Americans purchased about $1,181,000,000 of German securities, according to Commerce Department figures.[15]

Loan Standards and Latin America

Since the turn of the century the influence of the United States has been more pervasive in Latin America than in any other part of the world. Here lay an ideal testing ground for Hoover's investment and loan policies. To be sure, countries lacking a stable economy and sound financing were to be found in postwar Europe as well as in Central or South America. Poland, for

14. Henry M. Robinson, "Are American Loans Abroad Safe?" *Foreign Affairs,* V (Oct. 1926), 50-51, 56.
15. *American Underwriting of Foreign Securities in 1928 (Trade Information Bulletin, no. 613 ,1929), p. 1; American Underwriting of German Securities (Trade Information Bulletin, no. 648, 1929), pp. 1, 6, 8; Kuczynski, op. cit., pp. 11-12, passim.*

example, was forced in 1926 to accept the monetary reforms suggested by the United States Treasury Department as a condition for obtaining dollar loans.[16] But Latin American countries were, for many years before this, subject to the economic and political influence of their neighbor to the north.

Hoover, as Secretary of Commerce, was intensely concerned with Latin America as a huge market for United States products, a source of essential raw materials, and a fertile field for investment capital. Under his aegis, there developed an official corps of experts on Latin American economic affairs.[17] United States firms desiring to invest in South American oil lands, to export machinery, or to lend money to governments south of Panama were afforded the efficient and sympathetic services of the Commerce Department. Some of its fact-finding activities were summarized for the public in the Commerce Department's 1925 study by Fred M. Halsey, *Investments in Latin America and the British West Indies.*

Specific assistance to American bankers was extended in several forms. In some cases Commerce officials exercised their prestige in uncovering the true budgetary conditions or previous defaults of South American states. At times they were interested observers of legislative proceedings affecting United States investment bankers. For example, when the latter vied with the British Ethelburga Syndicate for the privilege of floating an Ecuadorian loan, they were informed promptly of local legislation favorable to the American banking interests.[18]

In some cases fiscal reports of South American state governments were considered by Commerce headquarters to be inade-

16. The financial plan for Poland was drawn up by Professor Donald Kemmerer and Charles S. Dewey (Assistant Secretary of the Treasury); both became financial advisers to Warsaw, and Dewey was appointed director of the Bank of Poland (1927-1931). See Emerson, *op. cit.,* p. 242; *Who's Who In America* (XXVII).

17. Myers, *The Foreign Policies of Herbert Hoover,* p. 41.

18. Ralph H. Ackerman (Chief, Latin American Division) to Fred G. Hoddick (Fincke, Bangert & Co., Philadelphia), March 13, 1922, NA, RG 151:640 (Brazil); Robert O. Hayward (Dillon, Read) to Jones, Dec. 6, 1922, *ibid.;* Jones to R. F. Loree, Bank of Central and South America (New York), Oct. 17, 1923, *ibid.* (Ecuador).

quate. Subsequently Commercial attachés would be ordered to "suggest" to the South American authorities that the flow of dollars might be held back for lack of "complete financial information."[19]

These services to United States investment bankers were continued throughout the 1920's, in bland obliviousness to growing protests by Latin Americans against financial "imperialism." The latter term embraced not only Washington's direct influence, but also the high initial discount and interest demanded by the North American bankers and the attachment of governmental revenues as security for the dollar loans. Some South Americans objected to what they considered useless public projects fostered by Yankee loan salesmen. Even if the fault lay largely with corrupt or inept local politicians, ill feeling was often aroused against United States interests.[20]

Brazil, the slumbering giant of South America, had by the 1920's a long history of defaults. Her British creditors threatened to bring suit, and financial circles on both sides of the Atlantic were convinced of the instability of her economy. Dillon, Read, nonetheless, floated substantial Brazilian loans in the United States (not for "Coffee Defense," but for general economic development). When these funds were misused, and "stabilization" in Brazil seemed as far away as ever, the local press — especially the influential *O Globo* — launched an anti-American campaign which aroused even the hitherto placid State Department. By the end of 1927, State, on behalf of American investors who refused to accept repayment in "paper" for Brazilian gold bonds, decided to bring suit against Brazil before the Court of International Justice.[21]

Hoover's objections to the flotation of foreign "paper currency" securities in the United States did not usually receive the backing of the State Department. Had his advice been acted upon, including the acceptance of firmer loan standards on a

19. Jones to the Bogoté Office, Oct. 17, 1927, *ibid.* (Colombia).
20. Harrison to Hoover, April 1, 1927, *ibid.*
21. Reports of Consuls-General Claude Dawson and Harry H. Morgan, July 6 and 18, 1927, NA, RG 59.

"business basis," American losses in foreign securities may have been lessened appreciably. Hoover believed that foreign loans should be "definitely tied to the gold standard" and looked back nostalgically to the prewar practice of stipulating repayment in "gold coin of [specific] weight and fineness." He doubted the stability of the "soft" foreign currencies of the 1920's.[22] As in the case of the Brazilian gold bonds, however, it was difficult to require repayment in gold, if at all, short of military intervention.

This possibility was ruled out by Hoover, who believed that it "ought not to be the policy of the United States to intervene by force to secure or maintain contracts between our citizens and foreign States and their citizens." Hoover opposed also the use of non-recognition as a form of pressure against recalcitrant Latin American governments.[23] In effect, his ideas actually ran counter to past United States policies, especially in Central America and the Caribbean.

It was these policies which came under the critical scrutiny of the Senate Committee on Foreign Relations in 1925 and 1927. The purpose of these hearings was to consider concurrent resolutions calling for the Commerce, State, and Treasury departments to desist from "engaging the responsibility of the Government . . . [in] supervising the fulfillment of financial agreements between citizens of the United States and sovereign foreign Governments." Many Senators intended also to prevent the kind of intervention on behalf of United States interests which led to the occupation of the Dominican Republic, Haiti, and Nicaragua.[24]

Witnesses such as Lewis S. Gannett, editor of *The Nation*, attacked the Hoover-inspired governmental system of loan approval as but a strengthening of economic imperialism. "Irresponsible bureaucrats," he maintained, were "setting a new precedent in the partnership between the United States Govern-

22. Hoover to the Secretary of State, April 13, 1922, *ibid.*
23. Hoover, quoted in Bemis, *The Latin American Policy of the United States*, p. 222.
24. *Hearings before . . . the Committee on Foreign Relations: Foreign Loans*, 68 Cong., 2 Sess., 1925; 69 Cong., 2 Sess., 1927, *passim.*

ment and the bankers." Part of Gannett's evidence were loan
contracts between Bolivia and the Equitable Trust Company
which, he attempted to prove, "turned over the Republic of
Bolivia to a group of New York bankers" (by pledging the
country's import and tax revenues). The approval of such loan
contracts, he proposed, implied that the American Government
was ready to enforce them militarily.[25]

Dr. Samuel Guy Inman, writer on political affairs, claimed
that the Foreign Service had become, by its own admission,
"largely a commercial agency." He and Dr. James Weldon
Johnson, a former diplomat and a public figure, cited cases of
United States "meddling" in Latin American affairs for "the
protection of the financial interests." Even John Dewey, the
philosopher, wrote the Senators that the "Government has other
business than that of acting as bill collectors in behalf of dubious
and highly speculative investments."[26]

The presence on the Senate committee of such stalwarts as
William E. Borah and Hiram W. Johnson was sufficient to add
to the excitement of what had already become a national issue.
Inman's article, "Imperialistic America," in the *Atlantic Monthly*
of July, 1924, was answered for the State Department in the
September issue by Sumner Welles. Welles disclaimed any government responsibility for "onerous [loan] contracts" signed by
countries unable to obtain better terms elsewhere.[27]

By contrast, Hoover displayed a far greater concern over the
quality of private dollar loans extended by American investment
houses to foreign governments. He admitted candidly that some
of the Latin American loans "had been particularly bad," and
recommended closer preventive governmental supervision.[28] The
latter was suggested by Hoover partly because, like the "anti-
imperialists," he opposed United States military intervention
abroad. Yet, the suspicion of all governmental involvement in
private loans fostered by Senator Glass and others weakened

25. Gannett's testimony, *ibid.* (1925), pp. 2-3, 6, 12.
26. *Ibid.*, pp. 15, 20, 81, 90.
27. Welles article quoted, *ibid.*, p. 43.
28. Hoover, *Memoirs*, II, 334.

further the prospects for qualitative supervision to assure the economic soundness of each loan.

Still believing, however, in the power of practical business advice — even if on a voluntary level — Hoover persisted in calling for loans "devoted to productive enterprise," and not for "military equipment or war purposes."[29] These remarks were aimed especially at Latin American loans.

But the State Department did not favor an outright ban on armaments loans, possibly for fear of weakening thereby the United States' influence south of the Rio Grande.[30] It raised no objection, for example, to a Bolivian loan for funding prior armaments obligations.[31] John Foster Dulles, as a private citizen, assumed that loan embargoes to control armaments were simply a convenient method of exerting United States pressure in Latin America. Recalling the "historic" American policy favoring a free flow of arms, Dulles doubted that proposed armaments loans could now be regulated governmentally by "some basic humanitarian objective."[32]

In the final analysis, policy differences between the Commerce and State departments lay mainly in the emphasis on economic versus political factors. Hoover opposed loans to Latin American countries for any but productive purposes intended to raise the capacity of those countries to buy manufactures and to repay prior debts. When the Commerce Department, however, applied these principles to proposed Bolivian and Colombian loans, asserting that both were already "over-borrowed," approval was not withheld by the State Department. The latter was still concerned primarily with such factors as non-recognition of Latin American governments and other traditional aspects of hemisphere politics.[33]

Yet, the tides of public opinion were turning away from the extension of direct United States political influence along the

29. Hoover, quoted in De Conde, *op. cit.,* p. 7; Hoover, *Memoirs,* II, 85.
30. De Conde, *supra., loc. cit.*
31. Madden, *op. cit.,* p. 244.
32. Dulles, "Our Foreign Loan Policy," pp. 39-40.
33. Angell, *op. cit.,* pp. 105-107; Madden, *op. cit.,* p. 247.

old lines of "dollar diplomacy." Hoover's emphasis on policies justified by the economic interest of the entire hemisphere and unencumbered by political considerations gained favor in postwar America.

This movement frowned on the use of "coercive measures" and, as a means of obviating their need, called for governmental "supervision over the terms and conditions of investments before they are made." Public opposition to the manner in which United States interests assumed important governmental functions in some parts of Latin America was evident even before the Senate hearings of 1925 and 1927. It was well-summarized by Henry Bruère, New York financier and civic leader.[34]

Hoover, of course, did not lose sight also of the national interest involved in capital exports. This was illustrated by his oft-repeated appeal for investments in oil and other strategic raw materials abroad. Related to these plans was the attempt, in 1926, to provide Federal tax exemptions for income received from certain foreign investments. United States government assistance in such forms as the legalizing of buying pools was acceptable to Hoover as simply another form of economic encouragement. But he would not sanction armed intervention, always preferring the pragmatic bargaining of the international market place. In comparison to the capital export policies of France before 1914, for example, American loans in the 1920's were indeed motivated to a greater degree by economic rather than political considerations.[35]

A somewhat paternal attitude may be deduced in Hoover's advice to Latin Americans to balance their budgets, refrain from unproductive loans, and eschew armaments and warfare.[36] This kind of counsel was given, however, to the great powers of Europe as well. The concept of "dollar diplomacy" in terms of

34. Henry Bruère, "Constructive vs. Dollar Diplomacy," *The American Economic Review*, XIII (March, 1923), 68, 71, 75.

35. Hoover, *Memoirs, passim.;* Earle, *op. cit.,* p. 49; Edwards, *op. cit.,* pp. 700-701.

36. Cited in "The Foreign Loan Policy of the United States," memorandum from Jones to the new Secretary of Commerce, Robert P. Lamont, July 13, 1929, NA, RG 151:640 (General).

sweeping political considerations for an entire region disinte-
grated during the late 1920's, in part because of the Hoover
policies. Official Washington tended to intervene only in the case
of those occasional loans which seemed obviously "undesirable"
for economic and, to a lesser degree, political reasons.[37]

The Open Door and Loans to Japan

One of the relatively few loans disapproved for both economic
and political causes involved Japanese interests in Manchuria.
The Commerce and State departments agreed on the major
issues confronting the American Government in these loan
negotiations.

The State Department was anxiously aware of the "delicate"
nature of Sino-Japanese relations, and of the expanding Japanese
influence on the Asian mainland. This expansion, threatening
to close the economy of Manchuria to all but Japanese interests,
was carried out partly by the government-financed Oriental
Development Company, in 1922 negotiated a $20,000,000
loan with the National City Company (New York) to pay
for "development work" in Manchuria and other parts of the
Far East.[38]

State and Commerce department strategists determined to op-
pose the loan, and the bankers were informed of this officially.
Diplomacy demanded, however, that the explanation exclude
the blunt mention of political or strategic considerations. Instead, the loan disapproval was based on an economic reasoning
developed previously within the Commerce Department; namely,
that loans aiding the foreign competitors of American enterprise
abroad were to be discouraged. The Oriental Development Company, it was argued, would compete with American firms
throughout the Far East. Permission for the loan was not granted
until pressure was brought by the Japanese, as well as National
City and the Riggs National Bank (its Washington agent),
claiming that the loan would be used only within Japan.[39]

37. Angell, *op. cit.,* p. 97; Madden, *op. cit.,* p. 241. It is not denied that the
borderline between the "economic" and "political" is often a moot question.
38. *Foreign Relations of the United States* (Washington, 1923), II, 503-506.
39. *Ibid.;* Feis, *op. cit.,* p. 35.

Subsequently, approval was refused for a loan to the Japanese-controlled South Manchurian Railway, even though National City suggested that all the proceeds might be spent in the United States. A similar Morgan and Company loan was disapproved in 1927. The official explanation maintained still that "the use of such American credit would tend to prejudice or circumscribe the opportunities for American enterprises or to further the . . . competition therewith."[40]

In the background of these negotiations, the Commerce Department's staff compiled valuable studies of Japan's capital needs and their bearing on international relations. With the demise of the Anglo-Japanese alliance *domestic* Japanese industry and utilities benefited increasingly from incoming American capital, whose flow was assisted by the informational media of the Commerce Department. As in other cases, Hoover's office was consulted before any Japanese loans received official approval. The Commerce Department retained also a constant chain of communications with National City, W. A. Harriman, and other bankers concerned with Japanese loans.[41]

Controversy over the Hoover Program

Did the United States during the 1920's demonstrate in certain aspects of its loan policy "an ignorance of both politics and finance?" So claimed Herbert Feis and other analysts of the period.[42] Several, moreover, have thrown the burden of error on the shoulders of Hoover as Secretary of Commerce. In the area of foreign loan controls, stated Dulles, policy "initiative" was maintained within the Commerce Department. The State Department was relegated, in Dulles's view, to the role of "cooperating" with the implementation of "economic theories" flowing from

40. *Foreign Relations of the United States, supra.,* 508-509; Feis, *supra.,* p. 36; NA, RG 151:602.2 (Oriental Development Co. file).
41. "Foreign Loan Policy of Japan" ("Special Circular" no. 14), Nov. 10, 1922; Hopkins to Hoover, Nov. 1, 1922; Harrison to Stokes, Aug. 1, 1924; Attaché Butts (Tokyo) to Klein, Sept. 4, 1924; Jones to Douglas W. Clinch (Harriman & Co.), July 30, 1925, and other documents in NA, RG 151:640 (Japan).
42. Feis, *op. cit.,* p. 45.

Hoover's offices. One example he cited was the acceptance of Hoover's ban on loans to foreign monopolies.[43]

Dulles believed, as did others, that American bankers should be allowed to exercise their own discretion, submitting for governmental approval only those loans which pertained to "some major policy in the field of international relations."[44] Hughes and Kellogg also were wary of government involvement in economic judgments to the extent suggested by Hoover. A possible exception may be found in Kellogg's warning concerning the safety of loans to a Germany saddled with reparations. This case, however, involved strong political as well as economic considerations.[45] At all times the State Department — unlike Commerce — refused to evaluate the quality of specific loans as a "business proposition," leaving that up to the investors themselves.

It was only after the stock crash of 1929 that the State Department — now under President Hoover — took more kindly to the old Commerce suggestion that the proceeds of foreign loans be earmarked for purchase of goods in the United States.[46] Before then it was argued that dollars loaned abroad would inevitably return to stimulate American industry and exports, although Commerce officials often had dismissed this view as leaving too much to fate alone, publicizing actively the advantages of "earmarking."[47] Similarly, the latter felt free to inform the leaders of finance and industry regarding excessive speculation in foreign investments and other economic trends uncovered by the Department's vast research network.[48]

Did the Hoover program of loan supervision and aid to busi-

43. Dulles, *op. cit.*, pp. 40-41.
44. *Ibid.*, p. 47.
45. *Foreign Relations of the United States* (1922), II, 764-766, cited in Feis, *op. cit.*, p. 9; Kellogg, "Some Foreign Policies of the United States," *Foreign Affairs*, IV (Jan. 1926, Special Supplement), xiii.
46. Cooper to Klein, Oct. 4, 1930; Klein to Lamont, Oct. 13, 1930 in NA, RG 151:640 (General).
47. Dulles, *op. cit.*, p. 43.
48. Klein predicted that the speculative mania would lead to a crash, "as always in the past"; *vide* his letter to Baltimore business leader Willoughby M. McCormick, May 6, 1929, NA, RG 151:640 (General).

ness involve the threat of bureaucratic paternalism? Dulles expressed the fear of some groups, presumably in banking, that government officials in charge of loan approvals already exercised "extra-legal" powers which could be extended to other areas of the economy. Control over foreign loans, as viewed by these private interests, could become a convenient method of implementing the pet economic theories of those who happened to head the executive departments.[49]

Democrats like Carter Glass, moreover, did not fail to remind the public that governmental loan controls were born at the time of the infamous Teapot Dome scandals. In view of the past record of corruption in government, they foresaw the possibility of new temptations and pressures arising out of the loan supervision machinery suggested by Hoover. In the Senate, Glass maneuvered the successful resolution advising the government to refrain from either approving or disapproving foreign loans. The resolution was the result of doubts regarding the legality of loan control, as well as alarm at the popular impression among investors that the government "guaranteed" the approved flotations.[50]

The venality of the Secretary of Interior, Albert Fall, in connection with the Teapot Dome oil lands could not be charged even remotely to Secretary Hoover. Yet, Hoover was caught in the cross-fire of two opposing camps concerned over capital exports. Some thought foreign lending was excessive and the controls ineffectual; others regarded official "advice" in many cases as an onerous affront to private interests and to foreign governments.

George W. Edwards, the economist, proposed that the United States was an "involuntary lender" exporting capital for the development of foreign areas in response to higher yields. This outflow of dollars, according to Edwards, was the result of foreign need rather than a reflection of American economic

49. Dulles, *op. cit.,* pp. 34, 38, 45.

50. Angell, *op. cit.,* p. 110; James E. Palmer, Jr., *Carter Glass: Unreconstructed Rebel* (Roanoke, 1938), pp. 200-202; De Conde, *op. cit.,* p. 68.

strength. Unlike Hoover, he recognized as valid the direct use of international loans for balancing budgets and stabilizing currencies. Edwards feared, however, that unrestrained export of surplus capital would impede America's own economic expansion. In this respect, he implied a position similar to Hoover's misgivings *à propos* the mushrooming branch factory movement.[51] Other analysts predicted that the staggering dollar obligations of Europe would force America to accept payment in goods by lowering import barriers. This, it was feared, would have an adverse effect on the entire economic structure of the United States.[52]

Did foreign loans stimulate American exports or did they finance foreign competitors while depriving domestic enterprise of required capital? As shown before, these doubts among nongovernmental critics influenced also the policies of the Commerce Department under Hoover in giving precedence to the expansion of American industry at home.[53]

There is little question that the program envisioned by Hoover could not be implemented effectively, partly because the "extralegal" governmental powers feared by some of his critics failed to materialize. In the midst of the embargo on French dollar bond flotations, for example, American capital was enticed into even riskier foreign currency mortgages, as well as privately issued stocks and bonds. Investments of this type were not subject to governmental approval. United States investors and foreign borrowers could thus get around the warnings or bans of the Commerce Department, toothless tiger that it was at times.[54]

To control loan flotations involving weak or unstable foreign governments was sometimes relatively easy. Similarly, some smaller domestic investment houses were in a less favorable position to disregard the "advice" of the Commerce Department.

51. George W. Edwards, "American Policy with Reference to Foreign Investments," *The American Economic Review*, XIV (March 1924—Supplement), pp. 31-35.

52. Paul M. Mazur, *America Looks Abroad; The New Economic Horizons* (New York, 1930), pp. 104-105.

53. Madden, *op. cit.*, p. viii.

54. Angell, *op. cit.*, pp. 108-110.

Under these circumstances it is not surprising to find occasional protests against "imperialism" or "favoritism" in connection with official loan policies.[55] Usually, however, informed critics could not find too much fault with Hoover's program for a "positive policy" of governmental supervision to reinforce investment bankers' "ethics" and to safeguard American interests threatened by economic nationalism abroad.[56]

Considering the great volume of foreign securities offered publicly — totalling $1,382,000,000 in 1924-25 alone — governmental "interference" was actually kept down to the barest minimum.[57] Secretary Hoover's convictions regarding the virtues of untrammeled private enterprise were an adequate safeguard against official usurpation of economic power. Thus, even Democratic leader Breckenridge Long, lecturing on the limitations restraining the executive branch in the control of foreign investments, could see no constitutional hazards with respect to the official loan approval procedure.[58]

The debate over investment controls, however, produced benefits other than the attempted crystallization of American policy. Foreign investments involved also "educational" aspects in terms of a greater public awareness of the world economy, even if often in such narrow terms as trade relations, tariff problems, and so on. These issues led, in turn, to specific Congressional moves, some of which have already been mentioned.

Congressman Emanuel Celler (D., N. Y.) led an energetic campaign to halt the flow of dollars to Rumania so long as that country refused to honor the postwar minority rights covenants. Other legislators, as well as the "grass roots," expressed more interest in the complexities of foreign affairs. Partly because of investments abroad, America was stirring from the slumber of

---

55. Senate Committee on Finance, *Hearings to Investigate the Sale of Foreign Bonds or Securities in the United States*, pp. 1610-1617, *passim*.

56. Culbertson, *op. cit.*, pp. 383, 388.

57. *Thirteenth Annual Report of the Secretary of Commerce*, p. 36, *passim*.

58. Breckinridge Long, "Limitations upon the Adoption of any Foreign Investment Policy by the United States," *The Annals*, CXXVI (July, 1926), 94.

"normalcy" toward a broader view of the world (only to recoil once more in the international chaos of the Depression).[59]

How did the foreign loan controversy affect Hoover personally? In the prosperous twenties Hoover's energetic policies no doubt contributed to his national prominence and popularity, culminating in the presidential election of 1928. But his record as Secretary of Commerce remained, this time in an unfavorable light, as a strong political issue after the crash of 1929. This was true especially with regard to the "evils" of speculative foreign loans. The question of American losses abroad, claimed Hoover, "was exaggerated out of all proportion in the Presidential campaign of 1932."[60]

In the midst of the campaign, Franklin Delano Roosevelt asserted that Hoover's credit policies as Secretary of Commerce fostered speculative foreign loans which helped bring on the depression. Hoover responded hotly by accusing his Democratic opponent of having engaged personally, "as a private promoter for profit," in the speculative activities of the "Federal International Banking Company," whose prospectus implied the "official blessing" of the Federal Government.[61]

Hoover defended also, with much justification, his own attempts to set up qualitative loan standards, claiming no defaults "where my proposed safeguards have been followed." The actual losses, furthermore, were far less than the figures claimed by the Democrats. Even these, Hoover asserted, were a "cheap method of unemployment and agricultural relief." He repeated his view of foreign loans as a stimulant to American exports and continued prosperity in the postwar decade.[62]

Some time before the 1932 election, liberals like Morris L.

---

59. Harry T. Collings, Rep. Henry R. Rathbone (R., Ill.), Rep. Franklin W. Fort (R., N. J.), Attaché Louis E. Van Norman, and George W. Edwards, Symposium on "The Investment of American Capital in Europe and its Probable Effect upon American Foreign Policy," *ibid.,* 71-94; *Congressional Record,* 70 Cong., 1 Sess. (April 5, 1928), pp. 5960 ff.

60. Hoover, *Memoirs,* II, 90-91.

61. *Ibid.,* III, 253-254; see footnotes 29-33 in chapter VIII of this study.

62. Hoover, *supra.;* Madden, *op. cit.,* pp. viii-ix, *passim;* Lewis, *op. cit., passim.*

Ernst, writing in *The Nation,* implied that Senatorial investigations of foreign loans cast doubts on the integrity of the Commerce Department under Hoover. Consequently, Ernst proposed such remedies as prohibiting Commerce (and State) officials from accepting private employment related to their previous government work for at least two years after quitting Federal service.[63]

Much more serious, however, was the continued attack on Hoover's tariff policies while he was Secretary of Commerce. His opponents protested that it was inconsistent to keep American tariff barriers high while expecting European countries to meet their war debt obligations to the United States. The result, they noted, was "bad feelings" on both sides of the Atlantic. Plans for a solution of the related reparations problem by floating a foreign loan to Germany, as proposed in the Hoover-backed Dawes scheme, were ridiculed by Keynes and his influential following. Hoover's own assertion that American cancellation of all but the postwar debts "would have strengthened our moral position," stood in strange contrast to his insistence, as Secretary, on repayment of all the European obligations.[64]

On this issue also Hoover never shirked from a defense of his policies. Ridiculing the notion of some "disastrous shift in our imports and exports of merchandise" resulting from protectionism, he explained that Europe did possess the "capacity to pay." Liberalizing United States tariff barriers to permit more imports from the debtor countries was unnecessary, he announced in 1926, partly because of huge dollar remittances by American tourists and European emigrants.[65]

Not tariffs, but "internal economic and social currents," such as the Bolshevik system within Russia, were responsible for

---

63. Morris L. Ernst, "Controlling Foreign Loans," *The Nation,* CXXXIV (Feb. 10, 1932), 168.

64. Hoover, *Memoirs,* II, 177-178; III, 248; Keynes, "The German Loan Delusion," *The New Republic,* XXXV (June 13, 1923), 62-64; Cooper to Jones, Sept. 27, 1927, NA, RG 151:640 (General).

65. Hoover, *The Future of Our Foreign Trade,* pp. 12-13.

widespread dislocations. In the United States, Hoover noted proudly, business-government cooperation to eliminate wasteful practices and improve economic operations brought prosperity to an entire nation. As a result, he affirmed, Americans increased steadily their purchase of foreign goods in spite of the high tariff laws.[66]

In a speech during the election campaign of 1928, Hoover defended his economic foreign policy by asserting that the European position was not so difficult as pictured by some over-sympathetic Americans. Their annual war debt settlement, for example, amounted to "less than 5 per cent" of their buying power, so talk of Europe's need for lower American tariffs was superfluous.[67] Hoover, moreover, regarded the European tendency toward economic nationalism and self-sufficiency as ample justification for protective measures by the United States. Republican tariff protection during the 1920's, he noted, still admitted 63 per cent of imports free of duty.[68]

Anyone wishing to deal justly with Hoover's policies regarding interallied debts, tariffs, and other relations with the world outside the United States, must not lose sight of the fact that Hoover was indeed an "exemplar of his age." On such issues as the war debts, Hoover was joined by Hughes and by most leading Americans. As recalled by the historian Dexter Perkins, the war debts issue and related problems were affected by the great "wave of postwar nationalism" sweeping the country in the 1920's. On certain issues, such as immigration quotas, Hoover represented the more "enlightened" opinion, at a time when the "spirit of xenophobia . . . [and] the virus of nationalism . . . [were] deep-seated."[69]

The political attacks of 1932 aimed at Hoover's policies as Secretary of Commerce were not only exaggerated but failed to appreciate Hoover in the context of "his times." Hoover, in spite

66. *Ibid.*, p. 11; Hoover, *Memoirs*, II, 61-78, 331.
67. Hoover, *The New Day*, p. 138.
68. Hoover, *Memoirs*, II, 291-292, 297. The *Memoirs* offer no satisfactory breakdown of Hoover's figures.
69. Perkins, *op. cit.*, pp. 119, 121-123.

of his efforts, was unable — even when he saw the need — to
stem the prevailing national tide of economic optimism and
feverish speculation.

This kind of optimism was exuded publicly as late as 1928-29
by "experts" like George P. Auld, international economist and
accountant-general of the Reparation Commission. Auld ridiculed the "fallacy" that high protective tariffs in the United
States could prevent Europeans from paying their governmental
and private dollar obligations. Moreover, he did not doubt that
the "debtor nations are thoroughly solvent." Loans to countries
like Germany were quite safe, Auld implied, basing his conclusion on a faulty analogy to the United States of prewar years.
Germany, like the young American colossus was simply developing her "productive facilities" to reach new levels of prosperity.
Taking account of world economic factors, as well as such problems as tariff protectionism coupled with a vast foreign indebtedness to the United States, Auld could still see no "threat either
to our investors or to our manufacturers." This was January,
1929.[70]

Long before this Hoover and his staff tied the national welfare
of the United States with the success of American industry and
finance. The latter benefited immensely from the services of the
Commerce Department at home and abroad. When ominous
signs of economic disaster appeared on the horizon, Hoover
could but warn and advise against the dangers of over-expansion
and over-speculation. The application of firm governmental controls against a business community so idealized in the America
of the 1920's seemed out of the question.

Even foreigners were encouraged by the Department of Commerce to acquire some stock in American business, "as in that
case they will be more interested in the welfare of this country."[71]
At first, sales of American securities abroad lagged, partly because British newspapers attacked them as "tribute" to "Uncle

70. Auld, *op. cit.*, pp. 181-185, 201.
71. Rufus S. Tucker (Acting Chief, Finance and Investment Division) to
Attaché Walter S. Tower (London), June 13, 1924, NA, RG 151:620 (U. K.).

Shylock," and partly because of rigid tax policies by the United States. But the Commerce Department stepped into the breach when its London attaché warned "that very big sums were involved [and, as usual,] that the people on this side expect relief . . . through the activities of the Department of Commerce."[72] These instances typified the Department's place in a business-oriented and nationalist era.

Conclusion

Historical studies developed around a central figure face the temptation of ascribing to that person sole credit for many achievements and then blending these into a characterization of almost heroic proportions. This study has endeavored to avoid such pitfalls of generalization and exaggeration by attempting to describe the policy-making process on the intra-departmental level, often analyzing the treatment of certain issues within the middle echelons of Commerce Department bureaucracy. Other major policy decisions have been traced from their origins in the disaffection or anxiety of certain business groups and their development studied on the governmental level, both within and outside the Commerce Department.

Rejecting the notion of a comprehensive governmental program emanating full-blown from the brow of a gifted departmental executive does not detract from Hoover's importance as an influential Commerce Secretary and formulator of national policies. His philosophy and general outlook pervaded all the activities of his Department. Consequently, they showed few traces of internal dissension or deviation from the policies he outlined.

A good part of the explanation lies in the fact that Commerce was then quite young in relation to other departments. Hoover's vast reorganization and expansion program included the appointment of an almost entirely new official staff, thus precluding the danger of an intrenched conservative clique. His personal con-

---

72. Tower to Klein, May 28, 1924; Lyon to Tucker, June 25, 1924, *ibid.*

ception of what was good for the country became popular among
both governmental circles and the public.

Efficient service to private American interests, patterned after
Hoover's view of the national welfare, became the keynote of
the Commerce Department's widespread operations. The path
to advancement in Commerce was a practical business background, as well as technical and professional competence. Qualities such as these were personified ideally by Hoover himself.
He possessed an intimate knowledge of business on the international level as well as proven administrative talent and
organizing skill. As Secretary, he rarely lost contact with his
Department's complex activities, even though he could depend
on the capable assistance of officials like Dr. Julius Klein, a
trusted lieutenant and Director of the Bureau of Foreign and
Domestic Commerce.

Hoover accepted the cabinet position in Harding's administration partly because of a desire to put into practice his own
economic and social principles. His experience as relief administrator in Europe convinced him more firmly than before that the
ways of "American Individualism" were superior to any other
system. Unlike European capitalism, private enterprise in the
United States fostered opportunity for all individuals and was
thus an expression of equality and "social justice." Belief in these
traditional American ideals was the truly "liberal" approach,
Hoover maintained, although he was himself attacked often by
progressive and international groups.

The Hoover policies were based on an ideological amalgam
of nineteenth-century classical economics with the needs and
wishes of twentieth-century business in the United States. A
"free" economy was revered by Hoover as the democratic force
on which depended the continued progress of all the American
people. Not merely the advancement of entrepreneurial interests
or material progress, but all the things which made America
great stemmed from the competitive business tradition.

Inconsistency in the application of these principles arose repeatedly out of the fact that Hoover preferred the more prag-

matic approach to specific issues. On the one hand, for example, he fought bitterly for free international access to raw materials, especially those the United States did not possess. Relying on nineteenth-century theories of free trade and "comparative advantage," he assailed the resort to "monopoly" control of such products as rubber, coffee, potash, and others. International amity was threatened, Hoover asserted, by foreign combinations to restrict prices and production. On the other hand, he defended American tariff protectionism as essential to continued prosperity, minimizing the opposition aroused at home and abroad by the Republican trade policies.

In dealing with such issues as the struggle against foreign "monopolies," Hoover stirred American national feeling and he kept himself in the forefront as the champion of American economic rights abroad. Against the uncooperative foreign interests he mobilized a counter-offensive which in some respects exerted greater pressure than the offending "monopolies." The Commerce Department effectively blocked loans to the Brazilian coffee interests and to the Franco-German potash cartel. British rubber interests, united behind the Stevenson price control scheme, were threatened continually with an American buying pool. The latter received valuable assistance under the Hoover program, which supported also Congressional legislation (the Newton Bill) to legalize all buying pools approved by the Secretary of Commerce.[1]

The vast public relations machinery developed by Hoover was utilized to its fullest during the anti-"monopoly" fight. In press releases, pamphlets, and fervent addresses, Americans were urged to conserve existing stockpiles of imported raw materials and to develop new sources of supply. The trade presses and general newspapers were caught up in the appeal to safeguard the interests of American industry and the American consumer against foreign "price-gouging." Hoover's efforts were supported

1. In April, 1928, shadows of the future were cast when a Democratic-Farm bloc coalition finally voted down the Newton Bill. This was partly the result of antagonism toward Hoover.

by friendly Congressional investigators. A partial result of his policies was the allocation of additional funds enabling the Commerce Department to conduct a world-wide search for independent supplies of raw materials under United States control.

The wide support for Hoover's program against foreign combinations was based on two prevailing forces: business and nationalism, each with its own ramifications, yet often intertwined. Anti-foreign feeling in the United States in the post-Versailles period may be traced to more than a disillusionment with the political results of World War I and the menace of new radical movements. Such difficult issues as the inter-allied debts also made Americans suspicious that their purses were to pay the costs of European folly. What's more, there seemed to be an attempt abroad to discriminate against American business by raising the price of raw materials, imposing special import quotas, and other phenomena of postwar economic nationalism.

Hoover was convinced that American business — the foundation of national progress — required Federal assistance to meet the foreign threat. His protestations against international monopoly were based, however, on aversion to governmentally-controlled combinations, rather than combination *per se.* Thus, he could devote his energies consistently toward fostering voluntary trade associations for greater efficiency and as a counter-balance against the "unfair" practices of hostile cartels. Organized American business could benefit most from the Commerce Department's informational services regarding competitive conditions abroad or the attitudes of foreign officials and even from occasional inter-governmental pressure on their behalf.

Official Washington pressure was brought to bear, for example, against the British control of rubber prices. These governmental controls were developed under the aegis of Winston Churchill, who was Colonial Secretary at the time they were adopted (1922). As a consequence of Hoover's attack on the rubber restrictions and his insistence on the repayment of war debts, the Secretary of Commerce became an unpopular figure in the British press. Most often, he was charged with hypocrisy in subscribing to American "monopolies" and protectionism, while begrudging foreign interests the benefits of closer organization. The Hoover policy of loan embargoes against foreign combinations and countries refusing to sign a war debt agreement was associated, particularly in France, with strong anti-American feeling.

Although Hoover probably enjoyed the support of most American newspapers and influential sections of public opinion, his policies were criticized in several quarters. The Democratic minority was in the opposition on such issues as the tariff, while the more internationalist groups — reflected in *The Nation* — objected to the intransigent stand on war debts. Congressman Fiorello La Guardia, a "liberal" Republican, charged Hoover with serving the interests of Big Business — such as the tire manufacturers — and with grasping for too much personal power.

John Foster Dulles, also a Republican and a prominent attorney with diplomatic and banking connections, joined in the anti-Hoover argument. Dulles maintained that Europeans should be allowed to adopt whatever economic organization they preferred. American attempts to exert pressure in the ways suggested by Hoover, he admonished, would only aggravate existing disturbances in international relations.

The dominant forces in American life during the 1920's, however, were neither the internationalist elements nor the farm-state progressives who were suspicious of Hoover's motives and deplored his ostensible presidential ambitions. Their opposition was more than amply counteracted by the apotheosis of Hoover among powerful business and trade associations. As the spokesman for business interests in the business-oriented Harding and Coolidge administrations, the influence and popularity of the Secretary of Commerce rose steadily toward the pinnacle of the Presidency.

It would be misleading to imply that Hoover's concept of the voluntary partnership between government and business was intended to serve only the interests of business. The Commerce Department was no passive partner sacrificing its own initiative either to Wall Street or Main Street. In spite of the opposition of many investment houses, Hoover promoted a program of governmental supervision over foreign lending so that the diplomatic and economic interests of the American people would be given due consideration. Hoover insisted on adequate loan standards, as a governmental responsibility, to prevent widespread losses to American investments abroad. These efforts were weakened by Wall Street's failure to heed the Commerce Department's warnings, by the general speculative mania, and by the opposition to controls of such administration stalwarts as Treasury Secretary Andrew W. Mellon.

Frequently, however, the Commerce Department attempted to steer the decisions of industry and finance along lines consonant with the national welfare. Its policy-makers, for example, sought to encourage "tying" clauses in loan contracts, whereby foreign borrowers of dollars would pledge to buy from American exporters. Likewise, the Department warned against the establishment of branch factories overseas unless warranted by specific conditions, such as foreign import quotas on United States products. These policies are traceable to Hoover's concern for an ever-increasing flow of American exports as a mainstay of domestic prosperity. The Department, like its Secretary, saw no reason for building up potential competition abroad and giving employment to foreign rather than native labor.

Hoover and his staff often suffered from an inability to see beyond the range of American interests, frequently ignoring diplomatic considerations for the narrow aims of economic nationalism. Thus, they failed to see the inconsistency of expecting the world to increase indefinitely its purchases of American products while demanding, at the same time, the payment of all debt obligations to the United States and the dissolution of "price-gouging" schemes. Some of these combinations, moreover, presented no significant threat to the United States. How much more conciliatory and realistic — if perhaps over-generous

— was the American policy after World War II toward European reconstruction and economic cooperation!

Diplomatic blundering as well as usurpation of power by the Commerce Department were charges repeated often by State Department personnel and their sympathizers. The Commerce Department, possessing a time-honored Foreign Service, resented the increasing superiority of Commerce in the ill-defined area of economic foreign relations. Though temporary compromises moderated the inter-departmental competition, for Secretaries of State Hughes and Kellogg were not personally antagonistic to Hoover, Hoover continued to gain in prestige and power. In a period when governmental agencies were ham-strung by budgetary limitations, the Department of Commerce successfully expanded its operations by publicizing its services to business and the national economy.

Being constantly in the limelight brought political benefits for Hoover, who could point proudly to his Department's achievements before and during the presidential election year of 1928. Ironically, Hoover's record as Secretary of Commerce was to be used against him, however, during his 1932 bid for a second term as president. At that time America's economic involvement abroad during the prosperous 1920's appeared to have ended in total failure, and the Democrats made political capital of this issue by blaming Hoover's pre-presidential policies. Much of this criticism was unjustified.

While it is true that Hoover encouraged the profitable expansion of American interests abroad, his Department did not possess the enforcement powers necessary to prevent what it often considered highly speculative investments. It is even probable that Hoover's proposal to halt loans for armaments, especially in Latin America, was primarily an attempt to halt the flow of dollars to "over-borrowed" countries.

No doubt Hoover promoted and assisted the expansion of American influence abroad, particularly in the underdeveloped areas he considered desirable for the production of essential raw materials (such as Latin America and Liberia). His efforts to modify the land laws of the Philippines to make possible large rubber plantations resulted in charges of "Imperialism." He opposed military intervention, however, as well as the old-style "dollar diplomacy," preferring economic bargaining on a "business basis."

A significant accomplishment of Hoover and his staff was to demonstrate — in a period of so-called *laissez-faire* — the valuable services which could be performed by governmental agencies in the sphere of business activity. The Department of Commerce became a great clearing-house of information and advice for American industry and finance. It served also as a buffer between private American interests and their foreign counterparts. By publicizing the economic "opportunities" abroad, Hoover demonstrated that America was as much as any other country a part of the world community — even if we did refuse to join the League of Nations. Had it not been for the shock of the Great Depression, the increasing economic participation of the United States in world affairs might have led to greater political cooperation as well.

BIBLIOGRAPHY

I. SOURCES

A. *Manuscript Sources* in the National Archives, Washington, D. C.

Record Group 59: General Records of the Department of State. These include memoranda by officials of the Department, as well as inter-departmental and other correspondence.

Record Group 151: Records of the Bureau of Foreign and Domestic Commerce. Included are letters to and from the Secretary of Commerce and other high officials of the Department, inter-departmental memoranda, *data* on economic developments, as well as general records of governmental activity.

B. *Printed Government Sources*

Congressional Record. 68 Cong., 1 Sess., LXV (Part 8). Washington, 1924.

————. 70 Cong., 1 Sess., LIXX (Part 6). Washington, 1928.

United States Congress, House, Committee on Foreign Affairs. *Hearings on the Foreign Service of the United States.* H. R. 17 and H. R. 6357, 68 Cong., 1 Sess. Washington, 1924.

————, ————, Committee on Interstate and Foreign Commerce. *Hearings on Crude Rubber, Coffee, Etc.* H. R. 59, 69 Cong., 1 Sess. Washington, 1926.

————, ————, ————. *Preliminary Report on Crude Rubber, Coffee, Etc.* 69 Cong., 1 Sess. Washington, 1926.

————, Senate, Committee on Finance, *Hearings . . . to Investigate the Sale of Foreign Bonds or Securities in the United States.* S. Res. 19, 72 Cong., 1 Sess. Washington, 1931-1932.

————, ————, Committee on Foreign Relations, *Hearings . . . on . . . Foreign Loans.* S. Res. 22, 68 Cong., 2 Sess. S. Res. 15, 69 Cong., 2 Sess. Washington, 1925, 1927.

United States Department of Commerce. These publications include the *Economic Series (E. S.),* the *Trade Information Bulletins (T. I. B.),* and the *Trade Promotion Series (T. P. S.).* All were issued by the Bureau of Foreign and Domestic Commerce in Washington, D. C.

————. *American Underwriting of Foreign Securities in 1928.* T. I. B. No. 613, 1929.

————. *American Underwriting of German Securities.* T. I. B. No. 648, 1929.

————. *Commerce Reports,* February 26, 1923 - July 6, 1925.

221

—————, Domeratzky, Louis. *The International Cartel Movement.* *T. I. B.* No. 556, 1928.

—————, Figart, David M. *The Plantation Rubber Industry in the Middle East. T. P. S.* No. 2, 1925. This thorough study deals with the areas in present-day Indonesia and the Malay Federation, as well as the rest of south-east Asia.

—————, Hall, Ray O. *The Balance of International Payments of the United States in 1927. T. I. B.* No. 552, 1928.

—————, Holt, Everett G. *Marketing of Crude Rubber. T. P. S.* No. 55, 1927.

—————, Hoover, Herbert. *Annual Reports of the Secretary of Commerce.* Washington, 1922-1928.

—————, —————. *Foreign Combinations Now Fixing Prices of Raw Materials Imported Into the United States.* This Commerce Library pamphlet contains Hoover's address of October 31, 1926.

—————, —————. *The Future of Our Foreign Trade.* Washington, 1926. This Commerce Library pamphlet contains Hoover's address of March 16, 1926.

—————, —————. *How the United States Department of Commerce Serves the Farmer.* Washington, 1923.

—————, —————. *A Merchant Marine Policy.* Washington, 1925. Hoover's address of November 16, 1925.

—————, Lary, Hal B. *The United States in the World Economy. E. S.* No. 23, 1943.

—————, Lyon, Charles E. *British Financial Conditions in 1924. T. I. B.* No. 336, 1925.

—————, —————. "Great Britain and the Gold Standard." *Commerce Reports,* I (March 16, 1925), 612-614.

—————. *Merchandising Methods and Trade Conditions in the Amazon Valley. T. I. B.* No. 320, 1925.

—————, Notz, William F. *Representative International Cartels, Combines and Trusts. T. P. S.* No. 81, 1929.

—————. *Possibilities for Para Rubber Production in the Philippine Islands. T. P. S.* No. 17, 1925.

—————. *Potash: Significance of Foreign Control and Economic Need of Domestic Development. T. P. S.* No. 33, 1926.

—————, Roper, Daniel C. *American Branch Factories Abroad.* Washington, 1934. *Senate Document* No. 120, 73 Cong., 2 Sess.

—————, Ryan, Franklin W. *The Balance of International Payments of the United States in 1925. T. I. B.* No. 399, 1926.

—————, Schurz, William L. *The Brazilian Iron and Steel Industry. T. I. B.* No. 6, 1922.

—————, Tucker, Rufus S. *The Balance of International Payments of the United States in 1924. T. I. B.* No. 340, 1925.

—————, Whitford, Harry N. and Anthony, Alfred. *Rubber Production in Africa. T. P. S.* No. 34, 1926.

United States Department of State. *Foreign Relations of the United States.* 1922, II; 1923, II. Washington, 1922, 1923.

C. *Autobiographies, Memoirs, and Speeches*

Coolidge, Calvin. *The Autobiography of Calvin Coolidge.* New York, 1929.

————. *The Mind of the President . . . Coolidge's Views . . .* (C. Bascomb Slemp, ed.). New York, 1926.

Hoover, Herbert. *The Memoirs of Herbert Hoover.* 3 vols. New York, 1952. As in most published memoirs, there is an occasional tendency to defend one's policies through the wisdom of hind-sight. The account is generally factual and forthright. Vol. II deals with the Cabinet period.

————. *The New Day; Campaign Speeches of Herbert Hoover, 1928.* Stanford, 1928. These indicate, in part, Hoover's reliance on his record as Secretary of Commerce.

Hughes, Charles Evans. *The Pathway of Peace; Representative Addresses . . .* New York, 1925.

II. SECONDARY WORKS

A. *Books and Pamphlets*

Adams, James T. *Big Business in a Democracy.* New York, 1945.

Adams, Samuel H. *Incredible Era: The Life and Times of Warren Gamaliel Harding.* Boston, 1939. This study contains useful insights into the role of Hoover in the Harding Administration.

Angell, James W. *Financial Foreign Policy of the United States.* New York, 1933. A publication of the Council on Foreign Relations, this work is an excellent summary of governmental loan standards in the 1920's.

Bemis, Samuel F. *A Diplomatic History of the United States.* New York, 1955.

————. *The Latin American Policy of the United States.* New York, 1943.

Browder, Robert P. *The Origins of Soviet-American Diplomacy.* Princeton, 1953.

Corey, Herbert. *The Truth About Hoover.* Boston, 1932.

Culbertson, William S. *International Economic Policies.* New York, 1925.

De Conde, Alexander. *Herbert Hoover's Latin American Policy.* Stanford, 1951. The author traces the origins of the "good neighbor" policy to Hoover's term as Secretary of Commerce.

Dexter, Walter F. *Herbert Hoover and American Individualism; A Modern Interpretation of a National Ideal.* New York, 1932.

Divine, Robert A. *American Immigration Policy, 1924-1952.* New Haven, 1957.

Dulles, Foster R. *The Imperial Years.* New York, 1956.

Emeny, Brooks. *The Strategy of Raw Materials.* New York, 1934. Subtitled "A Study of America in Peace and War," this is a scholarly presentation of the raw materials problem facing the United States.

Emerson, Edwin. *Hoover and His Times.* Garden City, New York, 1932. Popular-style social history.

Fainsod, Merle and Gordon, Lincoln. *Government and the American Economy.* New York, 1941. The economic and legal aspects of governmental promotion and regulation of business.

Faulkner, Harold U. *American Economic History.* New York, 1954.

Feis, Herbert. *The Diplomacy of the Dollar; First Era, 1919-1932.* Baltimore, 1950. This brief summary presents some cogent conclusions, by a former State Department official, concerning the development of American foreign loan policies.

Figart, David M. *America and Rubber Restriction.* New York, 1926. Private printing.

Freidel, Frank. *Franklin D. Roosevelt.* 2 vols. Boston, 1954.

Fuess, Claude M. *Calvin Coolidge, the Man from Vermont.* Boston, 1940. A little more light on Hoover's place in the 1920's Cabinet.

Greaves, Harold R. G. *Raw Materials and International Control.* London, 1936. Although written by an economist, the emphasis is on the political difficulties of control.

Grunder, Garel A. and Lwezey, William E. *The Philippines and the United States.* Norman, Okla., 1951.

Hexner, Ervin. *International Cartels.* Chapel Hill, 1945. An authoritative general study, with emphasis on combinations in manufacturing.

Higham, John. *Strangers in the Land.* New Brunswick, New Jersey, 1955.

Hinshaw, David. *Herbert Hoover: American Quaker.* New York, 1950.

Hoover, Herbert. *American Individualism.* New York, 1922. A valuable source for Hoover's basic concepts.

Hughes, Charles E. *Foreign Relations.* Washington, 1924. A pamphlet published by the National Republican Committee in defense of the Administration's foreign policy.

Irwin, Will. *Herbert Hoover; A Reminiscent Biography.* New York, 1928.

Jacob, Heinrich E. *Coffee; the Epic of a Commodity.* New York, 1935. Translated from the German by Eden and Cedar Paul. Colorful survey, in a "popular" style.

Kellogg, Vernon. *Herbert Hoover, the Man and his Work.* New York, 1920.

Keynes, John Maynard. *The Economic Consequences of the Peace.* New York, 1920.

Kohn, Hans. *Nationalism and Imperialism in the Hither East.* London, 1932.

Kuczynski, Robert R. *American Loans to Germany.* New York, 1927. Scholarly analysis under the auspices of the Institute of Economics.

Statistics are broken into types of lending, the role of specific investment houses, etc.

Lamartine-Yates, Paul. *Commodity Control*, London, 1943. A Fabian view of economic imperialism and the effect of commodity control on cyclical movements.

Lawrence, James C. *The World's Struggle With Rubber*. New York, 1931. An informative but biased presentation of the American side in the Stevenson Plan controversy.

Lay, Tracy H. *The Foreign Service of the United States*. New York, 1925. The work of a Consul General, this book focuses on the conflicts between the Commerce and State departments.

Lewis, Cleona F. *America's Stake in International Investments*. Washington, 1938. A thorough and authoritative publication of the Brookings Institution. Contains a wealth of data and interpretation.

Liefmann, Robert. *Cartels, Concerns and Trusts*. London, 1932.

Lyons, Eugene. *Our Unknown Ex-President; A Portrait of Herbert Hoover*. New York, 1948. A very friendly biography.

Madden, John T., *et al. America's Experience as Creditor*. New York, 1937. A factual analysis of United States financial policies in the inter-war period.

Mantoux, Étienne. *The Carthaginian Peace; or, The Economic Consequences of Mr. Keynes*. New York, 1946.

Marcosson, Isaac. *Caravans of Commerce*. New York, 1926. Deals mainly with the work of the commodity divisions and the commercial attachés.

Martin, Robert F. *International Raw Commodity Price Control*. New York, 1937. Published by the National Industrial Conference Board.

Mazur, Paul M. *America Looks Abroad; The New Economic Horizons*. New York, 1930. Popular account of America's great influence in the international economy of the 1920's.

McCamy, James L. *Government Publicity*. University of Chicago *Studies in Public Administration, X*. Chicago, 1939.

McFadyean, Sir Andrew, ed. *The History of Rubber Regulation*. London, 1944. For the International Rubber Regulation Committee.

Moon, Parker T. *Imperialism and World Politics*. New York, 1939.

Moulton, Harold G. and Pasvolsky, Leo. *World War Debt Settlements*. New York, 1926.

Myers, William S. *The Foreign Policies of Herbert Hoover: 1929-1933*. New York, 1940. This study, as well as the one below, casts some light on the pre-presidential period. Both are marked by a friendly bias.

————— and Newton, Walter H. *The Hoover Administration: A Documented Narrative*. New York, 1936.

National Conference of Business Paper Editors. *What the Department of Commerce is Doing for American Business*. Washington, 1924.

Nevins, Allan and Hill, Frank E. *Ford; Expansion and Challenge: 1915-1933.* New York, 1957.

O'Connor, Harvey. *Mellon's Millions.* New York, 1933.

Oualid, William. *International Raw Materials Cartels.* Paris, 1938. A moderate approach, prepared for the International Studies Conference of the League of Nations.

Parks, Wallace J. *United States Administration of its International Economic Affairs.* Baltimore, 1951.

Perkins, Dexter. *Charles Evans Hughes and American Democratic Statesmanship.* Boston, 1956.

Pollock, James K. and Thomas, Homer. *Germany in Power and Eclipse.* New York, 1952.

Pound, Arthur. *The Turning Wheel.* New York, 1934.

Prothro, James W. *The Dollar Decade; Business Ideas in the 1920's.* Baton Rouge, 1954.

Pusey, Merlo J. *Charles Evans Hughes.* 2 vols. New York, 1951.

Robinson, Edgar E. *The Roosevelt Leadership.* New York, 1955.

Rossiter, Clinton. *Conservatism in America.* New York, 1955.

Rowe, John W. F. *Markets and Men; A Study of Artificial Control Schemes in some Primary Industries.* Cambridge, 1936.

Schlesinger, Arthur M., Jr. *The Age of Roosevelt.* Vol. I, *The Crisis of the Old Order, 1919-1933.* Cambridge, 1957.

Schwarz, Sanford. *Research in International Economics by Federal Agencies.* New York, 1941.

Shwadran, Benjamin. *The Middle East, Oil, and the Great Powers.* New York, 1955.

Smith, Rixey, and Beasley, Norman. *Carter Glass.* New York, 1939.

Soule, George. *Prosperity Decade; From War to Depression: 1917-1929.* Vol. VIII of Henry David, *et al.,* eds., *The Economic History of the United States.* New York, 1947.

Southard, Frank A. *American Industry in Europe.* New York, 1931. A pioneering, scholarly study of branch factories and related problems.

Spykman, Nicholas J. *America's Strategy in World Politics.* New York, 1942. For the Institute of International Studies, Yale University.

Staley, Eugene. *Raw Materials in Peace and War.* New York, 1937. For the Council on Foreign Relations.

Sullivan, Mark. *Our Times; The United States, 1900-1925.* 6 vols. New York, 1926-1945.

Uribe, C. Andrès. *Brown Gold; the Amazing Story of Coffee.* New York, 1954.

Wallace, Benjamin B. and Edminster, Lynn R. *International Control of Raw Materials.* Washington, 1930. This publication of the Brookings Institution affords a comprehensive view of world controls and their effect on the United States.

White, William A. *A Puritan in Babylon.* New York, 1938. An excellent biography of Coolidge which sheds light also on Hoover's role in the 1920's.

Whittlesey, Charles R. *Governmental Control of Crude Rubber.* Princeton, 1931.

Wickizer, Vernon D. *The World Coffee Economy; with Special Reference to Control Schemes.* Stanford, 1943.

Wilbur, Ray L. and Hyde, Arthur M. *The Hoover Policies.* New York, 1937. Strongly pro-Hoover.

Williams, Benjamin H. *Economic Foreign Policy of the United States.* New York, 1929.

Williams, William A. *American-Russian Relations, 1781-1947.* New York, 1952.

Wolf, Howard and Ralph. *Rubber; A Story of Glory and Greed.* New York, 1936.

B.   *Articles and Essays*

"American Industry Acknowledges Its Debt to Herbert Hoover: A symposium of Appreciation of His Work, by Leaders of Industry." *Industrial Management,* LXXI (April, 1926), 199-212.

"An Opportunity Missed." *The New Republic,* XVII (July 27, 1921), 229-230.

"Artificial Rubber Again." *The Outlook,* CIL (August 8, 1928), 607.

Auld, George P. "Does High Protection Hamper the Repayment of our Loans and Investments Abroad?" *The Annals,* CIXL (January, 1929), 181-203.

Barnes, Julius H. "Herbert Hoover's Priceless Work in Washington." *Industrial Management,* LXXI (April, 1926), 193-198.

Bruère, Henry. "Constructive Versus Dollar Diplomacy." *The American Economic Review,* XIII (March, 1923), 68-76.

Bunuan, Vincente G. "Whose Land — Whose Rubber?" *The Nation,* CXXIV (January 5, 1927), 22.

Collings, Harry T. "The Foreign Investment Policy of the United States." *The Annals,* CXXVI (July, 1926), 71-79.

"Do Foreign Branch Plants Pay?" *The Business Week,* I (Oct. 19, 1929), 22-24.

Domeratzky, Louis. "American Industry Abroad." *Foreign Affairs,* VIII (July, 1930), 569-582.

Dulles, John Foster. "Our Foreign Loan Policy." *Foreign Affairs,* V (October, 1926), 33-48.

Durand, E. Dana. "Economic and Political Effects of Governmental Interference with the Free International Movement of Raw Materials." *International Conciliation,* No. 226 (January, 1927), 25-34.

Earle, Edward M. "International Financial Control of Raw Materials." *International Conciliation,* No. 226 (January, 1927), 46-53.

Edwards, George W. "American Policy With Reference to Foreign Investments." *The American Economic Review,* XIV (March, 1924 - Supplement), 26-35.

—————. "Foreign Investment Policies and their Relation to International Peace." *The Annals,* CXXVI (July, 1926), 95-97.

—————. "Government Control of Foreign Investments." *The American Economic Review,* XVIII (December, 1928), 684-701.

Ernst, Morris L. "Controlling Foreign Loans." *The Nation,* CXXXIV (February 10, 1932), 168-169.

Fess, Simeon D. "The Crude Rubber Monopoly — How It Can Be Met by America." *India Rubber and Tire Review,* XXVI (March, 1926), 16-18.

"Five Years of Rubber Restriction." *The Rubber Age,* XXII (December 25, 1927), 295-296.

Fort, Franklin W. "The Practical Side of America's New Foreign Investment Policy." *The Annals,* CXXVI (July, 1926), 84-86.

Harding, Warren G. "Less Government in Business and More Business in Government." *The World's Work,* XLI (November, 1920), 25-27.

"Herbert Hoover Praises Plan for American-Owned Rubber Plantations." *The Rubber Age,* XVIII (January 25, 1926), 271-273.

"Home-Grown Rubber." *The Outlook,* CIL (July 4, 1928), 367-368.

Hoover, Herbert. "America Solemnly Warns Foreign Monopolists of Raw Materials." *Current History,* XXIII (December, 1925), 307-311.

"Hoover Calls on Public to Save Rubber in Every Possible Way." *The Rubber Age,* XVIII (January 10, 1926), 219-20.

"Hooverizing the Department of Commerce." *The Weekly Review,* IV (March 9, 1921), 216.

Hyde, Charles C. "Charles Evans Hughes." Bemis, Samuel F., ed., *The American Secretaries of State and their Diplomacy,* X (New York, 1929), 221-401.

James, F. Cyril. "Benefits and Dangers of Foreign Investments." *The Annals,* CL (July, 1930), 76-84.

Joslin, Theodore G. "Eighty Thousand Weekly." *The World's Work,* LIX (July, 1930), 73-75.

Kellogg, Frank B. "Some Foreign Policies of the United States." *Foreign Affairs,* IV (Special Supplement, January, 1926), i-xvii.

Kellogg, Vernon. "Washington Five and Eight O'Clocks." *The Yale Review,* IX (April, 1920), 452-461.

Keynes, John Maynard. "The German Loan Delusion." *The New Republic,* XXXV (June 13, 1923), 62-64.

Klein, Julius. "Business." Beard, Charles A., ed., *Whither Mankind; A Panorama of Modern Civilization.* New York, 1929, pp. 83-109.

—————. "How Uncle Sam Stands on Foreign Trade." *System, the Magazine of Business,* IL (February, 1926), 205-208, 304-308.

—————. "International Cartels." *Foreign Affairs,* VI (April, 1928), 448-458.

—————. "Migrating Machinery." *The Saturday Evening Post,* CCIII (July 5, 1930), 21, 40, 42.

Long, Breckenridge. "Limitations Upon the Adoption of any Foreign

Investment Policy by the United States." *The Annals,* CXXVI (July, 1926), 92-94.

Marcosson, Isaac F. "Commercial Exploration." *The Saturday Evening Post,* CXCVIII (February 13, 1926), 8-9, 50-54.

—————. "The Franco-German Economic Entente." *The Saturday Evening Post,* CXCVIII (January 16, 1926), 16-17, 123-127.

May, George O. "Rubber: The Inquiry and the Facts." *The Atlantic Monthly,* CXXVII (June, 1926), 805-812.

"Mr. Hoover Stabs Russia." *The Nation,* CXVI (March 21, 1923), 327.

"Mr. Hoover's Warning to Foreign-Trade Gougers." *The Literary Digest,* LXXXVII (November 21, 1926), 12-13.

M. W. D. "The Search for Rubber: New Prospects in South America." *Foreign Affairs,* IV (January, 1926), 334-336.

"No Rubber Peonage." *The Outlook,* CIL (August 15, 1928), 607.

Rathbone, Henry R. "America's Present Need — A Strong Foreign Investment Policy." *The Annals,* CXXVI (July, 1926), 80-83.

Robinson, Henry M. "Are American Loans Abroad Safe?" *Foreign Affairs,* V (October, 1926), 49-56.

"Rubber and Mr. Hoover." *The Nation,* CXXII (January 20, 1926), 50.

"Rubber Company Profits Increase." *The Rubber Age,* XXII (March 25, 1928), 664, 666.

"Rubber Planting Possibilities in the Philippines." *The India Rubber World,* LXXII (September 1, 1925), 709-712.

Van Norman, Louis E. "Present Tendencies in the Investment of American Capital in Europe." *The Annals,* CXXVI (July, 1926), 87-91.

Viner, Jacob. "National Monopolies of Raw Materials." *Foreign Affairs,* IV (July, 1926), 585-600.

"What Washington Offers Business this Month." *System, the Magazine of Business,* L (July-December, 1926). Feature Series.

Whitford, Harry N. "The Crude Rubber Supply: An International Problem." *Foreign Affairs,* II (June 15, 1924), 613-621.

—————. "Rubber and the Philippines." *Foreign Affairs,* IV (July, 1926), 677-679.

—————. "The Search for Rubber: New Prospects in South America." *Foreign Affairs,* IV (January, 1926), 331-337.

Wilhelm, Donald. "Mr. Hoover as Secretary of Commerce." *The World's Work,* XLIII (February, 1922), 407-410.

Woodhouse, Henry. "America at the Mercy of British Rubber Monopoly." *Current History,* XVIII (April, 1923), 134-140.

III. NEWSPAPERS AND PERIODICALS

The India Rubber World (New York), October 1, 1922 - January 1, 1928.

The India Rubber and Tire Review (Akron, Ohio), 1926.

The New York Times, March 17, 1924 - April 7, 1928.

The Rubber Age (New York), December 25, 1927 - March 25, 1928.

INDEX